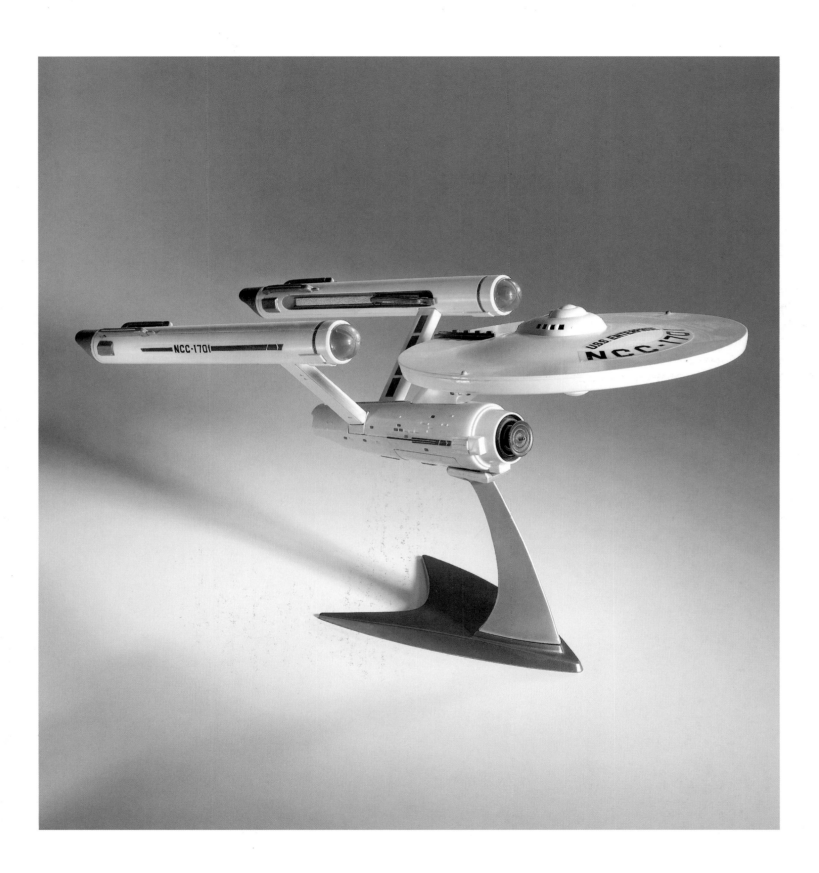

# STAR TREK

## THE COMPLETE UNAUTHORIZED HISTORY

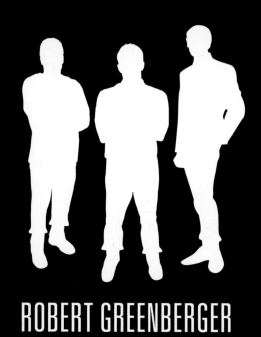

## ROBERT GREENBERGER

Voyageur Press

First published in 2012 by Voyageur Press, an imprint of MBI Publishing Company, 400 First Avenue North, Suite 300, Minneapolis, MN 55401 USA

The information in this book is true and complete to the best of our knowledge. All recommendations are made without any guarantee on the part of the author or Publisher, who also disclaims any liability incurred in connection with the use of this data or specific details.

This publication has not been prepared, approved, or licensed by CBS Television Studios, Paramount Pictures, or the Roddenberry Estate.

We recognize, further, that some words, names, designations, and screenplay quotes mentioned herein are the property of copyright and trademark holders. We use them for identification purposes only. This is not an official publication.

Voyageur Press titles are also available at discounts in bulk quantity for industrial or sales-promotional use. For details write to Special Sales Manager at MBI Publishing Company, 400 First Avenue North, Suite 300, Minneapolis, MN 55401 USA.

To find out more about our books, visit us online at www.voyageurpress.com.

ISBN-13: 978-0-7603-4359-3

10 9 8 7 6 5 4 3 2 1

Library of Congress Cataloging-in-Publication Data

Greenberger, Robert.
  Star trek : the complete unauthorized history / Robert Greenberger.
    p. cm.
  Summary: "A history of the Star Trek franchise from its beginning as a television show that barely lasted three seasons to a pop phenomenon approaching its fiftieth anniversary and comprising six TV series and soon a dozen movies, as well as hundreds of books and thousands of collectibles"--Provided by publisher
  ISBN 978-0-7603-4359-3 (hardback)
  1. Star trek (Television program) I. Title.
  PN1992.77.S73G74 2012
  791.45'72--dc23
                            2012018292

Editor: Scott Pearson
Design Manager: Cindy Samargia Laun
Designer: Simon Larkin

All memorabilia from the collection of Scott Pearson unless noted otherwise.

All pin-back buttons from the Voyageur Press collection unless noted otherwise.

**On the front cover:** Leonard Nimoy based the Vulcan salute on a Jewish ceremonial gesture forming the Hebrew letter "Shin." *Salute image created by Simon Larkin. Other photo elements from Harris Shiffman, Bill Frische, James Weston, and Malko at Shutterstock.com.*

**On the back cover:** Several comic book companies have published *Star Trek* over the years; represented here are DC, IDW, Marvel, Wildstorm, and Tokyopop's manga version. Playmates "Space Caps" were an attempt to get in on the pogs craze of the early 1990s. Even *Star Trek* can't avoid zombies, as evidenced by a promotional patch for IDW's *Infestation* series. *Buttons from the Scott Pearson collection; Bajoran ear ring from the Voyageur Press Collection; Salt and pepper shakers from ThinkGeek, Inc.*

**On the frontis:** The original *Starship Enterprise* from Playmates Toys.

Printed in China

# THIS IS FOR KATE

who can be assured that, should the Doomsday Machine actually near Earth,
Captain Kirk and the *Enterprise* will be there to defend us.

*Robert Greenberger*

# CONTENTS

# SIDEBARS

FOREWORD **REACHING FOR THE FINAL**

# *FRONTIER*

## AN ASTRONAUT'S PERSPECTIVE

Crew photo for STS-59, Thomas D. Jones's first shuttle mission, launched on April 9, 1994. Standing in rear, left to right: pilot Kevin P. Chilton and commander Sidney M. Gutierrez. Seated, left to right: payload commander Linda M. Godwin and mission specialists Jones, Jay Apt, and Michael R. Clifford.

# THOMAS D. JONES

When the first *Star Trek* episode aired on September 8, 1966, I was just eleven, already caught up in the excitement of the all-out race between America and the Soviet Union to put the first men on the moon. NASA's Project Gemini, launching two astronauts every other month to rehearse the major phases of a lunar landing mission, flew on Titan II boosters built in my hometown of Baltimore, Maryland. My town was living the Space Race, and my scrapbooks bulged with the latest news of rockets and astronauts.

*Star Trek* burst into my imagination as a "serious" sci-fi show with an expansive vision of human space exploration. Set nearly 300 years in the future, the series anticipated a future Earth society that had risen above national rivalries and established itself among the stars. The show's technological and societal optimism lent hope to my own dreams of spaceflight: if *Star Trek* was right, a young Boy Scout of 1966 might grow up with a decent chance of catching a ride on NASA's next generation of rockets.

Models of the starship *Enterprise* and a Klingon battle cruiser soon took flight in my darkened bedroom. Battery-powered bridge lights and warp engines lit up the linoleum-floored depths of interstellar space. With each new *Trek* episode, I wanted more than ever to be "out there" with Kirk and company.

Captain Kirk was my favorite character, a symbol of an America destined to open the space frontier as inexorably as the wagon trains of the pioneers raised the curtain on the American West. Like my favorite westerns, *Star Trek* projected America's independent character and courage into

Mission specialist Thomas D. Jones aboard space shuttle *Atlantis* during STS-98 in February 2001. *NASA*

a new world. The U.S. joined other nations in space, but there was no doubt who led. Americans would explore the galaxy, and I could be a part of that adventure.

*Star Trek*'s second season aired on Friday nights at around nine p.m., unfortunately just about the time when my weekly scout troop meeting was wrapping up. Every week, just after dismissal, I took off in a warp speed sprint for our living room, a couple of blocks away. Skidding to a landing in front of the TV, I'd usually make it just in time to hear Kirk intone " . . . where no man has gone before!"

At one of those Friday evening troop meetings, on January 27, 1967, I was preparing to bolt for home and the next *Trek* episode when I overheard the news of an accident at Cape Canaveral. Arms pumping, lungs burning, I gasped out a prayer on the run home that the astronauts were safe. That night, my optimistic view of spaceflight yielded to harsh reality as Walter Cronkite grimly announced the deaths of the Apollo 1 astronauts, killed in a flash fire on the launch pad.

Death made regular appearances on *Star Trek*, too (though usually sparing those outside the security division). But disaster never turned back Kirk and his crew. NASA was also undeterred—Apollo 11 would reach Tranquility Base just thirty months later. The Apollo 1 accident taught me that danger and death were inevitable elements of spaceflight. Yet true explorers forged on.

At the Air Force Academy in the mid-1970s, we cadets had no greater hero than the swashbuckling James T. Kirk, appearing daily in our TV lounge via the magic of syndication. The *Enterprise* crew still roamed the galaxy. There had to be a place there for me.

My dreams began to converge with reality as NASA christened its first space shuttle *Enterprise*. A decade later I'd completed six years in an Air Force jet cockpit and was wrapping up a science doctorate; my first astronaut application went to NASA the same year that *Challenger* broke up over the Atlantic. I was twice rejected, but partly

inspired by that decade's *Star Trek* films, I persisted. My third attempt got me a NASA interview, and I joined the U.S. astronaut corps in 1990.

The space shuttle was crude transportation compared to warp engines and transporter beams, but for me it was the fulfillment of a lifelong dream. Four times I was privileged to experience "standard orbit" around a Class M planet, this one our own Earth. My first two missions conducted extensive "sensor scans" of our home planet using the space radar lab payload mounted in the orbiter *Endeavour*'s cargo bay. On the second of those flights, STS-68, we filmed crewmate and laser physicist Jeff Wisoff launching small models of *Endeavour* and the starship *Enterprise* in a weightless race across our cabin's middeck. *Trek* was still with me, nearly thirty years after it first captured my imagination.

My third mission, aboard *Columbia*, found my crew falling silently around the nighttime face of the globe in a darkened cockpit. Our view out the windows was of a gaping hole in the stars, a darkened planet dappled by lightning flashes and starlit clouds. The swirl of the Milky Way and the star-filled cosmos stretched beyond, a universe so three-dimensional that we could project our imaginations outward into the galaxy. Kirk's viewscreen had nothing on this.

In 1966 even my eleven-year-old imagination could not guess that the *Enterprise*'s model of an international crew would be matched by NASA reality. My fourth mission took my crew—four men, one woman—to the International Space Station, where we joined an American and two Russians, the outpost's first residents. I'd arrived at "space dock" on spaceship *Atlantis*, and in the course of a week helped berth an American laboratory to a station with Russian living quarters and "escape pod." During three spacewalks, EVA partner Bob Curbeam and I outfitted the *Destiny* lab and scrambled over a space station that seemed to mimic Kirk's starship in flight. From my magnificent perch at the prow of the station, I drank in the incredible view of Earth, the glittering

silver and gold of the ISS, and above, the limitless expanse of "space, the final frontier." How many other dreams of spaceflight were propelled by the *Enterprise*'s warp engines, arriving decades later at breathtaking reality? I think the vision of *Star Trek* attracts us still, and it is our challenge to push our imaginations and abilities ever outward.

*Thomas David Jones went from* Star Trek *fan to NASA, joining the astronaut corps in 1990 and completing four space shuttle flights (STS-59 and STS-68 in 1994, STS-80 in 1996, and STS-98 in 2001) before retiring in 2001. His total mission time was 53 days 48 minutes. He is currently a science/space contributor for the Fox News channel. His website is www. AstronautTomJones.com.*

Jones performed three spacewalks on STS-98 while he and mission specialist Robert L. Curbeam attached the *Destiny* Laboratory Module to the International Space Station. *NASA*

# CHAPTER 1 GENE RODDENBERRY'S
# *DREAM*

Leonard Nimoy acknowledges a fan at an early convention appearance in New York, January 26, 1976. No doubt, the fire marshals had issues with the hordes of fans hanging on to his every word. *NY Daily News via Getty Images*

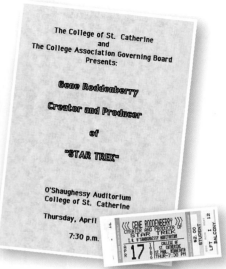

The College of St. Catherine
and
The College Association Governing Board
Presents:

Gene Roddenberry

Creator and Producer

of

"STAR TREK"

O'Shaughessy Auditorium
College of St. Catherine

Thursday, April

7:30 p.m.

*Above:* Program and ticket for a 1986 Gene Roddenberry speaking appearance. Roddenberry often spoke to college audiences, telling anecdotes about the show, running the pilot film and blooper reels, and taking audience questions.

*Left:* Las Vegas was host to the long-running *Star Trek: The Experience*, which became a must-visit destination for gamblers, Ferengi, and terran sightseers. *Time & Life Pictures/Getty Images*

The 850 fans attending Tricon, the 1966 World Science Fiction Convention held over the Labor Day weekend in Cleveland, Ohio, had no idea they were witnessing the birth of a phenomenon. In addition to appearances by author guest of honor L. Sprague de Camp and toastmaster Isaac Asimov, special screenings were scheduled. Among those was the pilot for a new NBC series, *Star Trek*, scheduled to debut days later, introduced by its creator, unknown Hollywood producer Gene Roddenberry.

The tall, stocky producer also brought some exotic costumes designed for the series by William Ware Theiss, hoping they'd be featured in the annual masquerade event, organized by John and Bjo Trimble. "There's no way I'm gonna let this damned Hollywood producer stick a couple of his damned costumes into my fashion show," Bjo Trimble maintained. But Roddenberry's persuasive charm overcame her resistance and the costumes made their appearance after all.

Other fan treats included screenings of 20th Century Fox's film *Fantastic Voyage*—the screenplay for which had been novelized by Asimov—and Irwin Allen's pilot for *The Time Tunnel*, a series set to debut a day after *Star Trek*. After the audience watched *The Time Tunnel*, Roddenberry introduced his series and said he was eager for feedback.

"We noticed people of varied races, genders, and planetary origins working together," convention attendee Allan Asherman wrote years later. "Here was a future it did not hurt to imagine. Here was a constructive tomorrow for mankind, emphasizing exploration and expansion. This was the science fiction television series we all wanted to see."

Roddenberry returned to the stage after the episode and was greeted with a standing ovation. He revealed that he had a second episode—the original series pilot, rejected by NBC—and it too was screened for the crowd, inaugurated as *Star Trek*'s first fans.

Five years earlier, Roddenberry was at a Los Angeles Dodgers game with his longtime friend, fellow writer Christopher Knopf. He told Knopf his idea for a series set in the late nineteenth century, aboard a dirigible that would take people of different races on worldwide adventures. He had been inspired by that year's *Master of the World*, a Vincent Price/Charles Bronson movie based on the works of Jules Verne, set aboard a fantastic airship.

Knopf later said, "There's no question in my mind this idea was absolutely the philosophical forerunner to *Star Trek*." Norman Felton, head of MGM-based Arena Productions, expressed interest in the concept, but there was no development money for such a potentially expensive proposition. Roddenberry liked to dream big.

*Above:* Gene Roddenberry poses with a model of the *U.S.S. Enterprise*, refit version, circa 1988. Originally designed by Matt Jeffries, the refit version introduced in *Star Trek: The Motion Picture* was designed by Andrew Probert working from Jeffries' own updates for the abandoned *Star Trek: Phase II* television series. © *Douglas Kirkland/Corbis*

*Above:* A B-17 bomber similar to the one that Roddenberry flew as copilot during World War II. *USAF*

*Right:* Jack Webb as Sgt. Joe Friday, the stone-faced police detective of *Dragnet*. Webb, the producer, creator, and star of the series, gave police officer Roddenberry his entre into Hollywood. *Associated Press*

E ugene Wesley Roddenberry was born on August 19, 1921, in El Paso, Texas, and was raised by his bigoted father, soldier-turned-railway-lineman Eugene Edward Roddenberry, and his mother Caroline. The family relocated to Los Angeles, where the elder Gene found work as a policeman. The younger Gene was a voracious reader, devouring 1930s pulp magazines filled with larger-than-life figures.

Uncertain of his future, despite his interest in writing, Roddenberry took police studies classes at Los Angeles City College. He joined, and soon led, the LACC Police Club, called the Archons, working as a liaison to the FBI. He also met and fell for Eileen Anita Rexroat.

While a student, Roddenberry trained as a pilot, enlisting in the United States Army Air Corps shortly before World War II. He married Eileen before being sent to the South Pacific where he was copilot on a B-17 Flying Fortress.

As the war ended, Roddenberry began flying for Pan Am even before his July 1945 discharge, making a smooth transition from military to civilian aircraft.

Gene and Eileen's first child Darleen was born in 1948. Soon after, Roddenberry left Pan Am and moved his family to California, determined to become a writer for the new medium of television.

Roddenberry joined the Los Angeles Police Department in February 1949, where new police Chief William H. Parker understood television's potential. Eventually, Roddenberry found himself in the Public Affairs Department, where he honed his skills writing speeches for Parker and articles for the in-house publication *The Beat*.

Jack Webb was paying $100 for good cop stories for his TV series *Dragnet*, so in 1951 Roddenberry offered his fellow officers a deal: they'd tell him their best stories and he'd write them up. If the stories were purchased, they would split the fee.

Roddenberry taught himself to write for television and he was hired in 1953 as a technical advisor when the popular radio crime show *Mr. District Attorney* moved to television. He sold his first script to producer Frederick W.

Ziv in March 1954. Now a sergeant, Roddenberry sold his first science fiction script, "The Secret Defense of 117" to *Four Star Playhouse*.

By this time, Roddenberry had also demonstrated a propensity for extramarital affairs and would have divorced Eileen had they not now been raising two daughters.

Roddenberry resigned from the force on June 7, 1956, to pursue writing fulltime. He wrote four pilots for Screen Gems hoping one would become a series. *333 Montgomery Street*, based on the book *Never Plead Guilty* by San Francisco criminal lawyer Jake Ehrlich and featuring DeForest Kelley as Jake Brittin, aired as part of *Alcoa Theater*. Another pilot pitch was *Hawaii Passage*, set aboard an ocean liner and focused on the ship's crew and their exploits. This unsold concept clearly resonated for Roddenberry and would be repurposed several times before someone actually bought the idea of a ship and its crew.

Roddenberry also borrowed from James A. Michener's *Tales of the South Pacific* for *The Wild Blue*, centered on two characters, Phil Pike and Eddie Jellicoe. Screen Gems backed the idea, renaming it *APO 923*, and CBS ordered a pilot filmed. The show included a supporting character, Lt. James T. Irvine, and demonstrated the first sketch of the later Kirk-Spock-McCoy triumvirate.

Roddenberry's writing deal at Screen Gems, housed at MGM, led to several momentous events, including his introduction to aspiring actress Majel Lee Hudec. Using the stage name Majel Barrett, she approached finding roles like a salesman going door to door, impressing the writer.

Desperate to sell a pilot, Roddenberry appealed to Arena's Norman Felton. His pitch merged themes from an episode of *Dr. Kildare*, his Michener idea, and his own wartime experiences. The script, written in January 1963, was quickly approved and MGM

*Left:* For every future member of Stafleet, a bib and spoon set for infants. *ThinkGeek, Inc.*

*Below:* The well-dressed baby geek can display his or her Starfleet career destination. *ThinkGeek, Inc.*

arranged to shoot at the Army's Camp Pendleton near San Diego, using soldiers as extras. Respected journeyman director Buzz Kulik was hired and Roddenberry's fledgling producer skills were immediately tested. Roddenberry didn't realize how many crucial decisions needed to be made quickly during production, and it was exacerbated by his drinking, rocky marriage, and self-promotion as he posed for the cameras. Kulik summoned Felton to the location to sort out the problems. The haphazard production ran late, forcing a rushed edit followed by a cross-country flight so MGM could screen the show for all three networks in a single day in New York; within twenty-four hours, NBC bought *The Lieutenant*.

Twenty-six-year-old Gary Lockwood starred as Marine Corps Second Lieutenant William Tiberius Rice, paired with Robert Vaughn, riding high from his work in *The Magnificent Seven*. Roddenberry's heavy rewriting of the scripts for the show angered many writers and taxed his time. Story editor Del Reisman functioned as stand-in producer, making

daily decisions for a show constantly behind schedule. Aspiring writer Dorothy Fontana was lured away from producer/writer Sam Peeples and joined Roddenberry and Reisman as secretary. Casting for *The Lieutenant* was done by newcomer Joe D'Agosta.

Citing growing public dissatisfaction with the military and the Vietnam War, NBC informed Felton that *The Lieutenant* would be canceled after just one season. Roddenberry wrote the final episode, "To Kill a Man," recycling themes from the unsold *APO 923* pilot as Rice arrived in Southeast Asia to replace a fellow soldier named Robert April.

As production ended on *The Lieutenant*, Roddenberry refined his earlier dirigible idea. The past became the future, the dirigible a starship, and character relationships gelled. On March 11, 1964, Roddenberry completed a sixteen-page premise for a series called *Star Trek*. He registered it with the Writers Guild on April 24, just as *The Lieutenant* ended.

His premise introduced the multiracial crew of the starship *U.S.S. Yorktown*: Thirty-four-year-old Captain Robert April, styled after novelist C. S. Forester's Captain Horatio Hornblower; the enigmatic female second-in-command; the South American navigator; the senior medical officer; the young, sexy yeoman; and the half-Martian/half-human first lieutenant, Spock, a red-hued man who ingested food through

Basque Nationalist Party candidate Juan Jose Ibarretxe (at podium) is flanked by other party members dressed for a "Mr. Spock Party" in the northern Spanish Basque city of Bilbao in February 2009. Ibarretxe is known as Mr. Spock for his resemblance to the character. *Rafa Rivas/AFP/Getty Images*

*Left:* Yoko Ono (center) and her son Sean and his girlfriend Bijou Phillips wait to be transported during their visit to a *Star Trek* convention at Hyde Park, London, in 2002. *Martyn Hayhow/AFP/Getty Images*

a plate in his stomach. Roddenberry included twenty-five brief story ideas to demonstrate the scope of the concept.

Roddenberry pitched *Star Trek* to MGM and then other studios. In early summer 1964, MGM turned down the project, ending Roddenberry's successful relationship with the studio. By then, he had received an interesting offer from Desilu, a production company formed by comedienne Lucille Ball and her husband Desi Arnaz.

Desilu wanted to produce dramatic television after years of producing situation comedies starring the couple. The company had bought the old RKO studios, adjacent to Paramount Pictures on Melrose Avenue and Gower Street. After their divorce, Arnaz was bought out as company president in November 1962, and Ball's first significant step was hiring twenty-six-year CBS veteran Oscar Katz as programming chief. Needing an exec who really understood television production, Katz then hired Herb Solow away from NBC.

Desilu had money to spend. Ball's contract with CBS provided Desilu with $500,000 annually for series development, with a guarantee that one pilot would be filmed, though not necessarily purchased. Ted Ashley of the Ashley-Famous talent agency agreed to represent the studio and Ashley agent Alden Schwimmer suggested to Katz he sign a drama producer and a comedy producer to long-term development deals. As a result, Roddenberry was contracted for three years.

Given all the existing relationships, Desilu pitched *Star Trek* to CBS first. Solow helped Roddenberry refine the premise into more of a continuing series. He also conceived the Captain's Log narration voiceover to set the stage and quickly launch stories.

Roddenberry and Katz pitched to CBS, where network President James T. Aubrey asked pointed questions, concerned that Desilu wouldn't be able to deliver a high-priced, special effects-laden drama. CBS ultimately passed, using their recent acquisition of Irwin Allen's *Lost in Space* as an excuse.

Katz, Solow, Schwimmer, and Roddenberry honed their approach. Recognizing Roddenberry's limitations as a salesman, Solow made the pitch to NBC Program Development Vice President Jerry Stanley and West Coast Programming chief Grant Tinker in May. Both were intrigued and Roddenberry outlined what would become "The Cage." Tinker's trust in former lieutenant Solow convinced him to commission a pilot episode.

Roddenberry crafted three varied but well-developed springboards—"The Women," "Landru's Paradise," and "The Cage." The network selected "The Cage," wanting Desilu to prove they could actually pull off Roddenberry's ambitious concept. Roddenberry worked diligently and had the outlines completed in late June, submitting the final one on the twenty-ninth. By then, the *Yorktown* had become the *Enterprise*.

# CHAPTER 2 THE PILOTS

The model *Enterprise* used for filming the original series
originally was on display amidst real world aircraft at
the Museum of Air and Space. *Howard Weinstein*

In time, the model would be refurbished and moved to the gift store, making it a must-visit destination for series fans making their pilgrimage to Washington, D.C. *Howard Weinstein*

NBC provided $435,000 toward the costs of the script and filmed episode, but the budget for "The Cage" was close to $600,000. Ball and the Desilu board of directors took a leap of faith and decided to deficit finance the difference. They believed in Roddenberry's concept, and they wanted a show on NBC.

But what would the *U.S.S. Enterprise* look like? Where would the captain sit? Roddenberry delved into the latest scientific theories and astronomical research. He used his Pentagon contacts to access the Air Force's Weapons Effects and Test Group, which in turn pointed him toward California's RAND Corporation think tank. There, Roddenberry met physicist Harvey P. Lynn, who consulted with Roddenberry for those crucial first eighteen months of the show's life. It was Lynn who first anticipated the shuttlecraft and shuttle bay, and he took Roddenberry's fuzzy sense of astro-geography and made it fit actual astronomical charts. Roddenberry, though, chose to give the planets distinct names as opposed to the dry combination of letters and numbers used by astronomers.

Lynn also helped Roddenberry envision energy-beam weaponry beyond the newfangled lasers just becoming commonplace in the world. After calling the weapons "laser pistols" in the pilot, Roddenberry later ignored Lynn's suggestions and chose "phaser," feeling that the similarity to the already familiar term laser would help audiences understand the futuristic weapon.

Roddenberry asked Desilu's production designer Pato Guzman to study the look of MGM's 1956 feature *Forbidden Planet*. That movie's design and approach to telling a humanistic science fiction story was quite influential on Roddenberry in those early days. Roddenberry soon met *Ben Casey*'s production designer Walter (Matt) Jeffries, a member of the Aviation Space Writers Association. Jeffries gave the series its streamlined look and the starship its identification number. International aviation agreements labeled United States planes with an N but Gene asked for more letters, so, thinking about visual clarity on a small screen, Jeffries added the CC. The *Enterprise* became NCC-1701.

In August, Roddenberry turned to Kellam de Forest, a researcher with offices at Desilu, hoping his team could help determine how the future might look. Such research would play a key role in the show's success and longevity, even if

One of the Talosians who captured Captain Pike in the first pilot, from the nine-inch-tall Playmates series of *Trek* characters.

Captain Christopher Pike, as represented in the Playmates Toys line of 4.5-inch action figures.

Madison Dylan as Vina the Orion slave girl with *Free Enterprise* writer/director Robert Meyer Burnett at WonderCon 2012 in Anaheim, California. Although the *Femme Fatales* actress was just introduced to *Star Trek* in the last year by Burnett and Mark A. Altman, writer/producer of *Free Enterprise*, she quickly became a die-hard fan. *Courtesy of Madison Dylan*

Thanks to the original TV pitch (and his eventual appearance in the animated series and various tie-in novels and comic books), Robert April is remembered as the first captain of the *Enterprise*, but for a brief time before the November 25 draft placed Christopher Pike in the center seat, James Winter was the starship's captain.

Roddenberry would eventually come to dread the nitpicking comments coming from de Forest.

William Ware Theiss, a costume designer with credits including *Spartacus*, was tasked with both exotic alien attire and starship crew uniforms.

Roddenberry liked ABC's SF anthology series *The Outer Limits*, and wound up hiring from their production ranks. Solow wanted Robert Justman to come over to work as associate director, but Justman refused at first, saying he didn't possess the requisite post-production knowledge. Solow appealed to *OL* creator Leslie Stevens and borrowed Justman for about a month's work.

Justman tapped *Outer Limits* colleague Fred Phillips to design the alien makeups, from Spock's pointed ears to the heads for the guest alien race, the Talosians. He also had to figure out how to turn an actress into a green Orion slave girl, which led to one of the most oft-told legends of the series. A shade of green was applied to Majel Barrett, and then filmed. The lab processed it, and everyone was shocked to see a Caucasian skin tone. The process was repeated with the same results, until a call revealed that since no one had told the lab technicians Barrett was supposed to be green, they kept correcting the "mistake" by adjusting the color resolution.

Budget and production realities forced some changes—originally conceived as crab creatures, the Talosians became big-headed humanoids, which incidentally helped separate *Star Trek* from the bug-eyed-monster science fiction films common in the 1950s. Prop genius Wah Chang left *The Outer Limits* long enough to work with Phillips to design and craft the Talosian head appliances, complete with tiny ears and throbbing veins. Janos Prohaska, who had designed alien beings for the ABC series, contributed the anthropoid ape from the episode "Fun and Games," and the humanoid bird from "The Duplicate Man" to fill Talos IV's alien zoo.

Even though Roddenberry read and liked science fiction, he wasn't steeped in its history. Early on, he sought out television-and-science-fiction writer Jerry Sohl to learn more about the current state of the genre. The two hit it off and became friends. Fellow screenwriter Samuel Peeples also served as a guide to the science fiction world. In many ways, it was Peeples who pointed Roddenberry toward a more literate take on the future, which resulted in several noted authors writing *Star Trek* stories.

By summer 1964, *Star Trek*'s core elements were taking shape. In September, a nearly complete draft went to NBC for their feedback. According to Solow, Roddenberry chafed at their "interference" regardless of the notes' validity, a portent of fights to come. Still, subject to minor revisions, NBC gave their approval to film the script and Robert Butler was hired to direct. Butler had already filmed dozens of TV episodes and would later attain a stellar record directing pilots beyond *Star Trek*.

From the start, Roddenberry wanted Majel Barrett to work on the show and she was the first person cast, as Number One, the stoic second-in-command. Roddenberry had hoped for Martin Landau to play Spock, but was turned down. Roddenberry's former star and regular drinking partner Gary Lockwood claims he suggested *The Lieutenant* guest star Leonard Nimoy to become the Vulcan. Marc Daniels recalled that Roddenberry had been off the set when that *Lieutenant* episode was produced, and it was Daniels, the director of the episode, who had hired Nimoy for the guest shot, a fortuitous event for Roddenberry.

Feature film actor Jeffrey Hunter was chosen to play Captain Pike. A serious man who'd already headlined one TV series, *Temple Houston*, Hunter was prepared for television's fast production pace. Butler rejected DeForest Kelley for Dr. Boyce and selected the older John Hoyt. Butler also chose Peter Duryea as navigator José Tyler and helped choose Susan Oliver in the guest role of Vina. Butler and Roddenberry agreed on casting women as the frail, telepathic Talosians, using male voiceovers to give them an otherworldly quality.

Laurel Goodwin, a child model turned actress, was the youngest member of the cast, playing Yeoman J. M. Colt.

Production commenced at Desilu's Culver City studios on November 27, 1964, with a scene between Dr. Boyce and Captain Pike.

Butler and Roddenberry may have been in synch during preproduction, but as the cameras rolled, they clashed over how gritty the sets should look. The producer prevailed, insisting on a spotless future, a *Star Trek* hallmark for decades to come. As a result, Butler was somewhat dismissive of his own efforts, telling interviewers that *Star Trek*'s future world was "too square-jawed, heroic" and "too worthy and clean" for him.

Alexander Courage was hired to score the episode in January 1965 and he created several audio special effects,

Some *Enterprise* crew members brought mess hall sporks on landing parties because you just never know when you might be stuck planetside during meal times. *ThinkGeek, Inc.*

*Above:* In the future, incoming cadets of Starfleet Academy will be issued towels (and sporks) on their first day in the dorms.

*Below:* The official Starfleet Academy spork. Some technologies never go out of style. *ThinkGeek, Inc.*

TM & © 2009 CBS

EX ASTRIS, SCIENTIA

STARFLEET ACADEMY™ snow peak

**Both Majel Barrett and Leonard Nimoy guest-starred in "In the Highest Tradition," an episode near the end of the first and only season of *The Lieutenant*, Roddenberry's first series.**

including the planet's "singing" plants. His stirring theme music added just the right touch to the sixty-three-minute film, using soprano Loulie Jean Norman to sing above an orchestra playing a somewhat jazzy beat. And that whooshing sound as the *Enterprise* streaks across the screen? That was Courage doing vocal sound effects. The composer also used a five-piece band to record various sounds, giving each planet distinctive, unearthly sounds.

The cast and crew were treated to a screening before it was shown to NBC and they recognized this was a unique production, a cut above typical television. There was other screenings as well, one of which was attended by DeForest Kelley, who had become friends with Roddenberry. He told the producer, "Well, I don't know what the hell it's all about, but it's either gonna be the biggest hit or the biggest miss God ever made."

NBC rejected the pilot in March, stunning Solow and Roddenberry—but not Butler. The cliché has been that the network called it "too cerebral," but the reality appears to be that it was too staid and serious, a little too-mind-bending with its themes of reality versus dreams. And despite network approval of the script, a woman in a command role apparently bothered them, while the pointy-eared fellow worried the sales department.

The execs still liked the premise and they were reluctant to walk away from their investment. On March 26, NBC's Mort Werner called Solow and surprisingly agreed to order a second pilot. Desilu had proven they could make a complex film, but now NBC wanted an action-oriented story, more representative of what the weekly series would be. Before they'd pay for a new script, NBC had several demands, the first of which was getting rid of Number One. They also wanted the alien off the bridge, but Roddenberry prevailed in keeping the character as a visual reminder that *Star Trek* presented a future populated by more than humans from Earth. Roddenberry also claimed years later that NBC attempted to whitewash the cast, while

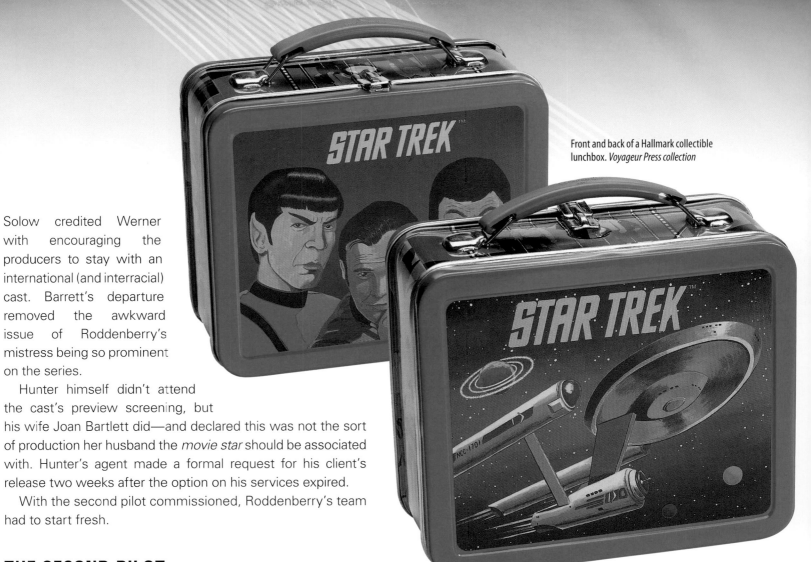

Solow credited Werner with encouraging the producers to stay with an international (and interracial) cast. Barrett's departure removed the awkward issue of Roddenberry's mistress being so prominent on the series.

Hunter himself didn't attend the cast's preview screening, but his wife Joan Bartlett did—and declared this was not the sort of production her husband the *movie star* should be associated with. Hunter's agent made a formal request for his client's release two weeks after the option on his services expired.

With the second pilot commissioned, Roddenberry's team had to start fresh.

## THE SECOND PILOT

NBC asked for more story springboards so Roddenberry revised "The Women" as "Mudd's Women," assigning the script to Stephen Kandel. He also crafted the somewhat hokey "The Omega Glory," which he scripted himself. Roddenberry then asked Samuel Peeples to generate story ideas, one of which was commissioned as a script.

Kandel took ill so his script wasn't completed in time to meet NBC's schedule, although it would be produced as part of the first season. That left a choice between "The Omega Glory" and Peeples's "Where No Man Has Gone Before." NBC preferred the conflict in Peeples's story for its tighter focus on the captain and a clear antagonist. In late May 1965, the script was reviewed and approved.

James Goldstone, a known quantity to Solow and Roddenberry, had been selected to direct before a script was chosen, enabling him to add his input. Sets were refurbished, costumes modified, and a new Starfleet cast was recruited.

Roddenberry already had his eye on some young, charismatic actors to replace Hunter. After being turned down by Jack Lord (who went on to fame in the original *Hawaii Five-O*) and Lloyd Bridges (star of *Sea Hunt*), the producer got third-time lucky.

Canadian-born William Shatner had been around Hollywood for a while, beginning with a role in *The Brothers Karamazov*. Around the time "The Cage" was shooting, he and future Batman, Adam West, were making their own unsuccessful pilot, *Alexander the Great*.

Roddenberry showed "The Cage" to Shatner, who liked the flawed, brooding lead, and recognized a terrific opportunity. He also thought everyone took themselves way too seriously

Above: Golden Trivia Games were available in many editions, covering such properties as Disney, *M*A*S*H*, and, of course, *Star Trek*.

Below: Modern-day office dwellers can be warned when visitors come by thanks to this replica communications device based on the original series. *ThinkGeek, Inc.*

and the second pilot needed to lighten up. Roddenberry agreed, but also planned to give his lead an obligatory action-star fistfight.

Rather than recasting Pike, Roddenberry created a new captain—James T. Kirk (a name selected as late as May 1965; the middle name Tiberius was lifted from *The Lieutenant*). Many of Number One's traits were transferred to Spock. In "The Cage," Nimoy's somewhat bombastic performance was a conscious attempt to counterpoint Hunter's brooding captain, so he appreciated playing a more fully developed character. Spock, still the science officer, would also become second-in-command.

The bridge also featured Lloyd Haynes at communications (a rare nonstereotypical role for a black actor) and Paul Carr at the helm. George Takei represented astrophysics and James Doohan was first seen as a nameless engineer with a Scottish accent. Doohan, a Canadian with a gift for dialect, auditioned using a variety of accents; when asked which he preferred, he told the producers that engineers are Scottish born so they went with his choice. Paul Fix was Dr. Mark Piper, a father figure reminiscent of the Pike/Boyce relationship. Roddenberry never warmed to Fix's portrayal and made a mental note to cast DeForest Kelley if the series got picked up.

The second pilot took nine days to shoot, between July 19 and 29, 1965. As the post-production process stretched into the fall, Roddenberry turned his attention to producing *Police Story*, another pilot for a thirty-minute drama, starring Steven Inhat, DeForest Kelley, and Grace Lee Whitney. Then Solow hired Roddenberry to produce *The Long Hunt of April Savage*, written by Sam Rolfe, a writer Roddenberry respected. However, Roddenberry infuriated one and all by informing ABC he'd be unavailable to produce the series should *April Savage* sell. The pilot starred Robert Lansing, and Justman, who served as associate producer, recalls it as a haphazard production—during which Roddenberry decided to flex his muscles by ordering Justman to throw ABC executive Harve Bennett off the set.

The cast of *Star Trek*, circa 1967: James Doohan as Scotty, DeForest Kelley as Dr. McCoy, Walter Koenig as Chekov, Majel Barrett as Nurse Chapel, William Shatner as Kirk, Nichelle Nichols as Uhura, Leonard Nimoy as Spock, and George Takei as Sulu. © *Sunset Boulevard/Corbis*

*Star Trek*'s second pilot originally had an alternate opening voiceover: "*Enterprise* log, Captain James Kirk commanding. We are leaving that vast cloud of stars and planets which we call our galaxy. Behind us, Earth, Mars, Venus, even our Sun, are specks of dust. The question: What is out there in the black void beyond? Until now our mission has been that of space law regulation, contact with Earth colonies, and investigation of alien life. But now, a new task: A probe out into where no man has gone before."

A musical score was belatedly added to the *Star Trek* pilot in late November, and the episode was screened for NBC. Before committing, the network did an audience test that yielded horrible scores. Solow pointed out the pilot had been screened for senior women, an odd demographic for testing a primetime series. NBC retested the pilot to a better sampling of men, women, and youth, which provided a truer and more positive score.

NBC bought the show on March 6, 1966, adding it to its 1966–67 schedule. Roddenberry and Desilu celebrated and then got to work adapting the pilot into an ongoing series. They had just six months to be up and running.

John D. F. Black, who had just won a Writers Guild of America award for an episode of *Mr. Novak*, was quickly hired as story editor. He was unfamiliar with science fiction, but was charmed by Roddenberry, who persuaded him to take the job hours after Black won his award. While the producer had a talented production crew in place, he needed writers.

Roddenberry had taken the new pilot to the Writers Guild and screened it for interested writers, pitching the series with the improved showmanship that became his hallmark in subsequent years. Jerry Sohl liked what he heard, as did Harlan Ellison, who'd just won an Emmy award for *The Outer Limits'* "Demon with a Glass Hand." As premises and early drafts arrived, Roddenberry read them and gave the writers detailed memos highlighting where things skewed from the bible, or had to be altered based on the evolving concept of the crew and their relationships. Tight budgets meant some grandiose concepts had to be scaled back or reconsidered entirely.

Alterations were also made to the cast. While Roddenberry felt Paul Fix just wasn't the actor he envisioned for the doctor, he decided the character of communications officer Alden was too boring, costing Lloyd Haynes his role. By May, Roddenberry conceived of a new communications officer, a sexy woman. He suggested they cast Nichelle Nichols, who by then was having an affair with him.

Justman took Roddenberry's vague notions of the planets visited and wrote an April 12 memo limiting the worlds visited to those with Earth-like conditions, later called M-Class.

For the first season, Roddenberry retained Harvey Lynn as his scientific consultant for $50 per episode. Lynn went on to suggest things that became the vocal shipboard computer and sick bay's diagnostic beds. In many ways, Lynn was the show's unheralded godfather.

CHAPTER 3

# *STAR TREK*

# THE FIRST SEASON

Chekov, Uhura, Spock, Kirk, McCoy, Scotty, and Sulu in their Playmates Toys incarnations.

Working with Roddenberry that frantic spring of 1966 were his secretary D. C. Fontana, and John D. F. Black, who arrived on April 19. Black was welcomed into the fold with what became a Roddenberry trademark: a sexually provocative practical joke. Majel Barrett, whom Black had never met, arrived at his office ostensibly to audition for the series—and proceeded to unbutton her sweater as she purred she would be willing to do *anything* for a role.

Gradually, a rhythm was established as Black and Roddenberry focused on scripts while Justman did the actual production work. Once scripts began coming in, it fell to Roddenberry to make them consistent with his vision of the future. Early episodes variously refer to the ship's authority deriving from the United Earth Space Probe Agency, Star Service, Spacefleet Command, and even Space Central. Only with the episode "Court Martial" do Starfleet and the United Federation of Planets get used regularly. To Roddenberry's credit, his conception of *Star Trek*'s setting quickly became fairly cohesive. In time, events from previous episodes were referenced, reinforcing the notion that what happened had consequences. At the time, not every primetime series could say the same thing.

NBC had just hired their first black programming executive, Stanley Robertson, and Werner and Tinker had concerns about how some of their producers might react. Roddenberry's request to work with Robinson eased some of that tension. Despite his public proclamations he had to fight the network to keep Uhura on the bridge, NBC was as in favor of racial integration as he was.

Surely an example of how far and wide *Star Trek* merchandise has spread: Kirk and Spock nutcrackers. *ThinkGeek, Inc.*

Justman arranged for Monday, May 23, 1966, as a rehearsal day, unusual for episodic television. That helped the cast and crew get prepared for the start of shooting the next day on Jerry Sohl's "The Corbomite Maneuver," directed by the veteran Joseph Sargent.

Despite Roddenberry and his crew prepping for months, the first three episodes each went over schedule and over budget, causing alarm among the production team. Things were set aright by director Marc Daniels who stepped in to helm "The Man Trap." When the scheduled director of the next episode took a feature film instead, the executives asked Daniels to stay on for a second straight episode, a highly unusual practice but one that allowed nerves to settle.

# WHAT NO FAN HAD SEEN BEFORE

*Maggie Thompson*

"The show you are about to see will top any science fiction experience you've had until now!" I'm paraphrasing here, but that was pretty much what the ABC representative told those of us at the preview. My guess is that the date was September 3, 1966; in any case, it was at some point during Tricon in Cleveland, Ohio.

Amid his fervent promises to the audience of hard-core science fiction fans was that the excellences of the episode would drive us en masse to discard our black-and-white television sets in order to substitute color sets so as to best savor the wonders of the new series.

All *right*, then! This could be cool!

And the assembled fans sat relatively quietly (though with increasingly sarcastic comments to one another) through "Rendezvous with Yesterday," the first episode of Irwin Allen's *The Time Tunnel*, starring James Darren. Attendees, at home with the ins and outs of time-travel fiction, found nothing out of the ordinary in either premise or execution. Moreover, many of us found considerable amusement at scenes in which supposedly smart characters were less than savvy in the midst of an expedition to the past. The rest of America got to see the episode less than a week later—but few of us in that preview audience bothered to give *The Time Tunnel* a second look.

As noted, the audience had become restive and unimpressed, despite the guest appearance of science fiction fan-favorite Michael Rennie as captain of the *Titanic*. In fact, such attendees as my late husband, Don, and I had become downright hostile to the idea that TV would do right by science fiction that season.

And then Gene Roddenberry addressed us.

He didn't promise that we would trot right out to buy a color TV set. He didn't say we'd be staggered by the wonders of what he was about to show us. He didn't compare or contrast his project to that of *The Time Tunnel*. As I remember it, he came across as self-effacing and simply said something along the lines of, "I know you are all experts on science fiction and I just hope you enjoy what I'm about to show you."

We saw "The Cage." I think we later saw "Where No Man Has Gone Before." In any case, in the course of the weekend, those of us in the convention's futuristic "fashion show" spent time with the professional model who wore the "straps" costume from "What Are Little Girls Made Of?" Throughout the convention, Roddenberry circulated among the fans, repeatedly reminding us of his project, engaging us in conversation and simultaneously feeding fans' egos and letting us feel that he loved science fiction as much as we did.

Don and I chatted briefly with him following the showings, when we commented to him that we thought that "the guy with the ears" would be "the next Illya Kuryakin" (referring to the popular *The Man from U.N.C.L.E.* character played by David McCallum). His response was something along the lines of, "Really? Well, I hope so, but it had never occurred to me."

Enjoy what we were about to see? Become a fan of the guy with the ears? Who'd have thought it? We were blown away.

On September 8, the rest of the nation was introduced to the series to which we'd had a delicious early introduction. And the rest, as they say, was the future.

*Maggie Thompson is senior editor of* Comics Buyer's Guide, *and the daughter of science fiction writer Betsy Curtis—who introduced her to the world of science fiction and conventions.*

# SHOOTING THE FIRST SEASON

Bob Justman asked Matt Jeffries to reassemble the bridge in six "wild" sections, any of which could be removed to allow a wider variety of camera angles. The two had used a scale model of Stage 9 to make the sets fit in the most economical manner. During the series' three seasons, permanent sets were often redressed to save construction costs—a conference room could double as a crewman's cabin. Justman subsequently built a four-foot-long scale model of the permanent sets so new directors could familiarize themselves prior to shooting their episodes.

Not only did a starship have to be constructed, but the crew needed to be outfitted. Roddenberry wanted the phaser pistols to be modular and the communicators more compact than those used initially. The producer had also thought of the tricorder, a scanning-recording device that the captain's yeoman would use during missions. Wah Chang and Gene Warren at Project Unlimited were hired to create these props. Replicating their sleek and futuristic creations in quantity gave Desilu's prop department fits, and their efforts ultimately were rejected by Roddenberry and Justman. When Project Unlimited got the contract to produce additional props, the studio's department filed a union grievance. Justman skirted this by claiming Wah Chang independently designed the props that *Star Trek* simply purchased.

Irving Feinberg designed the remainder of the props, finding innovative uses for everyday items that employed a modern design. Any number of these, notably medical tools, were actually salt and pepper shakers with a new paint job. In honor of his work, the medical scanner was finally dubbed a Feinberger.

Desilu was pressuring Solow, who pressured Justman, to find ways to stay on, or preferably under, budget. Producing a weekly science fiction mini-film for $193,000 each (the 2012 equivalent of approximately $1.3 million) tested the

*Above:* A set of decals featuring ships and characters of the original series, such as the giant spear-carrying Taurean of the episode "The Galileo Seven."

*Left:* A sticker set from Ambassador. Doubling up on Spock and Kirk left no room for Chekov and Sulu.

ingenuity of everyone involved. In order to keep the production on schedule, costumer Theiss resorted to operating a nonunion "sweatshop" in a nearby apartment, smuggling finished costumes through the show's mimeograph room window each morning. Theiss quickly gained a reputation for designing exceedingly sexy women's costumes, egged on by Roddenberry.

Ed Milkis, a former assistant editor on *The Lieutenant*, was hired to supervise special effects work. Effects Hollywood soon became the primary supplier—but *Star Trek* eventually had to employ five companies to meet all its special effects needs.

One key element wasn't sorted out until weeks before the show's premiere. On August 1, Justman insisted that Shatner

Who doesn't want to eat cookies out of Spock's torso? *ThinkGeek, Inc.*

record narration lasting no more than fifteen seconds for the title sequence. Justman took a stab at a draft, which Black refined. Nine days later, Shatner was called away from shooting to record the narration, which, with the addition of some reverberation, became an immortal introduction to an iconic series. Roddenberry himself sat a moviola editing machine to piece together the footage that went on to become the title sequence.

Roddenberry decided weeks before the series debuted that he needed production help to keep up with the grueling schedule and hired Gene L. Coon for the remaining thirteen episodes. Coon was a Korean War radio correspondent–turned–fiction writer who had established himself as a writing machine for prime time series across many genres. As a result, Roddenberry took the title Executive Producer. Around this time, he also started to be known as the Great Bird of the Galaxy, after Bob Justman started making joking references in the many memos that flew between offices during the show's production.

Coon was assigned Andee Richardson as his secretary, the first African-American in such a role at Desilu. She fit right into the manic production team and had such a good sense of humor; she would often answer the phone with: "Coon's office! Coon's coon speaking."

While the show featured strong character drama, and the trio of Kirk, Spock, and McCoy solidified, it also tackled contemporary issues through science fiction tales. Over the years, Roddenberry claimed more credit for elements in the series than documentation and collective memory would suggest. His reputation has been lionized, canonized, and brutalized as a result, but Nimoy told one biographer, "I remember very specifically a script we were having trouble with, I went to do a scene with [DeForest Kelley] and there were some new pages in it. We started to play it, and it was a pleasure to play. We looked at each other and said, 'This is Gene.' Gene had rewritten this scene. You could tell the difference. He had an attack, he had a use of language, he had a subtextual approach. When he was on his game, he was brilliant."

As scripts got stronger, they required less of Roddenberry's touch, but still the story editors would approach him with story problems and his writer's instincts

Uniform patches of the *Enterprise* NCC-1701, signifying the sciences division (left) and operations division. *Voyageur Press collection*

solved problems quickly. Roddenberry continued to try and elevate the status of women, although such efforts were often watered down or eliminated by the time rewrites, shooting, and editing occurred.

Roddenberry's obsessive control over scripts contradicted his agreement with Black, who had put his own reputation on the line to bring respected writers to the show. Black threatened to quit after Roddenberry rewrote the first script before the two could even compare notes. In time, more than a few writers felt burned by the production company and used pseudonyms, feeling Roddenberry sucked the originality from the stories, while the producer argued he was protecting his vision.

Harlan Ellison was one such writer, whose experiences with Roddenberry led to an extended feud between the two men, with Ellison continuing to tell his side even after Roddenberry's death. According to legend, Ellison repeatedly delayed delivery of his script. Between June 3 and February 1, 1967, Ellison, story editors Steven Carabatsos and D. C. Fontana, and Roddenberry himself all took turns rewriting and polishing. Ultimately, "The City on the Edge of Forever," with its doomed romance between Captain Kirk and Edith Keeler, would become perhaps the best-received episode of the series.

Black finally departed in August, to be replaced by Steven Carabatsos—but he too left after only a few months. Apparently, working for Roddenberry was an acquired taste; while he engendered loyalty from some, including Dorothy Fontana and Justman, many others were infuriated with his passive/aggressive manner.

Before leaving the production, Black found a way to save money and production time by writing a script for a framing story that would allow use of "The Cage" pilot that featured the *Enterprise*'s earlier captain. In time, Roddenberry did a polish and claimed sole script credit, which became a sore spot when the episode was up for Hugo and Emmy Award consideration.

"The City on the Edge of Forever" by Harlan Ellison is a fan-favorite episode of the original series. Playmates Toys issued special Kirk and Spock figures in the period clothing they wore after traveling back in time to Depression-era New York City, along with the twentieth-century woman Kirk fell for, Edith Keeler, played by Joan Collins.

The Guardian of Forever from "The City on the Edge of Forever" was re-created for "Star Trek: The Tour," on display here at the Queen Mary Dome in Long Beach. It was a prime photo op for fans visiting the exhibit. *Axel Koester/Corbis*

The Gorn, inspired by Fredric Brown's short story "Arena," has become one the original series' most recognizable alien life forms thanks to appearances in other media such as *The Big Bang Theory*.

Treylane, "The Squire of Gothos", was one of the original series' more colorful characters, thanks in large part to William Campbell's performance.

In late September, Fontana finally felt she could quit her day job and become a fulltime freelance writer. Soon after, Roddenberry asked her to revise Jerry Sohl's "The Way of the Spores." Her former boss dangled Carabatsos's soon-to-be-vacant story editor's role as a carrot and she agreed, turning the script into "This Side of Paradise." She thus became the first female story editor for an action-adventure primetime series, another barrier Roddenberry helped pierce.

Early on, the scripting tended to mirror contemporary 1960s dramatic writing, focusing on interchanges between the lead and one supporting player, as with Kirk and Spock's debate, or the captain's confrontation with Gary Mitchell in the second pilot. In time, there were exchanges between Kirk and McCoy, but the famed trio of Kirk, Spock, and McCoy—often seen as the Id, Ego, and Superego personified—didn't really start to appear until "Balance of Terror." Once Roddenberry saw his performers in action, he began writing to their strengths, leading to some of television's best character dynamics.

The cast also grew more comfortable with their characters. Nimoy introduced the Vulcan neck pinch early in the first season (inspired by a reference in Richard Matheson's "The Enemy Within") and later suggested the Vulcan salute (lifted from ancient Hebrew ceremonies). Shimon Wincelberg conceived the mind-meld in "Dagger of the Mind," and during the second season, Fontana filled in Spock's heritage, giving his parents names and personalities in the classic "Journey to Babel," while Theodore Sturgeon gave us a glimpse into Vulcan culture in "Amok Time."

As production continued, deals were revised and, in order to afford fuller cast commitments, one actor would have to be dropped. Given her character's background status in most stories, and her personal battles with diet pills and alcohol, Grace Lee Whitney, initially cast as the captain's yeoman, was cut.

Roddenberry's 1964 premise didn't include a recurring nemesis, but once the antagonistic Romulans arrived in "Balance of Terror," they seemed a natural fit. Written by

Paul Schneider, "Balance" owed a lot to *Run Silent Run Deep* and *The Enemy Below*, World War II movies released less than a decade earlier. It also featured the first shipboard wedding, with Kirk's opening lines later reused on both *The Next Generation* and *Deep Space Nine* as well as at countless real-world weddings.

Later, Gene Coon wrote "Errand of Mercy," a cautionary tale about two superpowers letting hostilities escalate into climactic conflict. The Klingons may have been stand-ins for the Soviets, but, thanks to Coon's script and John Colicos's charismatic performance as Kor, they proved an interesting return antagonist for Kirk and crew.

Recycling remained a part of *Star Trek* and Roddenberry's legacy. For example, in "The Return of the Archons," he borrowed the name from his college police club. Some lines echoed to the point of becoming clichés. McCoy first said "He's dead, Jim" in "The Enemy Within"—and many times after that. As a result, when McCoy had to make a similar

pronouncement in *Star Trek II: The Wrath of Khan*, Scotty got the line instead to avoid provoking unintended audience laughter. The oft-repeated "Beam me up, Scotty" was actually never said on the show and instead became a catch phrase representing the series.

*Star Trek* debuted on September 8, 1966, at 8:30 as part of "Sneak Peek Week." When the season formally began a week later, its competition was the long-running situation comedy *My Three Sons* on CBS and the very short-lived sitcom *The Tammy Grimes Show* on ABC. NBC hedged their bets, ordering just sixteen episodes, waiting to see the ratings before giving it a full-season order of twenty-six. By the season's fifth week, NBC was sufficiently encouraged to order a full season, even if the sales and marketing staff were lukewarm about *Star Trek*—especially Spock's pointed ears, to the "point" where early promotional materials showed Nimoy with airbrushed rounded human ears!

The Romulan Bird of Prey was rarely seen on the original series and it was difficult to discern the avian motif on the undercarriage of the starship, a problem remedied by the Playmates Toys model.

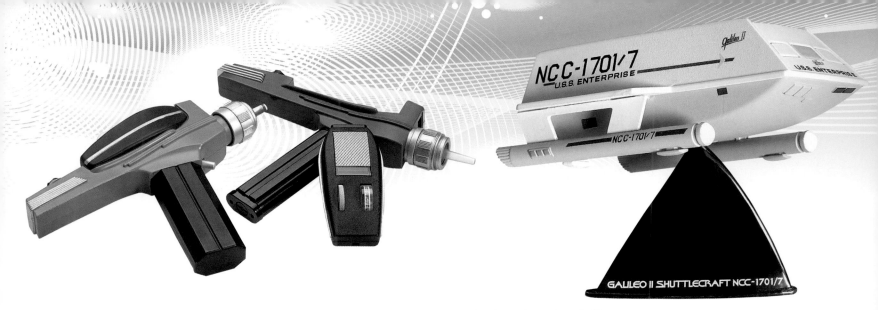

Playmates Toys issued a couple versions of the original series' Type 2 phaser. On the left is the simple one-piece model, while the version on the right allows the top-mounted Type 1 phaser to be detached and used separately.

From the Johnny Lightning "Legends of Star Trek" series, the *Galileo II* shuttlecraft of the third season episode "The Way to Eden."

Herb Schlosser, head of NBC's business affairs, remained worried that Spock's Satanic look could cost them network affiliates and audience. He begged Roddenberry to juggle the episode order to downplay shows featuring Spock until after the first thirteen weeks. However, by the time the fifth show aired and Spock had taken hold in the public mind, he changed course and ordered the Spock stories bumped up in order.

The reviews came in: the trade paper *Variety* found the show a little too high-minded for the typical audience, with too little action. The *Chicago Tribune* and the *Hollywood Reporter* offered positive assessments, but Percy Shain of the *Boston Globe* felt that the series was "too clumsily conceived and poorly developed to rate as an A-1 effort."

Isaac Asimov wrote a fairly negative piece for *TV Guide* criticizing scientific inaccuracies, prompting Roddenberry to write back in defense. A friendship began and Asimov later wrote a second, more positive *TV Guide* article.

The NAACP applauded the series for featuring a woman of color in command position on the bridge. Even though Uhura wasn't prominently featured, she was often visible diligently working.

*Life* magazine came to photograph Nimoy's ninety-minute transformation into Spock, igniting Shatner's jealousy. Though the two men competed for attention, they also forged a warm, enduring friendship. While Shatner apparently had an equity deal in the series (a fact that remains murky even today), he

considered himself the star and insisted on the lion's share of lines and being the focal point of scenes in which he appeared. As Spock-mania grew, Shatner became increasingly difficult, causing clashes with castmates. Decades later, several of them harshly criticized him in their own autobiographies. In his own memoirs, Shatner claimed to be unaware of the ruffled feathers, given how hard he worked to ensure quality television. Of course, Nimoy was the one complaining the most about the quality of the scripts and lack of a genuine part for the Vulcan science officer.

When it became obvious Spock was going to be hugely popular, Nimoy wanted to seize the opportunity to earn some significant money. He was being deluged with public appearances offers and even at this early stage in his career as Spock, he made it clear that the Vulcan was a character and Nimoy was a working actor. One instance required him to be done working early on a Friday so he could fly to a Connecticut appearance. Roddenberry explained to Nimoy that he and Majel Barrett were setting up Lincoln Enterprises to handle merchandise and personal appearances. He asked Nimoy to be the new company's first client but the actor refused, even though Roddenberry made it clear he controlled Nimoy's schedule.

*Star Trek* was being represented by the Licensing Corporation of America (LCA) and they cut a deal with scale-model manufacturer AMT. In addition to a model kit of the *Enterprise*, AMT wanted a shuttlecraft kit, but at

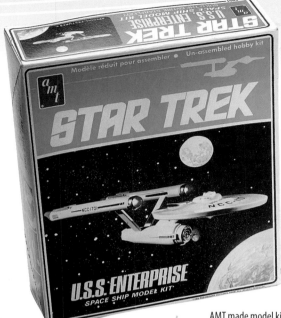

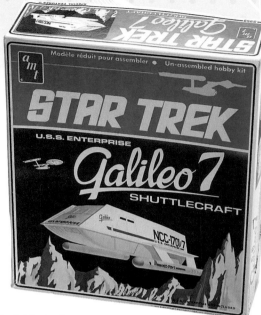

that point, no full-size shuttle existed. AMT offered to construct one and give it to the production in exchange for the rights. The full-scale *Galileo* was built for $24,000 in Arizona and trucked to the studio. AMT sold nearly one million *Star Trek* model kits in 1967, although Roddenberry chose not to share his profit participation with Matt Jeffries, the man who solved the ship design dilemmas years earlier. AMT national advertising and promotion director Stephen E. Whitfield befriended Roddenberry, and the two would go on to write *The Making of Star Trek*, a detailed if rather Roddenberry-centered history of the show's first two seasons.

AMT made model kits for *Star Trek* for decades. In the episode "The Doomsday Machine," the wrecked *U.S.S. Constellation* was an off-the-shelf AMT kit with battle damage added by the effects crew.

Lincoln Enterprises was eventually launched in 1968 and concentrated on things not handled by LCA. Roddenberry's attorney, Leonard Maizlish, advised them on which items Lincoln could sell without angering LCA and its clients. To initially run the company, Roddenberry turned to John and Bjo Trimble. They opened an office on Sunset Boulevard from which they helped answer fan mail and fill orders. After spending nine months getting the company up and running, they were fired without notice, replaced by AMT's Whitfield, who had taken office space next door.

Such business dealings demonstrated the dark side of Roddenberry, a man portrayed in numerous interviews and "tell-all" books as someone ready to take advantage of coworkers and friends to advance his own position. It later led to Eileen Roddenberry successfully suing her ex-husband's estate for millions of dollars in hidden profits.

Even though Spock had caught the public's attention within weeks, the early ratings were mediocre. That November, Roddenberry began executing a stealth campaign to ensure his baby survived. With Harlan Ellison's enthusiastic support, Roddenberry and Fontana drafted letters, one aimed at the media, and one for the small but growing fan movement. On December 1, Ellison issued a third letter, cosigned by fellow writers Theodore Sturgeon, Richard Matheson, A. E. Van Vogt, Robert Bloch, Lester del Rey, Phil Farmer, Frank Herbert, and Poul Anderson under the umbrella title of "The Committee," urging members of the science fiction community to rally behind the fledgling series and write to NBC.

Despite being one of only nine new shows to rank in the top fifty in the Nielsen ratings, by January, *Star Trek* was getting trounced by ABC's *Bewitched*, finishing third in its time slot. Still, the Committee's effort helped the series get renewed—although, according to at least one report in the *Chicago Tribune*, the network never seriously considered dropping the show. Word spread that NBC's executives didn't appreciate the letter writing campaign and Roddenberry's involvement. They had no idea what was coming next.

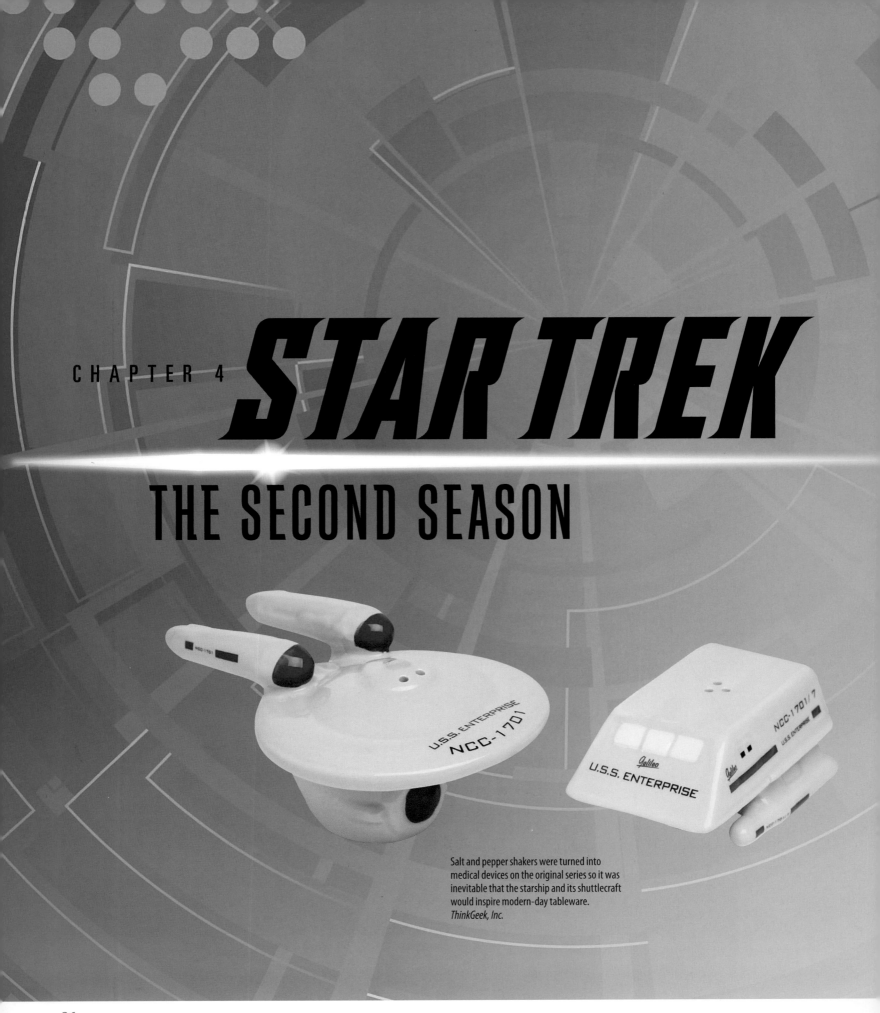

# CHAPTER 4

# *STAR TREK*

# THE SECOND SEASON

Salt and pepper shakers were turned into medical devices on the original series so it was inevitable that the starship and its shuttlecraft would inspire modern-day tableware. *ThinkGeek, Inc.*

U. S. S. ENTERPRISE
**BRIDGE**
BLUEPRINTS

SHOWS EVERY BUTTON OF EVERY STATION
AND THEIR FUNCTIONS

COMPLETE SET OF 10 ACC⌐⌐⌐TE 17"x22"
BLUEPRINTS OF THE PRI⌐

DRAWN BY:
MICHAEL McMASTER
DESIGNER OF THE ROMULAN BLUEPRINTS
AND THE KLINGON BATTLECRUISER BLUEPRINTS

**ROMULAN**
"BIRD OF PREY" CRUISER
BLUEPRINTS

COMPLETE SET OF 18"x24" BLUEPRINTS
OF THE ROMULAN CRUISER

DRAWN BY:
MICHAEL McMASTER
DESIGNER OF THE BRIDGE BLUEPRINTS
AND THE KLINGON BATTLECRUISER BLUEPRINTS

$6.0

Michael McMaster designed detailed blueprints of the Romulan Bird of Prey, Klingon D-7 battle cruiser, and *Enterprise* bridge. The bridge blueprints show functions for the buttons of every station, a monumental effort in extrapolation.

The renewal announcement on March 17, 1967, came less than a month after production ended on the first season. After brief consideration as the Tuesday night lead-off, *Star Trek* was moved from Thursday at 8:30 to the same time on Fridays. Its competition would be another Desilu production, CBS's *Gomer Pyle, USMC*, and ABC's new Western drama *Hondo*, which failed to last the season.

The show's hiatus gave Roddenberry and the creative staff a chance to make refinements. An April 1967 memo showed Roddenberry asking for greater efficiency among the bridge crew, both to demonstrate crew competence and to get stories moving faster.

As early as September 1966, Roddenberry had considered adding a youthful recurring crewman to the show to appeal to young viewers. He first thought of "an English-accent 'Beatle' type" like Davy Jones of NBC's Beatlemania-inspired *The Monkees*. But following January 1967 criticism from official Soviet newspaper *Pravda* over *Star Trek*'s lack of a Russian crewman, Roddenberry decided to make the new kid Russian, and Chekov was born. Walter Koenig, a serious actor and younger than the other regulars, was cast after being recommended by director Joseph Pevney. Koenig hated the unconvincing mod wig he had to wear until his hair grew to the right length.

His addition came at a good time because helmsman Sulu was about to be MIA. George Takei had booked a role in John Wayne's hawkish Vietnam movie *The Green Berets*. With Takei absent from several episodes, the writers modified scripts to feature Chekov and solidify him in the audience's mind.

Nimoy's popularity led his agent to repeatedly ask for higher compensation. On April 1, 1967, Roddenberry informed Coon, Justman, and Fontana that he was thinking of recasting Spock. Joe D'Agosta supplied a list of possible replacements, headed by Mark Lenard, who would play a Vulcan later that year. When NBC learned of the contract stalemate, they insisted on Nimoy's retention. He received a raise, better billing, and a promise of more script input.

In April, Justman got permission to upgrade DeForest Kelley to a lead, gaining a place in the opening titles when the show returned that September. Kelley had grown to adore his role and was eager to explore the character.

Though the first season left everyone exhausted, their efforts also earned five Emmy Award nominations: best dramatic series, outstanding supporting performance by a dramatic actor (Nimoy), special photographic effects, special mechanical effects, and film and sound editing. However, at the June 1967 ceremony, they went home empty-handed.

With NBC only firmly ordering sixteen episodes for the second season, producer Herb Solow decided to give as many directing assignments as possible to Marc Daniels and Joe Pevney to avoid commitments to directors for shows that might not get made.

Scripts were written all spring long with NBC programming executive Robertson complaining that the themes and plots of stories, such as "Return to Tomorrow," were too "cerebral," a word that the series should have worn with pride.

The Andorian (left) and Tellarite were introduced in "Journey to Babel" and have since become fixtures in the *Star Trek* universe, said to be among two of the Federation's founding members.

The sleek design of the tricorder and communicator have been widely admired and oft-imitated but nothing beats the originals.

Season two production began with Robert Bloch's "Catspaw," which didn't air until Halloween week. It demonstrated many of the show's budget constraints, leaving an episode that should have been drenched in atmosphere anything but spooky.

Perhaps the biggest challenge was shooting another season with a smaller budget. Although NBC's per-episode payment had increased, cast raises ate that up, and Desilu wanted to begin recouping studio investment in the first season, rather than wait for syndication. This required even tighter preplanning and more "bottle" stories—episodes that could be filmed on existing sets with fewer guest stars.

A new wrinkle developed when a pending deal to sell Desilu to Gulf+Western became a reality on July 28. As "Mirror, Mirror" was filming, Lucille Ball departed and G+W chairman Charles G. Bluhdorn took over, eventually merging Desilu with its next door neighbor, Paramount Pictures, which G+W had bought the previous year.

Apparently a week after the deal closed, Bluhdorn was made aware of Desilu's deficit financing for *Star Trek* and its stablemate *Mission: Impossible*. *Trek* had been shooting on a six-day schedule, often running over by half a day or more. Now the schedules called for episodes to be filmed in five-and-a-half days, six at the most.

Such lunacy led Herb Solow to resign not long after. An exhausted Gene Coon also decided to leave in early September. Coon remained as a highly valued writer and was replaced by John Meredyth Lucas as producer. Lucas also wrote three episodes for the season and lasted on staff through "The Omega Glory" at the end of 1967. He also made his directing debut that season with "The Ultimate Computer," and he directed three more episodes the following season.

Lucas immediately observed it was far from a happy set. There were constant complaints by actors about their castmates, with most aimed at Shatner's perceived camera-hogging—and his monopolizing the sound stage's one phone. Eventually, Roddenberry forbade all onstage personal calls.

Even though NBC initially ordered only sixteen episodes, Justman crafted a full-season budget. One casualty was the art department, given less than $10,000 per episode. Matt Jeffries therefore got creative, resulting in such sights as aluminum foil wrapped around a wooden frame for the temple of Vaal in "The Apple."

When NBC finally gave the full-season order on October 18, Robertson insisted the episodes be delivered in a timely manner and threatened that there would be no pre-emptions to allow more post-production time.

During this uncertain period, Nichelle Nichols received an offer for stage work in New York at a time when she was increasingly dissatisfied with her role and feeling harassed by racism within Desilu. She seriously considered leaving the series after discovering that employees were keeping her fan mail from being delivered. One Friday, as production ended for the week, she told a

This fun coffee mug has the *Enterprise* officers "energize" and fade away when hot liquid is poured in.

Hallmark has produced countless *Star Trek* holiday ornaments, including this representation of Dr. McCoy in his least favorite place, the transporter.

The Mugato, originally called the Gumato according to the end credits of "A Private Little War."

stunned Roddenberry she wanted to leave. He insisted she think about it over the weekend.

The next day, Nichols was a celebrity guest at an NAACP fundraiser at UCLA. She was asked to meet a big fan, and it was her turn to be stunned when the visitor turned out to be Dr. Martin Luther King Jr. He was effusive with his praise but shocked to hear she had decided to leave. Dr. King insisted she remain on the series, telling her, "You are the first nonstereotypical role in television! Of intelligence, and of a woman and a woman of color?! That you are playing a role that is not about your color! That this role could be played by anyone? This is not a black role. This is not a female role! A blue-eyed blond or a pointed-ear green person could take this role!"

Back at work Monday, she recounted the conversation with Roddenberry, who was delighted to retain his performer and moved to hear his vision of a unified future was actually getting noticed. About that same time, a young viewer watching the show in Los Angeles called out to her mother, "Come quick! Come quick! There's a black lady on TV, and she ain't no maid!" That girl grew up to be actress Whoopi Goldberg. Nichols's influence and her own long-lasting love of *Star Trek* led her to play the wise Guinan twenty years later in *Star Trek: The Next Generation*.

The season fell into some bad habits, repeating gimmicks and plot lines. Kirk outsmarts rogue computers in "The

Harcourt Fenton Mudd was a colorful rogue who could go toe-to-toe with Captain Kirk, brought to lovable life by Roger C. Carmel.

including one called "A Fuzzy Thing Happened." Fontana and Justman both saw enough in it to allow continued development. In the end, Coon did a massive polish that moved the story toward production. "The Trouble with Tribbles" became an episode that usually ranks first or second on all-time-favorite *Star Trek* episode lists, perhaps because the cast were allowed to play more broadly than Roddenberry normally allowed.

The tight budget and production schedule forced the show to visit Earth-like planets multiple times. Roddenberry raided his leftover 1964 story proposals, including the failed pilot pitch, "The Omega Glory." A heavy-handed story of a parallel Earth, right down to the races being named "Yangs" (Yankees) and the "Kohms" (Communists), it underwent several rewrites. Roddenberry liked it enough to lobby NBC in February 1968 to hold it back for use as the third-season opener. He also wrote the business affairs department suggesting an ad campaign to nab the episode an Emmy Award nomination. Both ignored the requests and the weak installment aired March 1 as scheduled.

The show managed only mediocre ratings, but Spock's popularity remained high. As a result, Leonard Nimoy donned the ears for a guest appearance on *The Carol Burnett Show*, airing on rival network CBS. The skit had Carol as a new mother confusing Spock with the famed baby doctor of the same name—a problem Nimoy constantly faced.

The final episode of the season was actually a backdoor pilot for a new series conceived by Roddenberry. "Assignment: Earth" had been a thirty-minute pilot written in November 1966 that did not sell; a year later, it was repurposed into a *Star Trek* episode. Robert Lansing played Gary Seven, a human agent trained by unidentified aliens, and Teri Garr appeared in her first major role as naïve secretary Roberta Lincoln introduced to a fantastic world of possibilities. The episode left the door open to a spinoff that never materialized on screen.

Return of the Archons," and then again in "The Changeling," "I, Mudd," *and* "The Ultimate Computer"—possibly indicating the toll of the weekly grind on the writing staff.

It wasn't all recycled themes, though. Jerome Bixby's brilliant "Mirror, Mirror" introduced *Star Trek*'s parallel universe. Under Daniels's sure hand, the cast portrayed their baser selves, and Fred Phillips gave Spock a wonderfully sinister goatee. By mid-season, *Star Trek* lightened up with the return of Harry Mudd, with countless androids. Then came the tribbles.

David Gerrold, fresh out of college, was a fan of the show and began pitching stories to Roddenberry in early 1967,

An April Fools' Day product from the twisted minds at ThinkGeek.com. *ThinkGeek, Inc.*

## STAR TREK LIVES!

The "Save Star Trek" campaign has become part of American folklore, but its true origins remained clouded for years.

Before the second season began airing, the show's fans had already begun to make their presence felt. During the early weeks of production, John and Bjo Trimble asked Roddenberry for some props to use in a charity auction to bring Japanese science fiction fan Takumi Shibano to NyCon3 over Labor Day weekend in New York City. Roddenberry's secretary sent several boxes containing rare items such as Kirk's torn shirt from "Amok Time," pairs of Spock's ears, copies of the series bible, and a whole box of tribbles, long before anyone knew what they were. The $5,000 for Shibano's airfare was raised in under three hours. John Trimble later identified this as a key moment "when *Star Trek* fandom first came together and became a force in and of itself. People who met each other at the convention went off and started producing fanzines and formed clubs."

NyCon3 was also where the first *Star Trek* fanzine appeared. *Spockanalia* was edited by Devra Langsam and Sherna Comerford, and it featured news from Justman about "Amok Time" as well as a letter of encouragement by Nimoy. While fanzines had existed since the 1930s, they were devoted predominantly to science fiction and only in the 1960s were there any about comic books. *Spockanalia* was the first devoted to a single science fiction concept. Sold for a mere fifty cents, it sparked a profusion of zines for decades to come.

However, weeks after the second season began, rumors circulated that the show was in trouble. According to Nielsen, some sixteen million people were watching the show weekly but that wasn't enough to command advertising rates high enough to allow NBC to profit from their expensive series.

Roddenberry shared his fears for the series' life with the Trimbles, enlisting their support that fall in an organized campaign to save the series. They wrote hundreds of letters, urging recipients to write to ten of their friends plus a letter

If you don't recognize these as tribbles, you should be ashamed of yourself.

to NBC. The chain letters grew, as did petitions, which the Trimbles felt would have less of an impact.

Five hundred students from California Institute of Technology marched on NBC's West Coast headquarters on January 7, 1968. Roddenberry witnessed the movement he helped spawn and covertly supported. He spent over $300 on 5,000 "Mr. Spock for President" bumper stickers, which were plastered on cars on the NBC Burbank lot two days later.

New York fans got into the action, armed with the same stickers. Fanzine editor Devra Langsam was on hand as was Wanda Kendall, representing the West Coast fans. She told the *New York Post* she had been sent out there after funds were raised by her peers—although Roddenberry had actually footed her bill. Kendall earned her money, dropping bumper stickers on corporate desks at NBC's headquarters and affixing several onto cars in the underground parking lot.

The *Hartford Courant* had reported on November 1 that the show was safe and the network had ordered the full twenty-six-episode season. By January 1968, though, as the sticker campaign was at its height, the paper ran a story headlined "*Star Trek* Doomed, Renewal Is Unlikely." The alarm bells were loud enough that the studio got in touch and the paper ran a retraction, adding a quote from Nimoy, "We've gotten no word yet one way or the other. And at this point we seem

*Above:* This Hallmark *Enterprise* can be hung as an ornament or displayed on the base. When the button at the back of the base is pressed, the theme music plays and the ship lights up.

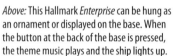

*Right:* The *Galileo* Hallmark ornament contains a voice chip with Leonard Nimoy as Spock wishing you "Happy holidays" and, of course, "Live long and prosper."

to be in a better position than we were a year ago."

NBC reported receiving 114,667 letters between December 1967 and March 1968, including 52,151 in February. The final tally? No one can confirm an actual count, though it was probably under 200,000—far fewer than the million letters sometimes claimed, but still a significant number. NBC was not amused and they called Herb Solow at Paramount to complain, but no one realized the trail ended at Roddenberry's office. In all, to salvage a third season, it cost Roddenberry $977.12.

The campaign proved successful and the network announced in February that *Star Trek* would be back for a third season. A move to Monday nights was all-but-assured, although it would mean Captain Kirk versus Marshal Dillon and John Steed as *Star Trek* would be pitted against *Gunsmoke* on CBS and ABC's British import *The Avengers*. In exchange for the favorable time slot, Roddenberry agreed to return as showrunner.

Finally, NBC took an unprecedented step and during the end credits of "The Omega Glory," viewers were told, "And now an announcement of interest to all viewers of *Star Trek*. We are pleased to tell you that *Star Trek* will continue to be seen on NBC Television. We know you will be looking forward to seeing the weekly adventure in space on *Star Trek*."

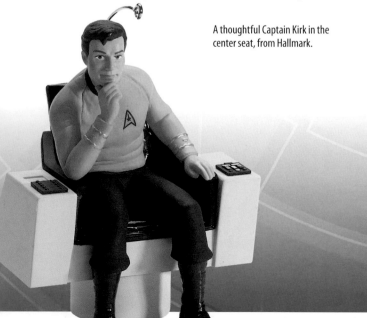

A thoughtful Captain Kirk in the center seat, from Hallmark.

# THE BIRTH OF TREKZINES

*Devra Langsam*

In the days of the original *Star Trek*, there were no VCRs, no instant reshowing of episodes, no computer feed access. If you missed an episode, you had to wait for the summer reruns, and not all episodes were actually reshown. In this desert, we thirsted for more *Trek*, more stories about the people and situations we loved. There were no professional novels except James Blish's and the books that summarized episodes. Our answer was to write our own stories—and to share them with our friends and coaddicts. To do this, we needed to distribute them. Conventions where you could sit and talk story to people who understood your references were few and far between; there were no chat rooms or blogs or Live Journals.

With no spell check or grammar check, we were obliged to vet our own stories, unless we were lucky enough to have a friend who could read and edit them, checking the facts that we'd been given in the episodes, the cultural attitudes characters had demonstrated and, oh, yes, spelling and grammar. A good editor was a gem, and a fearful taskmaster; no one wanted to distribute a story with an obvious gaffe, contradicting the canon as expressed on the shows—unless you were writing a "mirror" story.

It was exhilarating and scary to write your stories and pray that they wouldn't be invalidated by material in the next aired episode. People developed enormous skill in not only inventing the coat from the button, but also in finding a way to weave the cloth of the coat—the culture, the interactions of aliens—from the button we had been given.

These stories, once written, cried out to be shared beyond one's own small pool of fellow fans. Professional science fiction magazines refused *Trek* stories. They were concerned about copyright violations, and many decent stories were vignettes and would not stand on their own without the background material found in the show. If you said "The Captain," you didn't have to describe him. Even when an attempt had been made to de-*Trek* these stories, they were not easily disguised, and found no market.

So we published our own stories. We used school mimeographs and church ditto machines, typing our stencils on manual typewriters and hand-cutting the artwork that we pasted onto the stencils. We depended on the small size of our print runs, Roddenberry's personal tolerance (I have a newspaper clipping showing him holding a copy of *Spockanalia*, my fanzine), and the fact that we were not taking any income from them to keep Paramount from bothering us.

In the beginning, our mentors were general SF fan publishers and authors like Juanita Coulson, Bjo Trimble, and Ruth Berman. We grew and expanded; there was a zine devoted to listing available Trekzines, and a multivolume index listing stories and poetry. We got technological wonders: electric typewriters, electro stencils to copy pictures, computers, and the internet. Hundreds of zines, thousands of stories, were published. Many printed stories are lost now, but fanzines still thrive online.

*Devra Langsam helped pioneer both* Star Trek *fanzines and conventions, continuing her work as a librarian and fan.*

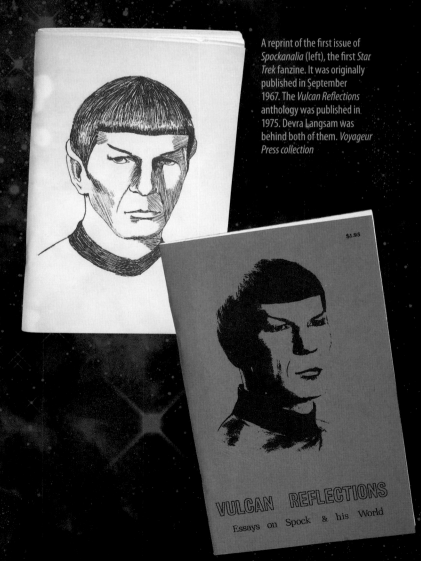

A reprint of the first issue of *Spockanalia* (left), the first *Star Trek* fanzine. It was originally published in September 1967. The *Vulcan Reflections* anthology was published in 1975. Devra Langsam was behind both of them. *Voyageur Press collection*

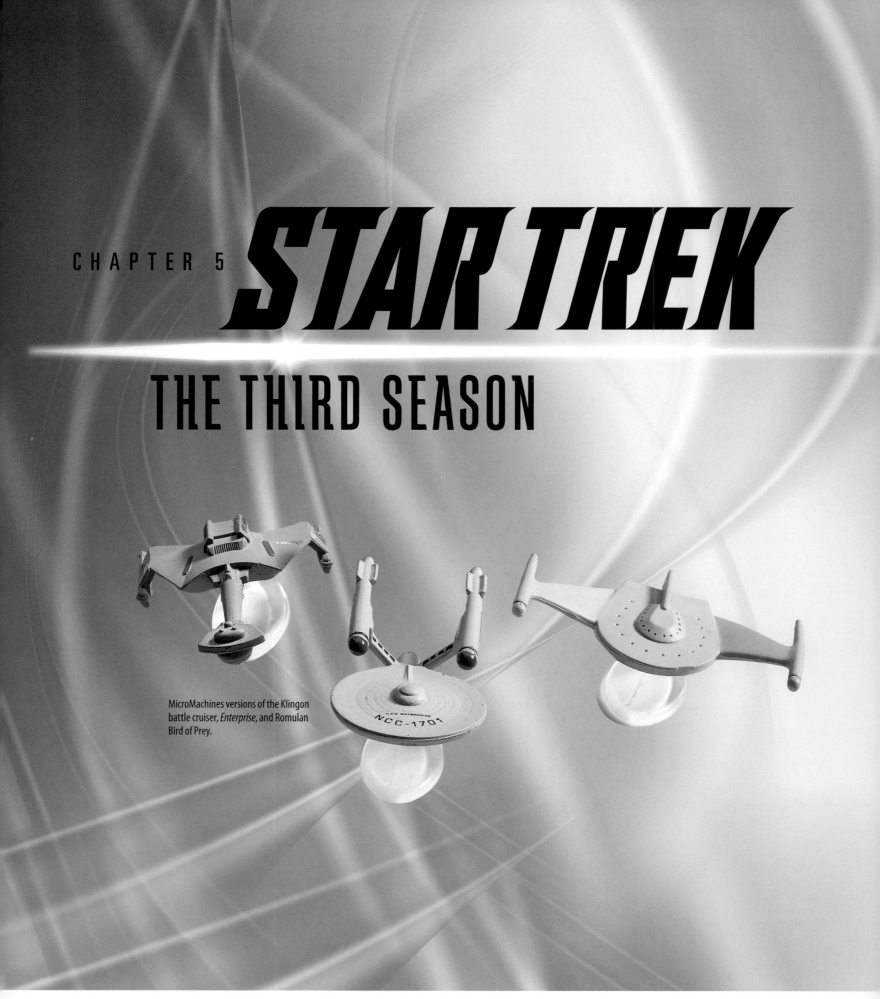

# CHAPTER 5

# *STAR TREK*

## THE THIRD SEASON

MicroMachines versions of the Klingon battle cruiser, *Enterprise*, and Romulan Bird of Prey.

Although NBC announced *Star Trek*'s renewal in March, there was diminishing network affection for the show and Roddenberry. While NBC verbally promised him a move to Mondays at 7:30 p.m., their plan to shift mega-hit *Rowan & Martin's Laugh-In* to 8:30 so angered its producer George Schlatter that he threatened to take his trend-setting—and far more popular—show elsewhere.

NBC felt they had little choice, so they stuck Roddenberry's show on Fridays at 10:00 p.m. claiming it was the last available hour-slot. Roddenberry felt betrayed and made threats of his own, none of which moved NBC. So Roddenberry left the Paramount lot and set up shop at National General Pictures, where he signed a deal to write a *Tarzan* film, which never materialized.

Despite being promised a promotion to sole producer, Justman was named coproducer; without explanation, John Meredyth Lucas wasn't invited to take on a larger role so he departed. Fred Freiberger stepped in as the new showrunner, on the recommendation of Alden Schwimmer, who represented both Freiberger and Roddenberry. Freiberger was greeted by the news that the per-episode budget had been trimmed again, from $185,000 in the previous season to $180,000, despite contractual raises to the cast.

Soon after arriving April 1, Freiberger recognized the need for a story consultant to replace Fontana, who had left late in the second season, and hired his old colleague, Arthur Singer. Failing to steep himself in *Trek* lore, Singer couldn't bring the same level of detailed attention to the scripts. Familiar names and pen names did appear throughout the season's credits.

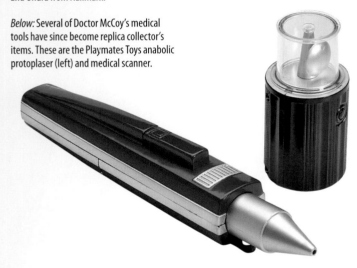

Still, without Roddenberry, Coon, or Fontana polishing them, the scripts remained lesser works.

In order to help the newcomers, Roddenberry wrote a memo on April 18 musing on the core crewmen and what should happen over the third season, including beefed up roles for Sulu and Uhura. Just about everything suggested by the Great Bird was ignored. Roddenberry's only significant contribution that season was the script to "The Savage Curtain," a weak effort that indulged his affection for Abraham Lincoln, but did it give us our first glimpses of the great Vulcan philosopher Surak and the Klingon legend Kahless.

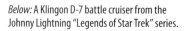

*Below:* A Klingon D-7 battle cruiser from the Johnny Lightning "Legends of Star Trek" series.

*Above:* William Shatner in costume as Captain Kirk with soapbox derby members rides a float during the 1968 Macy's Thanksgiving Day parade. *NBC via Getty Images*

KLINGON D7 BATTLECRUISER

Freiberger and Singer's lack of knowledge soured the mood on set. Nimoy continued to write memos arguing Spock was being ill-used, while the supporting players continued to chafe under Shatner's diva-like behavior. A frustrated Freiberger summoned Roddenberry, Shatner, and Nimoy for a meeting to try to deal with the actors' conflicting needs and demands. When pressed, Roddenberry finally said Shatner was the sole star of the show. This permanently damaged the relationship between creator and Nimoy.

Even Justman had enough of a sinking starship and bailed after "Let That Be Your Last Battlefield." He was hired by Solow, now an executive at MGM, to produce NBC's newly purchased *Then Came Bronson*. Freiberger was left to fend for himself while cost-conscious Paramount and NBC began to approve older premises that had been previously rejected, lowering the bar for quality storytelling.

"Spock's Brain," often regarded as the single worst episode of the entire *Star Trek* canon, was selected as the season premiere—an omen of bad things to come. As that final season began, *Star Trek* was being aired on only 181 of NBC's 210 affiliate stations, slashing the potential audience and affecting ratings. Only two other NBC series failed to appear on the full roster of affiliates. With the youngest fans already in bed when the show aired, and the next generation of viewers likely out on dates, the ratings suffered badly.

Despite all the production difficulties, the show gained a sheen and polish it lacked earlier. James Doohan's Scotty got his first good haircut and a kilt for his dress uniform, while the

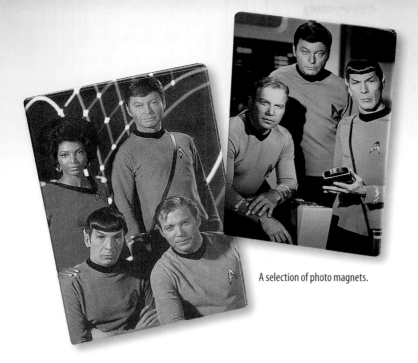

A selection of photo magnets.

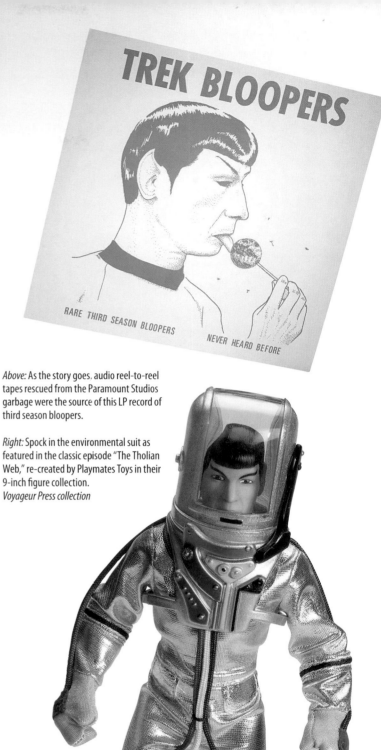

TREK BLOOPERS

RARE THIRD SEASON BLOOPERS

NEVER HEARD BEFORE

crew uniforms were now double-knit polyester in lieu of the shrinking Velour. Matt Jeffries contributed a newly designed Klingon D-7 battle cruiser, and some of the *Enterprise* sets were modified and sharpened.

"Let That Be Your Last Battlefield" was based on a story pitched for the first season, "Portrait in Black and White." Although Roddenberry adored Gene Coon's idea, it was rejected by NBC exec Stanley Robertson on August 26, 1966. Two years later, Robertson had learned his job well enough to allow the story to finally be filmed.

"Plato's Stepchildren" saw Shatner and Nichelle Nichols share the first highly visible interracial kiss on primetime television. Whether there may have been earlier examples, this one has received the most attention and Nichols swears all the mail was positive, despite NBC's qualms that southern stations might object to airing it. To hedge their bets, the network insisted that the two actors' lips not touch, although the performers confirm there was plenty of contact. Additionally, a nonkiss moment was to be shot as an alternative, but Shatner deliberately marred the shot, leaving the producers no choice but to use the actual kiss.

With severely limited budgets, many episodes were glorified bottle shows. One expensive exception was "The Paradise Syndrome," which also required a massive obelisk to be built on location. Perhaps the best of the bottle shows was "The *Enterprise* Incident," an espionage caper that saw Kirk don pointed ears to infiltrate a Romulan vessel. This fairly gripping episode was based in part on the capture of

*Above:* As the story goes, audio reel-to-reel tapes rescued from the Paramount Studios garbage were the source of this LP record of third season bloopers.

*Right:* Spock in the environmental suit as featured in the classic episode "The Tholian Web," re-created by Playmates Toys in their 9-inch figure collection.
*Voyageur Press collection*

Leonard Nimoy managed to parlay his incredible international celebrity into a series of heartfelt albums, covering popular tunes of the day. Sales were remarkably strong, helping him avoid being lumped in with other "golden throats."

the U.S.S. *Pueblo* by North Korean forces, which led to the captain and crew charged with espionage.

Other issues raised that season included overpopulation and hippies. "The Way to Eden" may be the most reviled episode among the cast. Jimmy Doohan claimed it was the only one he objected to. Originally intended to bring Dr. McCoy's daughter Joanna aboard the ship, it was heavily rewritten so the character became Chekov's ex–Starfleet Academy lover. Apparently, Freiberger was sufficiently unfamiliar with the series bible that he felt McCoy was a contemporary of Kirk's, not old enough to have a twenty-one year old daughter. Writer D.C. Fontana wanted to explore the theme of rules versus freedom, and pitted the younger carefree Joanna against Kirk. Much to the doctor's discomfort, the captain would find himself attracted to his daughter. After repeated revisions, Fontana grew frustrated and used her Michael Richards pseudonym on the final script. She later developed a new story to introduce Joanna McCoy, "Stars of Sargasso," intended for a fourth season which was not to be.

Another sour note was hit when Roddenberry reappeared to insist the Vulcan IDIC medallion be worked into the script of "Is There No Truth in Beauty," so replicas of the William Ware Theiss design could be sold through Lincoln Enterprises. This was the only example of product placement in the original series.

Meantime, other forms of merchandise had become available. In time for the third season's debut, *The Making of Star Trek* was released by Ballantine Books. Written by AMT's Whitfield (sharing coauthorship with Roddenberry), it paved the way for "making of" books to become a standard within publishing. For the first time, readers got an inside look at how a TV series develops from initial pitch to final product. Roddenberry pressured Whitfield to cede half the credit and revenues to him, stating he needed to get his money wherever he could because he doubted he'd ever see profits from the show itself. In the end, Roddenberry

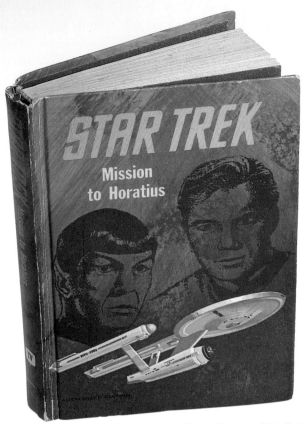

delayed reading the manuscript until it was already typeset, so most of his corrections and annotations failed to make it into print.

This wasn't *Star Trek*'s only foray into print. The first original *Trek* novel came out during this final season. *Mission to Horatius* was a juvenile work by Mack Reynolds, from Whitman Books. Roddenberry and John Meredyth Lucas had serious issues with its quality and adherence to the series' premise, requiring numerous rewrites and delaying its release. Whitman also had the license for comic books and in 1967 had begun one of their countless media tie-in works.

*Mission to Horatius*, published by Whitman, was a young adult novel, the first original licensed *Star Trek* fiction.

*Right:* Red shirts have become synonymous with "marked for death" and "expendable." It also appears to be the smell of fear, which has since been bottled. *ThinkGeek, Inc.*

*Below:* In addition to Red Shirt, the scent-conscious *Star Trek* fan can wear the essence of the Vulcan mating drive with Pon Farr, or the commanding fragrance of a despotic starship captain with Tiberius. *ThinkGeek, Inc.*

Unfortunately, the studio provided scant visual reference and with artist Alberto Gioletti living in Italy where it was not yet broadcast, the comic barely resembled the show. The worst offense may have been smoke contrails emerging from the *Enterprise*'s nacelles. Apparently, Roddenberry was less concerned with the comic version.

A more accurate interpretation emanated from Bantam Books, which in January 1967, had released *Star Trek*, a paperback containing eight prose episode adaptations. Acclaimed British science fiction writer James Blish based them on early draft scripts, leading to some glaring and interesting differences from the televised episodes. *Star Trek 2* and *Star Trek 3* followed in 1968 and 1969. The television series didn't air in England until 1969 so Blish was working with minimal information. Still, the first book went through five printings in under a year, another early sign of *Star Trek*'s popularity with fans, and spawned an industry of *Star Trek* publishing that continues to this day.

There were also some trading cards from White Leaf but little else in the way of collectibles.

*Above:* The much-coveted Franz Joseph blueprints of the original *Enterprise* featured both interior and exterior plans.

NATIONAL BROADCASTING COMPANY, INC.

THIRTY ROCKEFELLER PLAZA, NEW YORK, N.Y. 10020, CIRCLE 7-8300

June 5, 1969

Mr. Howard Weinstein

Dear Mr. Weinstein:

Thank you for your thoughtful letter regarding STAR TREK. Naturally, we regret any displeasure you may have felt over the cancellation of this program.

We too believe that STAR TREK is an attractive show with a fine cast. It was for these reasons that it found a spot in our schedule in the first place.but, unfortunately, the program failed to develop the broad appeal necessary for keeping it in our schedule.next season.

We are happy to be able to tell you that STAR TREK repeats are now being seen on Tuesday evenings at 7:30 p.m. and will remain in this time slot for the duration of the summer.

We very much appreciate the interest which prompted you to write and hope that NBC will continue to merit your attention.

Sincerely yours,

Bruce Terrence
Information Department

By Christmas 1968, it was clear NBC was not going to renew *Star Trek* for a fourth season. An unhappy cast, declining ratings, and Roddenberry's absence sealed the show's fate despite an enthusiastic fan following.

During the January production of "Turnabout Intruder," word came from NBC that they were passing on the option of filming two additional episodes for a complete twenty-six episode season. That stung Shatner because he had been given permission to direct the anticipated final story, ahead of Nimoy who had been lobbying for a chance the previous year. It left the show with a final episode featuring the body swapping of Kirk and Janice Lester, a vengeful former lover and Starfleet officer. The inauspicious finale was nicknamed "Captain Kirk, Space Queen" by the crew.

Production wrapped on January 9, 1969. The crew began dismantling sets without ceremony. The three-season voyage was officially completed and was now part of television history.

In March, weeks before the final new episode was due for broadcast, librarian and fanzine editor Sherna Comerford Burley held a *Trek* gathering at the Newark Public Library. Her program offered attendees a slide show of aliens from the series, skits, and one panel discussion of "The *Star Trek* Phenomenon." This library program could arguably be called the first *Star Trek* convention. Her coeditor, Devra Langsam, dreamt bigger.

As it was, "Turnabout Intruder" was pre-empted March 28 with a news special on the death of former President Dwight D. Eisenhower. It finally aired June 3, well after the official primetime season ended. After the leftover finale, *Star Trek* reruns replaced *The Jerry Lewis Show* until September 2, then faded out without fanfare.

But *Star Trek*'s second life was about to begin.

*Left:* The original cast of *Saturday Night Live* had some fun with *Star Trek* fans with this now-classic skit imagining the day an NBC executive (guest host Elliott Gould) appeared on the bridge to deliver word of the series' cancellation. A disbelieving Captain Kirk (John Belushi) and McCoy (Dan Aykroyd) stand by as Spock (Chevy Chase) tries the Vulcan neck pinch on the suit (Gould) without effect. *NBC via Getty Images*

*Below:* The head of the stage crew (Garrett Morris) was there to start dismantling the set. *NBC via Getty Images*

# CHAPTER 6
# THE ANIMATED
# SERIES

A collectible animation cel of Lieutenant Arex. Although not an actual painted cel, the character is printed on a piece of clear plastic similar to what was used in traditional cartoon animation, allowing the character to be photographed over the background illustration. Lieutenant Arex's triple-limbed arms and legs must have made sitting at the navigation station difficult. He was voiced by James Doohan.

From left, director Roger Vadim, star Rock Hudson, and producer Gene Roddenberry at a press conference announcing *Pretty Maids All in a Row*. © Bettmann/Corbis

As production wrapped in the early weeks of 1969, everyone went their separate ways. The tight-knit camaraderie seen in later years was nowhere to be found.

Almost immediately after the cancellation, Paramount considered a spinoff that would focus on Spock and life on the planet Vulcan. Roddenberry refused the invitation to produce and the project died.

Nimoy replaced Martin Landau on *Mission: Impossible* while the others took guest roles where they could. Doohan was the only one Roddenberry hired at MGM for the awful feature film *Pretty Maids All in a Row*. It proved another failure in a long line that would eventually lead Roddenberry to cling to *Star Trek* tighter than anyone thought possible.

Before the series ended its network run, it was clear the show was particularly popular with college students, who began inviting Roddenberry to come speak. He enjoyed the amiable atmosphere and the nice pay day for minimal work,

but later, after the box office failure of *Pretty Maids*, it became his chief source of income for a period of time. He turned his attentions to television, where he was seen as merely a science fiction guy, so he made a variety of pilots as movies-of-the-week throughout the 1970s. None sold.

Kaiser Broadcasting had recognized the value of *Star Trek* well ahead of Desilu or NBC. As a result, in 1967 they negotiated to obtain rerun rights when the series left the air. Two years later, as the show ended its network run, Kaiser scheduled the uncut reruns to run during the dinner hour, providing homes with a choice between the network news or action. Sure enough, the ratings soared.

Paramount controlled the show's fate, splitting revenues with Roddenberry's Norway Productions and Shatner. As the strong ratings were recorded, Roddenberry sensed there might be some life left in the property, and he approached the studio in 1970 asking to gain control of the rights.

The Gold Key adaptation was typical for its era, barely resembling the source material, written and drawn initially by people unfamiliar with the television series.

After analyzing rerun revenue, international sales, and merchandising, Paramount said they would let him have the series for $150,000. Roddenberry couldn't raise the funds and lost his best chance at owning his creation.

*Star Trek*, meanwhile, was building a brand new audience: families watching it with their dinners were enthralled by the storytelling and promise of a brighter future. The first syndicated reruns proved inspiring to countless fans who were stirred by the show to turn passions into professions.

The first real convention about *Star Trek* was conceived by fans Elyse Pines and Devra Langsam. In 1971 they decided there needed to be a gathering of the series' fans to talk about the show. The pair reached out to television executive Joan Winston, who had visited the set and knew Roddenberry.

That November, Pines and pop culture historian Allan Asherman addressed students at Brooklyn College, with the *Star Trek* seminar packing in twice as many students as the room was supposed to hold.

The trio recruited friends and fellow fans, loosely forming what became known as The Committee (not connected in any way with the group of science fiction writers who had helped Roddenberry achieve the show's renewal). One of the more active was Al Schuster, who had the most business acumen of the bunch.

After selecting January 21–23, 1972 as their date, they contracted with the Statler-Hilton Hotel, conveniently across the street from Penn Station and a regular home to comic book conventions. Pines invited Isaac Asimov, and Winston put in a call to Roddenberry, who agreed to come, bringing Majel Barrett, by then his wife. Roddenberry, in turn, invited D. C. Fontana to accompany them. Paramount graciously provided fifteen 16mm episodes for screening while NASA sent their touring lunar module exhibit.

Winston spoke with a reporter from *Variety*, hoping to generate a little professional news interest, and was stunned to see the resulting page one story.

The trio had no idea of the depth and passion of the fan community being tapped. Hints were there, with bags of mail arriving, requesting weekend tickets for $2.50 apiece. Ticket orders were coming in from the Midwest and Canada. A charter bus had been arranged to bring people from Montreal. Among those attending from far away were Bjo Trimble and a St. Louis fan named Richard Arnold. I also trekked in from Long Island for a day.

That Friday morning, the organizers arrived to find two hundred fans already standing on line, many having waited up to six hours in advance.

A few hundred people were expected, but over three thousand attended. They were treated to not only a talk by the series' creator, but also screenings of "The Cage" and, for the first time in public, the infamous "blooper reel." Most series saved their flubs and gaffes for a compilation reel screened during a wrap party, but never intended for the general audience. Few knew they existed when Roddenberry screened the *Trek* bloopers, and they became a mainstay at conventions for the next decade. The cast, notably Nimoy, later objected to the screenings, especially since cast members were not receiving compensation for the perceived embarrassment.

Roddenberry indulged the fans with many stories about the making of the series, hogging plenty of credit for himself, burnishing the impression that he regularly tilted at NBC's windmills. He also allowed the throng to believe him a well-read futurist, when he was largely a fanciful dreamer, spinning yarns for an eager audience.

Former Desilu executive Oscar Katz was in attendance and stunned by what he saw, as were executives from all three

A crowd of fans at the registration desk of the first *Star Trek* convention on January 21, 1972. *NY Daily News Archive via Getty Images*

*Above: Star Trek* didn't become a licensing bonanza until decades after the show initially aired. During the 1970s, though, it did spawn a handful of products, including jigsaw puzzles. *Steve Roby collection*

*Left:* Chuck Weiss and Sandy Sarris are dressed like characters of the television show *Star Trek* inside a "Trekkie" store in Berkeley, California. December 14, 1975. © *Ted Streshinsky/Corbis*

networks who weren't sure what they were witnessing.

The press latched on to the colorful story and queried whether Roddenberry thought there was more life to *Star Trek* on screen. He told *TV Guide*, "I didn't think it was possible six months ago. But after seeing the enthusiasm here I'm beginning to change my mind." Paramount, though, still needed some convincing.

While The Committee had all attended cons, none had been involved in the planning and execution, so there was a steep learning curve. Unanticipated expenses were matched by unprecedented attendance, leaving the organizers exhausted. To their credit, it worked so well that just weeks later, plans for a second show began. By the time that it took place, *Star Trek* was heading back to the small screen, but not perhaps in the way that its fans—and its creator—might originally have hoped.

## SELLING THE ANIMATED SERIES

In March 1972, Roddenberry first mentioned trying to turn *Star Trek* into a feature film. The studio was not at all interested despite the clear popularity of the series. Science fiction as a genre was not performing well in theaters; the last two hits— *2001: A Space Odyssey* and *Planet of the Apes*—were both 1968 releases. Additionally, Paramount was only interested in Roddenberry's involvement as a writer not a producer, while the creator wanted total control.

Eventually, Roddenberry took an unused premise from the 1964 outline and developed a story. Solow agreed to come on as producer and began discussing details with studio president Frank Yablans. Then Roddenberry and his lawyer Leonard Maizlish asked for too much money and the project stalled.

Instead, *Star Trek* found new life on Saturday mornings via Filmation's adaption of the series. Roddenberry had previously been approached about an animated project, but the simplistic alien monster of the week premise did not interest him.

Small animation studio Filmation was born less than a decade earlier, headed by partners Lou Scheimer and director Hal Sutherland, alongside former radio disc jockey Norm Prescott, with *The Adventures of Superman* marking their first foray into the competitive Saturday morning field in 1966. By 1972 they were producing numerous programs for all three networks. Scheimer was a fan of *Star Trek*, aware of the growing audience thanks to years of syndication, and Filmation prevailed against animation behemoth Hanna-Barbera for the rights. Their kid-friendly approach meant their first pitch featured young cadets aboard the training ship *Excalibur* working alongside our familiar crewmen. Each

Letraset produced many media tie-ins in their action transfer series, including DC and Marvel Comics, *Star Wars*, and *Star Trek*. Various characters and props could be placed on the background illustration to create a scene. *Steve Roby collection*

episode would have an educational component, prevalent at this time for animated fare.

Roddenberry wouldn't approve the juvenile concept. Paramount, though, liked the idea and, according to Prescott, they offered the series creator plenty of cash to relinquish his creative control. Despite needing the money, Roddenberry refused. (Filmation later recycled the concept into their 1977 live-action show *Space Academy*, starring *Lost in Space* veteran Jonathan Harris.)

Roddenberry saw the animated series as a bridge between syndication and films or a new television series, so wanted the integrity of the concept maintained. He modified the series bible for the animators, hired Fontana as story editor, and let Filmation get to work. He took the title Executive Consultant while Fontana was given the title Associate Producer, even though she did a producer's work. It was no surprise that NBC bought the show, and it debuted on September 8, 1973, exactly seven years after the parent show's first broadcast, with an episode written by Samuel Peeples. Given its older approach, the show was scheduled at 10:30 a.m., late enough for high school and college fans to probably be awake. For its second,

*Above:* Lieutenant Arex and Lieutenant M'Ress were added to the animated series in the 1970s and were warmly embraced by fans, going on to be included in comics, novels, and role-playing games. Although official action figures were never produced, Australian fan Ian McLean created custom figures of his own. *Ian McLean*

*Right:* Diamond Select Toys Minimates versions of McCoy, Kirk, Spock, and the Gorn.

shorter, season, the show moved an hour later, ending its run on October 12, 1974. The more mature approach to animated storytelling earned the show kudos from parenting advocates and more importantly, the fans. Roddenberry told *Show* magazine, "That was one of the reasons I wanted creative control. There are enough limitations just being on Saturday morning. We have to limit some of the violence we might have had on the evening shows. There will probably be no sex element to talk of either. But it will be *Star Trek* and not a stereotype kids cartoon show."

The animated style allowed for more alien worlds and civilizations in addition to new crewmembers. Still, the show was produced on a tight budget and hiring the original cast to provide voices was a strain. When the decision was taken to transfer Chekov off the ship, Roddenberry and Fontana each thought the other was going to make the heartbreaking phone call. Unfortunately, Walter Koenig learned of the show and his lack of participation at a convention. He was, though, invited to write a script, which became "The Infinite Vulcan." Chekov was replaced at the helm by Lieutenant Arex, a three-armed, three-legged crewman. Uhura was occasionally spelled by Lieutenant M'Ress, a distinctly feline lifeform.

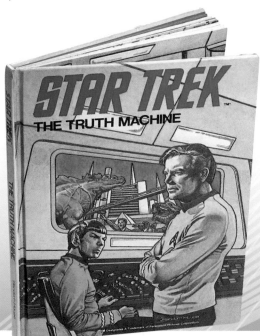

*Above:* Leonard Nimoy felt his career as a performer was being hamstrung by the audience's continued fascination with Spock. He tried to distance himself from the character with his first memoir. Twenty years later, he reversed himself with a second volume, *I Am Spock*.

*Left:* An original illustrated children's book by Christopher Cerf published by Random House in 1977.

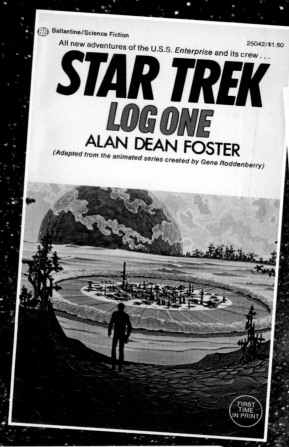

**Ballantine/Science Fiction** 25042/$1.50

All new adventures of the U.S.S. *Enterprise* and its crew . . .

# STAR TREK
## LOG ONE
### ALAN DEAN FOSTER
(Adapted from the animated series created by Gene Roddenberry)

**Ballantine/Science Fiction** 24260/$1.25

All new adventures of the U.S.S. *Enterprise* and its crew . . .

# STAR TREK
## LOG THREE
### ALAN DEAN FOSTER
(Adapted from the animated series created by Gene Roddenberry)

FIRST TIME IN PRINT

**Ballantine/Science Fiction** 25046/$1.50

All new adventures aboard the U.S.S. *Enterprise* . . .

# STAR TREK
## LOG FIVE
### ALAN DEAN FOSTER
(Adapted from the animated series created by Gene Roddenberry)

FIRST TIME IN PRINT

Ballantine made the unfortunate choice to update their cover design with just two books left to publish in the original run, swapping out images from the cartoons for generic shots of the *Enterprise*.

**Ballantine/Science Fiction** 25043/$1.50

All new adventures of the U.S.S. *Enterprise* and its crew . . .

# STAR TREK
## LOG TWO
### ALAN DEAN FOSTER
(Adapted from the animated series created by Gene Roddenberry)

FIRST TIME IN PRINT

**Ballantine/Science Fiction** 25045/$1.50

All new adventures aboard the U.S.S. *Enterprise* . . .

# STAR TREK
## LOG FOUR
### ALAN DEAN FOSTER
(Adapted from the animated series created by Gene Roddenberry)

FIRST TIME IN PRINT

BB Ballantine/Science Fiction/24965/$1.50

All new adventures aboard the U.S.S. Enterprise...

# STAR TREK
## LOG SEVEN
### ALAN DEAN FOSTER
*(Adapted from the animated series created by Gene Roddenberry)*

FIRST TIME IN PRINT

ALL NEW ADVENTURES ABOARD THE U.S.S. ENTERPRISE

# STAR TREK
## LOG NINE
### ALAN DEAN FOSTER
*(ADAPTED FROM THE ANIMATED SERIES CREATED BY GENE RODDENBERRY)*

DEL REY
Ballantine
Science Fiction
27165
$1.50

BB Ballantine/Science Fiction 24655/$1.50

# STAR TREK
## LOG SIX
### ALAN DEAN FOSTER
*(Adapted from the animated series created by Gene Roddenberry)*

FIRST TIME IN PRINT

BB Ballantine/Science Fiction/25141/$1.50

# STAR TREK
## LOG EIGHT
### ALAN DEAN FOSTER
*(Adapted from the animated series created by Gene Roddenberry)*

FIRST TIME IN PRINT

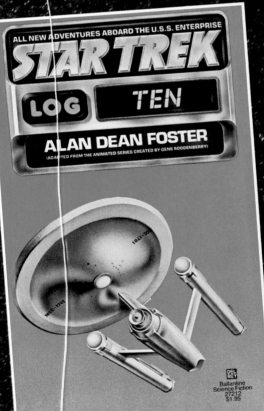

ALL NEW ADVENTURES ABOARD THE U.S.S. ENTERPRISE

# STAR TREK
## LOG TEN
### ALAN DEAN FOSTER
*(ADAPTED FROM THE ANIMATED SERIES CREATED BY GENE RODDENBERRY)*

DEL REY
Ballantine
Science Fiction
27212
$1.95

# A SPACE PIRATE STORY AND A DREAM

*Howard Weinstein*

It all started with one little story, and a dream: to be a writer—though I wasn't exactly sure how to do that. Fortunately, when we're young, we try things we'd never do if we had *any* common sense. Writing came naturally to me. In high school, while memorizing *Star Trek* reruns, I scribbled some *Star Trek* short stories on notebook paper to share with friends. And—inspired by Stephen Whitfield's great behind-the-scenes book *The Making of Star Trek*—I taught myself to write television scripts. When I tried to submit a *Mission: Impossible* script, I discovered studios only accepted submissions through agents—and found an agent who happened to be my father's childhood friend. As a favor, he agreed to look at my scripts.

When NBC's animated *Star Trek* series debuted in 1973, I was a college junior, determined to give it a shot. I chose my best short story, wrote "The Pirates of Orion" script, and sent it to the agent, who mailed it to Filmation Associates—addressed to Associate Producer Dorothy Fontana. Dorothy had departed by that time, so Filmation forwarded the script to her, and (for legal reasons) she returned it to my agent unopened: it traveled 6,000 miles and nobody even peeked at it. The show was renewed, the script resubmitted—and they bought it in April 1974, when I was nineteen. There's a lesson about perseverance in there somewhere.

Filmation honcho Lou Scheimer was surprised to learn I was a college junior selling my first script (which made me *Star Trek*'s youngest scriptwriter, at least until a high school kid sold a *Star Trek: The Next Generation* story). I was back at college when "Pirates" opened the show's second season on September 7, 1974, days before my birthday. Dorm-room televisions weren't common then, so I invited friends over to watch on my little black-and-white. Thirty kids (and one dog) crammed into our

room and cheered my name in the credits. Kind of like a very-mini-convention.

Speaking of conventions, I'd been among those mobbing the first *Star Trek* convention, in New York City in January 1972. After "Pirates" aired, I sent a letter to the FebCon '76 con committee (including my registration fee) and volunteered to do a talk, if they'd like. They quickly returned my check and invited me as a guest speaker.

I was pretty nervous for my solo talk in the big ballroom. I'd done radio, but it's scarier facing several hundred actual humans. I'd scribbled some prompt notes, just in case I froze. The notes helped—for fifteen minutes. So I gulped, and croaked out four fateful words: "Anybody have any questions?" Mercifully, they did (enough to fill my hour) even though I was an unknown nobody.

But I was more than that: I was a young fan-turned-professional. Selling that *Star Trek* script vaulted me onstage, and I've been there ever since. And if I could do it, maybe they could too. David Gerrold and I were probably the first *Trek* fans to become professional writers by selling *Star Trek* stories, but many have followed our trail. *Star Trek* remains uniquely inspirational, attracting creative fans for whom the show opened up careers in both arts and sciences, and too many lifelong friendships to count.

I'm lucky to have been aboard for this continuing journey. And it all started with one little story . . . and a dream.

*Howard Weinstein's* Star Trek *fiction credits include seven novels, short stories, sixty-five comic books and graphic novels, and story development assistance on* Star Trek IV: The Voyage Home.

Alan Dean Foster wrote several of the adventures for the Peter Pan series of audio adventures that came complete with comic books, executed by Neal Adams's Continuity Associates.

The producers were also thinking of saving cash by not using George Takei and Nichelle Nichols (while retaining Barrett, which was a financial boon to the married couple), but Nimoy used his star power to reject the notion. If Takei and Nichols were not hired to voice their characters, he would refuse to participate. Of course, Nimoy prevailed since Spock remained essential to the series.

In June 1973, Roddenberry and the cast were reunited for the first time in years to announce the new animated show. Whatever animosities between individuals were hidden behind the beaming smiles. It didn't hurt that the spread of conventions meant they were seeing one another in laudatory, social settings, allowing friendships to deepen between most of the performers.

Recording the voices proved a challenge, given that the cast was scattered around the country. Shatner was recorded wherever he was at the time. As a result, he was given scant direction, leading to a relatively flat performance. Kelley was the most comfortable performing, given his experience decades before in radio. And Doohan, with his mastery of accents, contributed multiple parts in almost every episode, as did, to a lesser extent, Takei, Nichols, and Barrett.

Fontana and Roddenberry were blessed with good timing since scripts were being commissioned during an eight month Writers Guild of America strike. Guild rules allowed their members to write one episode of an animated television series. The strike's end in summer 1973 also meant opportunities for new writers for the show's abbreviated second season after NBC ordered six more episodes.

The stories were a mix of strange new worlds and decidedly familiar ones, replete with recurring characters. Lieuenant Kyle gained a mustache while the color-blind Scheimer approved a pink shade for the Klingon tunics. A "Shore Leave" sequel was written by Chuck Menville and Len Janson. Fontana weighed in with another visit to Vulcan and Spock's childhood in the

warmly regarded "Yesteryear," some of whose scenes were revisited in the 2009 *Star Trek* movie. Two scripts originally written for the third season wound up being revised for the new format: Larry Brody's "The Magicks of Megas-Tu" and Gerrold's second Tribbles tale.

Larry Niven, who developed "The Pastel Terror" but never pitched it (although it did run in the *T-Negative* fanzine), did get associated with the franchise, trying several approaches. "I feared (groundlessly) that nobody at Filmation would see their chance to use real aliens rather than actors in rubber suits. So I wrote a story treatment using Outsiders (built like a black cat-o'-nine-tails, using photoelectric metabolism at near absolute zero) and quantum black holes. Dorothy Fontana was right: I was aiming over the audience's heads." While that concept later became his Hugo Award-winning novelette "The Borderland of Sol," Niven went on to write "The Slaver Weapon" incorporating his Kzinti race as antagonists on the show.

Filmation did not receive NBC's order until well into the spring

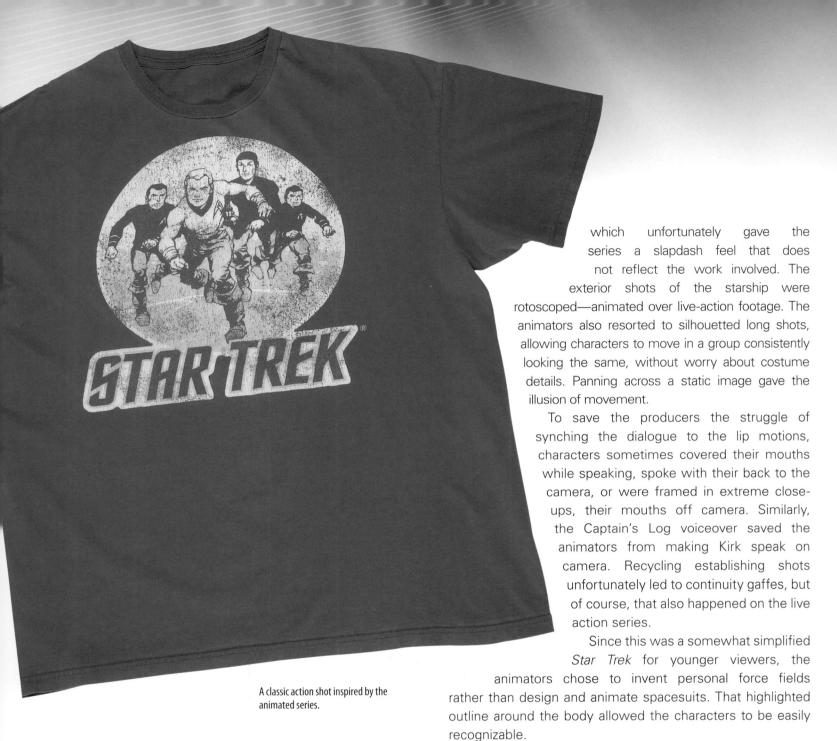

A classic action shot inspired by the animated series.

which unfortunately gave the series a slapdash feel that does not reflect the work involved. The exterior shots of the starship were rotoscoped—animated over live-action footage. The animators also resorted to silhouetted long shots, allowing characters to move in a group consistently looking the same, without worry about costume details. Panning across a static image gave the illusion of movement.

To save the producers the struggle of synching the dialogue to the lip motions, characters sometimes covered their mouths while speaking, spoke with their back to the camera, or were framed in extreme close-ups, their mouths off camera. Similarly, the Captain's Log voiceover saved the animators from making Kirk speak on camera. Recycling establishing shots unfortunately led to continuity gaffes, but of course, that also happened on the live action series.

Since this was a somewhat simplified *Star Trek* for younger viewers, the animators chose to invent personal force fields rather than design and animate spacesuits. That highlighted outline around the body allowed the characters to be easily recognizable.

of 1973, with the show on air in September. For the sixteen-episode first season, the price per episode was estimated to be $75,000, once again making *Star Trek* the most expensive production of its kind. To make the air dates, Filmation hired seventy-five artists who produced upwards of 7,000 drawings per episode, needing to complete nearly eight hours of animation in just five months.

Filmation also resorted to a handful of tricks and shortcuts,

Robert Kline, who got his start in comic book fanzines, was hired to do a lot of the alien design work, and with a trained eye you can tell his efforts. Less obvious is the early work of Glen Keane, who went on to a celebrated career twenty years later as a lead animator for Disney's renaissance films *The Little Mermaid* and *Beauty and the Beast*.

Fans debated almost from the beginning whether the series was considered part of the canon, given some continuity

errors and the use of Niven's alien Kzinti. Still, it was where we first met Robert April, Pike's predecessor as captain of the *Enterprise*; heard Kirk's middle name of Tiberius uttered; and saw the first use of what evolved into the holodeck. Visually, this bridge had two entrances, a touch added to the *Motion Picture* bridge and subsequent films.

The *Los Angeles Times* critic Cecil Smith wrote on September 10, 1973: "NBC's new animated *Star Trek* is as out of place in the Saturday morning kiddie ghetto as a Mercedes in a soapbox derby. Don't be put off by the fact it's now a cartoon. . . . It is fascinating fare, written, produced and executed with all the imaginative skill, the intellectual flare and the literary level that made Gene Roddenberry's famous old science fiction epic the most avidly followed program in TV history, particularly in high I.Q. circles. NBC might do well to consider moving it into prime time at mid-series." However, Tom Zito in the *Washington Post* questioned whether the show might be too cerebral for the four- to eight-year-olds watching.

Ballantine Books won the adaptation rights and hired the young Alan Dean Foster to turn these thirty-minute scripts into prose. He was challenged to pad out the material and initially expanded three scripts per volume under the *Star Trek Logs* umbrella title. The final four *Logs* were each based on a single episode, with Foster adding completely new adventures for the crew. It was many years before any of the episodes were referred to in the comics and novels, and later still before any of the new characters were used in the licensed product. Still, the show would resurface in reruns, first on Nickelodeon in the 1980s and later on the Sci Fi Channel a decade later.

The show's ratings were respectable but not record-setting, and once more, given the expense in producing the high quality series, NBC was not encouraged to continue. Despite praise from parents groups and winning the Emmy Award for Best Children's Series for the 1974–75 season, the show was canceled.

By then, though, Paramount had a new idea.

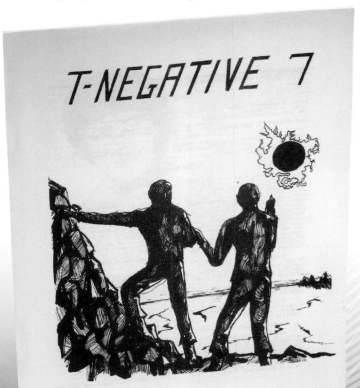

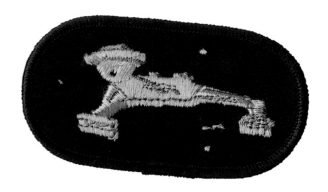

*Left: T-Negative* was one of the longest-running and most popular of the *Star Trek* fanzines.
*Voyageur Press collection*

# CHAPTER 7 *THE FANS*

## TAKE OWNERSHIP

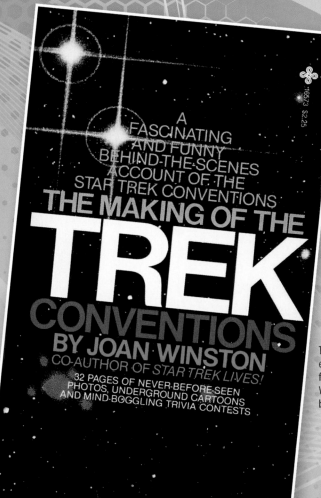

A FASCINATING AND FUNNY BEHIND-THE-SCENES ACCOUNT OF THE STAR TREK CONVENTIONS

## THE MAKING OF THE

# TREK

## CONVENTIONS

### BY JOAN WINSTON

CO-AUTHOR OF *STAR TREK LIVES!*

32 PAGES OF NEVER-BEFORE-SEEN PHOTOS, UNDERGROUND CARTOONS AND MIND-BOGGLING TRIVIA CONTESTS

16573 $2.25

The chaotic behind-the-scenes action of the early *Trek* conventions was captured in book form by veteran convention organizer Joan Winston, coauthor of *Star Trek Lives!*, published by Doubleday in 1977.

Once upon a time there was a man whose idea was not to change the world, but to show what it could be: that we could live with and love people different from ourselves, and that we could learn so much if we didn't fear the unknown.

That idea became STAR TREK. People liked this man's idea so much that they began to get together to discuss it, to explore the unknown themselves if only in words, and to communicate with strangers who became friends.

STAR TREK became a picture of a future we could hope for, a group of people we could fall in love with, and an experience we could share. We hope this memory book will help keep it alive for you.

We dedicate this book to the man who single-handedly brought the word 'trek' back into the language - to Gene Roddenberry, with love and devotion, from all his STAR TREK fans and fiends.

Maureen B. Wilson,
President,
GENE RODDENBERRY APPRECIATION SOCIETY

Photos courtesy of NBC and Paramount Studios

A section of the photo booklet handed out at the first New York *Star Trek* convention in January 1972. *Howard Weinstein*

The success of the January 1972 New York *Star Trek* convention led to *Trek* being a part of that fall's Detroit Triple Fan Fair, which celebrated comics, science fiction, and the series.

The Committee that organized the first New York convention in 1972 each earned $92.46 after all the expenses were covered. They were enthusiastic about trying again and took the hard-learned lessons to heart. They needed more space and for the 1973 convention headed uptown to the Commodore Hotel, adjacent to Grand Central Station. The show moved from January to Presidents' Day weekend in February, where it remained through 1976.

In her innocence, The Committee's Elyse Rosenstein (nee Pines) wrote to the original cast, inviting them to attend. Doohan and Takei accepted, as did author Gerrold. There was a more expanded trivia contest and a masquerade. Two fans from Poughkeepsie, Art Burmaghim and Mike McMaster,

had spent the previous two years building a bridge replica and spent countless hours reassembling it as part of the show. Jeff Maynard, who went on to a successful career in film, began his annual slide and multimedia shows. The legendary Phil Seuling, who ran the most successful New York Comic Conventions of the time, was in charge of the packed dealers' room, featuring a growing selection of *Star Trek* merchandise, from glossy stills to tribbles. Programming included episodes of television shows starring the cast or written by members of the staff, and Katz was back, this time teasing Roddenberry's latest project, CBS's *Genesis II*.

The highlight of the second con, called the International *Star Trek* Convention, was the unannounced appearance of Leonard Nimoy that Sunday. I was on hand as a helper (unpaid volunteer) and, along with future comics writer Paul Kupperberg, was part of the flying V-formation of security to get Nimoy from the entrance to the stage. We then stood in

Abby Uhlan was one of the most recognizable of the New York area fans thanks to her button-festooned hat. She was a fixture at the conventions through the 1970s. *Andrew Scholnick*

position to form a human wall between shrieking fans and a smiling actor.

Anticipating between 5,000 to 6,000 fans, the organizers were pleasantly surprised with a total head count of 6,200.

That same year, Bjo Trimble organized The *Star Trek* West Coast Convention as a part of her Equicon event, which she had started two years earlier.

For the third New York show in 1974, the guest roster grew to include Kelley, Nichols, and Koenig, along with returning visitors Fontana, Gerrold, and Takei. Makeup artist Fred Phillips rounded out the guest list; Al Schuster was turned into a Klingon on stage thanks to Phillips's ministrations.

Needing more room, The Committee moved the convention a little further uptown to the Americana Hotel. When Kelley, Nichols, and Takei arrived on the same plane, luck had it that "All Our Yesterdays" guest star Mariette Hartley was also on the flight. The Committee gave her a ride into Manhattan, which resulted in an impromptu invitation to speak at the con, and she became a well-received surprise guest.

It should be noted that while these memorable affairs made people happy and brought in huge crowds, most cons ended without anything in the way of a profit. After three cons, The Committee went to work on their fourth effort without profits from the previous show to bolster them. Instead, members used their personal resources to get things rolling until membership fees arrived. Everyone from the executives on down to the helpers worked for little beyond pizza, soda, and camaraderie. By then, those helpers grew to include future publishing professionals Claire Eddy, Patrick Daniel O'Neill, and Diane Duane.

Following the 1974 show, Schuster had a falling out with The Committee and decided to run his own show in New York, one month before the usual convention. The bad blood was the talk of fandom as people wrote to the growing number of fanzines, taking sides. Schuster's The International *Star Trek* Convention ran January 10–12, 1975, at the Statler

Fans took it upon themselves to re-create the bridge nearly life size for their own amusement or fan films. This bridge was taken apart from upstate New York and brought to Manhattan and reassembled for the original Committee conventions. *Andrew Scholnick*

Hilton with The Committee's *Star Trek* Convention following February 14–17, 1975, once more at the Commodore. Schuster scooped his former partners by signing Shatner to make his first convention appearance even though the star had already signed to appear in February. In the end, both did good business, but the good will engendered by The Committee's efforts won out in the end.

The Roddenberrys returned to the convention as did Gerrold and Takei, along with first-timer William Ware Theiss, who of course brought along some of his costumes. A surprise guest was "Assignment: Earth" guest star Robert Lansing, who demonstrated to me he was quite adept at doing magic coin tricks despite being inebriated in the wee hours of the morning. Unfortunately, that was the year the show was besieged with fans using counterfeit tickets, which crowded the show floor and confounded The Committee.

It was here that Roddenberry told the fans that a feature film was on Paramount's schedule and he was optimistic this would actually happen.

After Shatner's appearance at the February show, Committee member Thom Anderson was asked the difference between Shatner and Nimoy's interaction with the fans. Anderson explained that while the audience wanted a piece of Shatner, and there was a sexually charged atmosphere, they treated Nimoy more like an appearance by the Pope. Everyone hung on his every word in hushed silence.

The Committee was tired and worn out from the exhausting grind. It was decided 1976 was going to be their last hurrah, knowing full well that others would fill the gap. Sure enough, six months later, there was a Labor Day NYC show, Bi-Centennial 10.

New Yorker Linda Deneroff was a typical fan of the show, a contributor and reader to the fanzines who ended up working with The Committee. "I was an assistant at the second through fifth New York *Star Trek* conventions. My job was to prescreen the questions that people asked the celebrities and to make sure everyone got a turn asking a question. I almost had a heart attack the time Jimmy Doohan jumped off the stage into the audience and started shaking everyone's hands. I was afraid he was going to be mobbed, but everyone was nice and patient, and we both survived.

"By the time of the final convention, I had become a quite good photographer, and I had asked Majel Barrett if I might take her picture. She agreed, and I held up my 35mm camera with its hand grip, telephone lens, and a strobe light. Even though the photo came out great and she's smiling brightly, for just a second I could see the terror on her face before she realized I was holding a camera.

"We must have had a hundred entrants in the masquerade, and each one went through a prejudging

A fan-built miniature of the bridge from an early convention, showing incredible detail and talent. *Andrew Scholnick*

## THERE'S AN AMOEBA BY MILDRED TORGERSON

(HAVA NAGILA)

THERE'S AN AMOEBA STALKING THE STARSHIP
AND IF IT CATCHES US, WHAT SHALL WE DO?

THERE'S AN AMOEBA STALKING THE STARSHIP
AND IF IT CATCHES UP, STAR TREK IS THROUGH!

FIRE THE PHASER BANKS
RAISE THE DEFLECTOR SHIELDS
SEND OUT THE SHUTTLECRAFT
WE WILL NOT YIELD!

MR. SPOCK MUST GO OUT
IN THE SHUTTLECRAFT ALL BRAVELY
AS THE CAPTAIN COWERS KNAVELY
IN THE SHIP, IN THE SHIP
MR. SPOCK MUST MAKE THE TRIP.

## TREK AROUND THE CLOCK BY PAT & JUDY MOLNAR

(ROCK AROUND THE CLOCK)

ONE, TWO, THREE O'CLOCK, FOUR O'CLOCK SPOCK.
FIVE, SIX SEVEN O'CLOCK, EIGHT O'CLOCK SPOCK.
NINE, TEN, ELEVEN O'CLOCK, TWELVE O'CLOCK SPOCK.
WE'RE GONNA TREK AROUND THE CLOCK TONIGHT.

PUT YOUR PHASERS ON AND JOIN ME HON
WE'LL WATCH STAR TREK TIL THE CLOCK STRIKES ONE

(CHORUS)
WE'RE GONNA TREK AROUND THE CLOCK TONIGHT
WE'RE GONNA WARP, WARP, WARP TIL THE BROAD DAYLIGHT
GONNA TREK, GONNA TREK AROUND THE CLOCK TONIGHT.

WHEN THE CLOCK STRIKES TWO, THREE AND FOUR
WE'LL BE MEETING AT THE COMMODORE.

CHORUS

WHEN THE CHIMES RING FIVE, SIX AND SEVEN
WE'LL WATCH PIKE FIGHT ON RIGEL SEVEN.

CHORUS

WHEN IT'S EIGHT, NINE, TEN, ELEVEN TOO,
WE'LL MASQUERADE THE WHOLE NIGHT THROUGH.

CHORUS

NOW WHEN THE CLOCK STRIKES TWELVE
WE'LL YELL OUT THEN
TO SHOW THE BLOOPER REEL AGAIN.

CHORUS

## THE 12 DAYS OF CHRISTMAS AT STAR FLEET LOST & FOUND

BY MARY SCHAUB

ON THE FIRST DAY OF CHRISTMAS, THE FLEET TURNED IN TO ME
A FAT TRIBBLE IN A FIR TREE

ON THE SECOND DAY OF CHRISTMAS, THE FLEET TURNED IN TO ME
TWO GIANT EEL-BIRDS AND
A FAT TRIBBLE IN A FIR TREE

THREE FLAME GEMS...

FOUR BORGIA PLANTS...

FIVE WHEEZY GORNS...

SIX KLINGONS SCHEMING...

SEVEN KELVANS KNITTING...

EIGHT NOMADS BEEPING...

NINE VULCANS THINKING...

TEN HORTAS DIGGING...

ELEVEN SEHLATS TEETHING...

TWELVE BOWLS OF PLOMIK...

## THE FEDS WE ARE RAIDING TONIGHT BY ANN NICHOLS

(CAISSONS GO ROLLING)

KLINGONS HERE, KLINGONS THERE,
ALL GOOD KLINGONS EVERYWHERE
THE FEDS WE ARE RAIDING TONIGHT!
PHASERS OUT, SET ON 'KILL'
JUST THE THOUGHT GIVES US A THRILL
FOR THE FEDS WE ARE RAIDING TONIGHT!

WE'RE WORKING STEADILY
FOR FEDERATION ANARCHY
WE'RE GONNA BLAST THEM OUT OF SIGHT!
AIMING HIGH AND AIMING LOW
WE'LL BE LOOTING AS WE GO
FOR THE FEDS WE ARE RAIDING TONI
KEEP 'EM SHOOTING!
FOR THE FEDS WE ARE RAIDING TONI

## STAR FLEET LIFE BY DUSTY JONES & CHRIS BALDERSON

(ARMY LIFE)

CHORUS,
OH, I DON'T WANT NO MORE OF STAR FLEET LIFE
GEE MA, I WANNA GO
VULCAN'S THE PLACE YOU KNOW
GEE MA, I WANNA GO HOME

THE PAY OUT HERE IN STAR FLEET THEY SAY IS MIGHTY FINE
THEY GIVE YOU A HUNDRED CREDITS AND TAKE OUT 99.

CHORUS

THE NURSES HERE IN STAR FLEET, THEY FILL YOU FULL OF FEAR
YOU WALK AROUND THE CORNER, THEY KISS YOU ON THE EAR

CHORUS

COMMUNICATIONS PEOPLE, THEY MAKE A LOT OF DOUGH
YOU ASK TO CALL A STAR BASE, THEY TELL YOU WHERE TO GO

CHORUS

THE ENGINEERS IN STAR FLEET THEY SAY ARE MIGHTY FINE
THEY LIVE ON SCOTCH AND WATER AND JUST A DROP OF WINE

CHORUS

THE HELMSMEN HERE IN STAR FLEET BRING LETHAL THINGS ABOARD
YOU GIVE A SIMPLE ORDER, THEY STAB YOU WITH A SWORD

CHORUS

THE STAR FLEET NAVIGATORS HAVE
YOU ASK THEM FOR DIRECTIONS, TH

CHORUS

TRANSPORTERS OUT IN STAR FLEET
YOU BEAM DOWN TO A PLANET, YOUR

CHORUS

THE SHUTTLECRAFTS IN STAR FLEET
YOU ACTIVATE THE SENSORS, THEY

CHORUS

THE PHASERS OUT IN STAR FLEET,
YOU FIRE AT A KLINGON, THEY BLO

CHORUS

THE UNIFORMS IN STAR FLEET THEY
YOU ASK TO FIT A VULCAN, THEY F

CHORUS

THE MEDICAL EQUIPMENT, I'D LIKE
MY FATHER'S CORONARY WAS DIAGN

CHORUS

These lyric sheets are some of the earliest filk songs written about *Star Trek* and were used for sing-a-longs during the original Committee conventions. During a lull one day, David Gerrold took to leading an impromptu concert until the scheduled guest arrived. *Robert Greenberger*

## A MOST ILLOGICAL SONG BY SHIRLEY MEECH, KATHY BUSHMAN, & SHERNA COMERFORD

(I WISH I WAS A BUSY LITTLE BEE)

I WISH I WAS ON BOARD THE ENTERPRISE.
I WISH I WAS ON BOARD THE ENTERPRISE.
IF I WAS ON THE ENTERPRISE,
I'D LOOK INTO THOSE VULCAN EYES.
I WISH I WAS ON BOARD THE ENTERPRISE.

I WISH THAT I WAS CAPTAIN JAMES T. KIRK.
I WISH THAT I WAS CAPTAIN JAMES T. KIRK.
IF I WAS CAPTAIN JAMES T. KIRK,
THEN WITH THAT VULCAN I WOULD WORK.
I WISH THAT I WAS CAPTAIN JAMES T. KIRK.

I WISH I WAS A DOCTOR NAMED McCOY.
I WISH I WAS A DOCTOR NAMED McCOY.
IF I WAS A DOCTOR NAMED McCOY,
WHAT ARGUMENTS I WOULD ENJOY.
I WISH I WAS A DOCTOR NAMED McCOY.

I WISH I WAS AN ENGINEER NAMED SCOTT.
I WISH I WAS AN ENGINEER NAMED SCOTT.
IF I WAS AN ENGINEER NAMED SCOTT,
I'D GET TO TALK TO SPOCK A LOT.
I WISH I WAS AN ENGINEER NAMED SCOTT.

I WISH THAT I WAS SULU WITH A SWORD.
I WISH THAT I WAS SULU WITH A SWORD.
IF I WAS SULU WITH A SWORD,
BY SPOCK I WOULD NOT BE IGNORED.
I WISH THAT I WAS SULU WITH A SWORD.

I WISH I WAS UHURA WITH HER SONG.
I WISH I WAS UHURA WITH HER SONG.
IF I WAS UHURA WITH HER SONG,
I'D SING OF SPOCK THE WHOLE TRIP LONG.
I WISH I WAS UHURA WITH HER SONG.

I WISH I WAS A GAME OF THREE-D CHESS.
I WISH I WAS A GAME OF THREE-D CHESS.
IF I WAS A GAME OF THREE-D CHESS,
THEN SPOCK WOULD WANT TO WIN ME, YES!
I WISH I WAS A GAME OF THREE-D CHESS.

I WISH I WAS A VILLAIN WITH A WRENCH.
I WISH I WAS A VILLAIN WITH A WRENCH.
IF I WAS A VILLAIN WITH A WRENCH,
THEN SPOCK MIGHT USE THE VULCAN PINCH.
I WISH I WAS A VILLAIN WITH A WRENCH.

I WISH THAT I COULD HOLD SPOCK IN MY ARMS.
I WISH THAT I COULD HOLD SPOCK IN MY ARMS.
IF I COULD HOLD SPOCK IN MY ARMS,
HE'D FIND EMOTION HAS ITS CHARMS.
I WISH THAT I COULD HOLD SPOCK IN MY ARMS.

I WISH I HAD SOME SPORES FROM MIRA THREE.
I WISH I HAD SOME SPORES FROM MIRA THREE.
IF I HAD SPORES FROM MIRA THREE,
THEN SPOCK MIGHT BE TURNED ON BY ME.
I WISH I HAD SOME SPORES FROM MIRA THREE.

I WISH I WAS A HORTA MADE OF ROCK.
I WISH I WAS A HORTA MADE OF ROCK.
IF I WAS A HORTA MADE OF ROCK,
I'D GET TO SHARE MY MIND WITH SPOCK.
I WISH I WAS A HORTA MADE OF ROCK.

I WISH THAT I COULD JOIN AND TOUCH SPOCK'S MIND.
I WISH THAT I COULD JOIN AND TOUCH SPOCK'S MIND.
IF I COULD JOIN AND TOUCH SPOCK'S MIND,
JUST THINK OF ALL THE THOUGHTS I'D FIND.
I WISH THAT I COULD JOIN AND TOUCH SPOCK'S MIND.

I WISH THAT SPOCK COULD HEAR MY MELODY.
I WISH THAT SPOCK COULD HEAR MY MELODY.
IF SPOCK COULD HEAR MY MELODY,
HE'D RAISE ONE EYEBROW JUST FOR ME.
I WISH THAT SPOCK COULD HEAR MY MELODY.

## BATTLE HYMN OF THE HELPERS BY THE HELPERS, 1975 STC

(BATTLE HYMN OF THE REPUBLIC)

MINE EYES HAVE SEEN THE GLORY OF THE ENDING OF THE CON.
THEY WERE TRAMPLED ON THE CARPET WHEN THE MOVIES WERE
NOT ON.
THEY WERE TEARING DOWN THE WALLS THE GUESTS HAD RESTED
HANDS UPON.
PRAISE GHU, THEY ARE ALL GONE!

CHORUS,
GLORY, GLORY RODDENBERRY,
GLORY, GLORY RODDENBERRY,
GLORY, GLORY RODDENBERRY,
PRAISE GHU, THEY ARE ALL GONE!

THEY WERE LURKING IN THE CORRIDORS WHERE GENE AND MAJEL
LIVED.
OUR SECURITY ARRANGEMENTS WERE AS LEAKY AS A SIEVE.
ROOM NUMBERS COMMITTEE DIDN'T KNOW THE TREKKIES WOULD
GLADLY GIVE.
PRAISE GHU, THEY ARE ALL GONE!

CHORUS

BILL SHATNER OWES HIS LIFE TO FEN WHOSE NAMES HE'LL
NEVER KNOW.
THEY ARE PLACING THEIR FRAIL BODIES WHERE THE TREKKIES
WANT TO GO.
AND WE ALL ARE DEEPLY THANKFUL LEONARD NIMOY DID NOT SHOW!
PRAISE GHU, THEY ARE ALL GONE!

CHORUS

OUR GUESTS WERE WONT TO WANDER WHERE OUR HELPERS FEARED
TO GO.
DEAR GEORGE ONCE TRIED TO ROAM AROUND AND THOUGHT NO
ONE WOULD KNOW.
WE PICKED UP WHAT WAS LEFT OF HIM AND PUT HIM IN THE SHOW.
PRAISE GHU, THEY ARE ALL GONE!

CHORUS

IKE ASIMOV MADE SPEECHES WHERE HE TOLD ALL HE DID KNOW.
JEFF MAYNARD SET UP SIX DAYS TO PUT ON HIS LIGHT SHOW.
ROBERT LANSING GAVE US EXTRA WORK, HE KNOWS WHERE HE
CAN GO!
PRAISE GHU, THEY ARE ALL GONE!

CHORUS

THERE WASN'T MUCH OF DESTINY HER COSTUME DIDN'T SHOW.
THE VULCAN HOOKER PATIA MATCHED AGAINST HER BLOW FOR BLOW.
BUT HELPERS DIDN'T NOTICE, THEY WERE BUSY CLEARING ROWS.
PRAISE GHU, THEY ARE ALL GONE!

CHORUS

DAVE GERROLD BROUGHT SOME FUR WITH HIM A TRIBBLE IT
WAS CALLED.
DICK HOAGLAND GAVE HIS SPEECH ON THE SPACE PROGRAM, NOW
STALLED.
AND BILL THEISS SHOWED US SOME COSTUMES THAT WE ALL
THOUGHT WOULD FALL!
PRAISE GHU, THEY ARE ALL GONE!

CHORUS

HAL CLEMENT FIXED THE SCIENCE ERRORS THAT GENE'S WRITERS
MADE.
AND RESHAPED WORLDS TO BE THOSE WHERE THE ENTERPRISE
HAD STAYED.
THIS YEAR HE TOLD OF THE PLANET WHERE TO VAAL MEN PRAYED.
PRAISE GHU, THEY ARE ALL GONE!

CHORUS

BOB LANSING, GENE AND MAJEL WERE ALL DRINKING IN THE
SUITE.
THE COMMITTEE AND ASSISTANTS WERE ALL NURSING BLISTERED
FEET.
WE'LL DISCUSS OUR PLANS FOR NEXT YEAR'S CON, BUT NOT
BEFORE WE EAT!
PRAISE GHU, THEY ARE ALL GONE!

CHORUS

before the masquerade, and then a judging when they were on stage. Majel was one of the judges. Unfortunately, she had enjoyed the masquerade so much, she had neglected to judge or take notes, and everyone had to do a quick run back on stage before the winners could be announced. It was a *long* evening."

The final Committee con was bittersweet on several levels, but it was also knocked flat by the virulent Victoria flu, which reduced the twenty-four person costume show to seven and incapacitated the majority of The Committee. Anyone in the lower ranks with experience was pressed into service, myself included, and it was a tremendous amount of fun. Anne Meara, then starring in CBS's *Kate McShane* series, made a surprise appearance since she was a huge fan. She brought along her children, Amy and Ben. Young Ben Stiller was such a fan that he later wound up naming his company Red Shirt Productions.

The after-con Dead Dog Party was especially poignant as people came to the realization an era was ending. The Roddenberrys, Takei, and other guests stopped in to pay their respects and thank the assembled staff for making the effort. Roddenberry, in particular, was welcomed back with a singing of "Glory Glory Roddenberry" to the tune of "Battle Hymn of the Republic" that had him blushing. Months later, there was a thank you party as The Committee acknowledged the hard efforts that everyone had spent years investing in the cons.

## CONVENTIONS GO GLOBAL

In time, *Star Trek* conventions would become a global phenomenon, with Britain holding the first overseas event in 1974.

The 1975 West Coast convention was held in San Diego, folded into Trimble's Film Con, organized by Jean Graham. Other major cities, including Chicago, had caught convention fever and were running their own events, modeled after The Committee's shows. Others tried for distinct touches or doing cons on a smaller scale, such as Rich Kolker's August Party in 1975, held at the University of Maryland. Like the other shows, he planned on a few hundred and wound up with 1,100 people on hand. Without big-name guests, he began a tradition of having Roddenberry call the show and regale attendees with a private chat.

Al Schuster may have been the first to try turning conventions into big business, but he wasn't the only such entrepreneur. In time, other regional promoters got into the act and for stretches of time, they controlled portions of the country. At the time of this writing, the only one with a national presence is Creation Conventions, which began operations as a comic convention in November 1971. They have since turned Las Vegas into a mecca for *Star Trek* fans every August.

The shows have continued around the world. Explains German journalist Christian Humberg, "Since the 1970s, Germany had its own fan clubs, most of which were inspired by international (i.e., American) ones, which—in the days before the internet—often provided them with news from overseas. The German clubs worked like their foreign counterparts: through fanzines, penpal-ships, and regional meetings like the so-called Trekdinners. One group of German fans even influenced the *Star Trek* movies: frustrated by the way the original series and its movies were being dubbed, a Bavarian fan organization intervened. With the personal support of Leonard Nimoy and Harve Bennett, they contacted the German Powers That Be and became script advisors for the German dialogue.

"Seen from an international perspective, Germany's *Star Trek* scene may be best known for FedCon, Europe's largest SF/media convention. FedCon started in 1992 and celebrated its twentieth convention in 2011. It still attracts thousands of fans each year, who come from all over the world. It is organized by Dirk Bartholomä, the man behind the German branch of the Official *Star Trek* Fan Club.

*Below:* "Trouble with Tribbles" author David Gerrold mugs for the camera. On the bottom right is Devra Langsam, editor of the first *Star Trek* fanzine, *Spockanalia*. *Andrew Scholnick*

*Above:* Walter Koenig talks to the fans from a podium, a far more formal presentation than convention appearances evolved into in later years. *Andrew Scholnick*

*Left:* James Doohan and a fan at the 1973 *Star Trek* convention. *Andrew Scholnick*

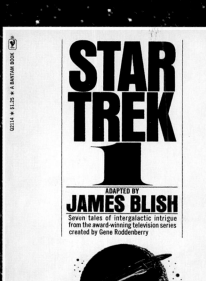

STAR TREK 1
Q2114 ★ $1.25 ★ A BANTAM BOOK

ADAPTED BY
JAMES BLISH
Seven tales of intergalactic intrigue
from the award-winning television series
created by Gene Roddenberry

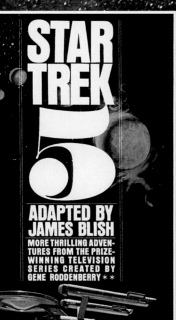

STAR TREK 2
Q2171 ★ $1.25 ★ A BANTAM BOOK

ADAPTED BY
JAMES BLISH
THE ULTIMATE TRIP TO WORLDS
BEYOND TIME, FROM THE
AWARD-WINNING TELEVISION
SERIES CREATED
BY GENE RODDENBERRY

BANTAM BOOKS ★ SPECIAL EDITION!

ALL NEW
AWARD-WINNING
STAR TREK 3

ADAPTED BY
JAMES BLISH

A MIND-REELING JOURNEY!
EERIE EXCURSIONS INTO
GALAXIES OF PROBABILITY!
BASED ON THE EXCITING
NBC-TV SERIES CREATED

A BANTAM BOOK
N6179 ★ 95¢ ★

ALL NEW
AWARD-WINNING
STAR TREK 4

ADAPTED BY
JAMES BLISH
MORE DAZZLING EXPLOITS BY
THE DYNAMIC CREW OF THE
ENTERPRISE ● BASED ON THE
EXCITING TELEVISION SERIES
CREATED BY GENE RODDENBERRY

STAR TREK 5
Q8150 ★ $1.25 ★ A BANTAM BOOK

ADAPTED BY
JAMES BLISH
MORE THRILLING ADVEN-
TURES FROM THE PRIZE-
WINNING TELEVISION
SERIES CREATED BY
GENE RODDENBERRY ★★

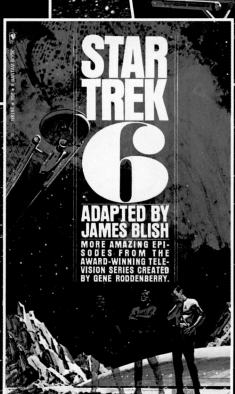

STAR TREK 6
N8184 ★ 95¢ ★ A BANTAM BOOK

ADAPTED BY
JAMES BLISH
MORE AMAZING EPI-
SODES FROM THE
AWARD-WINNING TELE-
VISION SERIES CREATED
BY GENE RODDENBERRY.

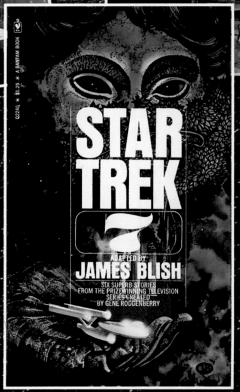

STAR TREK 7
Q2240 ★ $1.25 ★ A BANTAM BOOK

ADAPTED BY
JAMES BLISH
SIX SUPERB STORIES
FROM THE PRIZEWINNING TELEVISION
SERIES CREATED
BY GENE RODDENBERRY

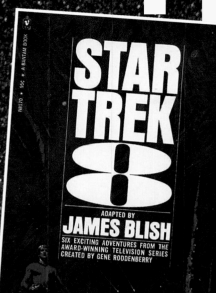

STAR TREK 8

ADAPTED BY
JAMES BLISH

SIX EXCITING ADVENTURES FROM THE
AWARD-WINNING TELEVISION SERIES
CREATED BY GENE RODDENBERRY

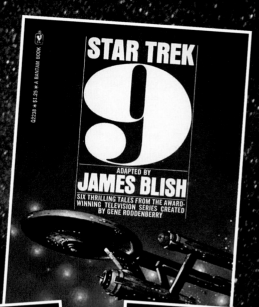

STAR TREK 9

ADAPTED BY
JAMES BLISH

SIX THRILLING TALES FROM THE AWARD-
WINNING TELEVISION SERIES CREATED
BY GENE RODDENBERRY

STAR TREK 10

ADAPTED BY
JAMES BLISH

SIX FASCINATING NEW EPISODES FROM
THE AWARD-WINNING TELEVISION
SERIES CREATED BY GENE RODDENBERRY
FIRST TIME IN PAPERBACK

STAR TREK 11

ADAPTED BY
JAMES BLISH

SIX AMAZING ADVENTURES FROM THE
AWARD-WINNING TELEVISION SERIES
CREATED BY GENE RODDENBERRY.

FIRST TIME IN PAPERBACK

STAR TREK 12

BY
JAMES BLISH
WITH
J.A. LAWRENCE

FIVE MIND-DAZZLING ADVENTURES
FROM THE AWARD-WINNING
TELEVISION SERIES CREATED BY
GENE RODDENBERRY.

FIRST TIME IN PAPERBACK

CORGI

A STAR TREK ADVENTURE
MUDD'S ANGELS

ADAPTED BY
J.A. LAWRENCE

THRILLING EXCURSIONS FROM THE AWARD-WINNING
TELEVISION SERIES CREATED BY GENE RODDENBERRY

A
STAR TREK
NOVEL

SPOCK
MUST DIE!

BY JAMES BLISH

AN EXCITING NEW STORY OF
INTERPLANETARY ADVENTURE

BASED ON THE
TELEVISION SERIES CREATED
BY GENE RODDENBERRY

James Blish and his wife, J. A. Lawrence,
adapted the original series scripts into a series
of short story collections for Bantam Books.
*Mudd's Angels* (represented here by the British
edition published by Corgi) included both of the
TV appearances of Harry Mudd plus an original
Mudd story by Lawrence. *Spock Must Die!* was
an original short novel by Blish. *Star Trek 1–11
courtesy of Becky Pagel*

*Above:* DeForest Kelley speaks with the press at the 1974 *Star Trek* convention. *Andrew Scholnick*

*Right:* Nichelle Nichols is at a press conference prior to taking the stage at the 1974 *Star Trek* convention. *Andrew Scholnick*

"FedCon is the only one of the big media conventions that survived the end of the *Star Trek* boom of the 1990s. Rival yearly events like the popular Galileo VII and Nexus conventions have since ceased to exist."

Architect and fan Marc B. Lee began attending Baltimore-based conventions and eventually became an international impresario, hosting events in Germany. The gregarious Lee explains the difference between events in the two countries. "Although I am a huge fan of the fan-run conventions here in my own country, and pay homage to groups such as Farpoint (formerly Clippercon/Oktobertrek) and Shore Leave, who both continue to produce untouchable fan-dedicated events, the cons in America have two exceptions as standouts in comparison to the European cons: Comic-Con International, which in my opinion is a waste of fandom as we have known it but provides the celebrity level expected, and Dragon*Con which in a mere word is 'mecca.'

"All other cons in this great country couldn't hold a match to the European cons. Why? Passion. Electricity. Production. Creativity. Visual overload. Loud. Imagine a high school fair or dance and add a little of Halloween and you'd have an American convention. Then think of the Academy Awards, add Mardi Gras and an Aerosmith concert, with Oktoberfest and beautiful locales, along with beautiful women, and you'd have a European event. The sheer money that goes into one of their cons would be the operating budget of ten conventions in the U.S."

## FANDOM GROWS

Fans found each other through fanzines. After *Spockanalia* debuted, *Star Trek*-related zines grew from a trickle to a torrent over the next three decades. They were mimeographed with stenciled artwork, hand-collated and stapled, and mailed first class, charging whatever was necessary to cover expenses and postage. Zines were labors of love, and never meant to make the editor rich.

The pages were filled with editorials, articles, letters, poetry, and lots of fan fiction. *ST-Phile 1*, published in January 1968, was coedited by Juanita Coulson, one of many to find their fan passions become careers. This zine had the privilege of printing the complete *Star Trek* series pitch, provided by Roddenberry. As had become habit, members of cast also sent along letters of greeting and best wishes. The second issue featured fiction from Lois McMaster, known today as Hugo and Nebula Award–winning Lois McMaster Bujold. Already a pro, Marion Zimmer Bradley also contributed to the zines, enticing many *Trek* fans to read her *Darkover* stories. Others who got their start in the zines include Allan Asherman, who went on to write many books about the series; novelist Jean Lorrah; and Hugo Award–winning artist Phil Foglio.

Bjo Trimble channeled her passion in 1969 to write *Star Trek Concordance of People, Places, and Things*, covering the first two seasons of the original series. That year, a variety of zines began featuring recurring authors, with a lot of the fan fiction trying to fill in gaps in the characters' backgrounds or provide sequels to the more compelling episodes. Fans soon started debating the future of the show, teased with the success of the reruns.

Interviews with cast, crew, and writers began to appear, and fans got a glimpse into the world behind the camera, and learned of shows that almost were. Whatever scant news there was to be had could be found in these zines, such as the announcement of the gathering of fans in New York City in January 1972. There were also critiques aplenty, including one in 1971 that was already complaining about the volume of stories featuring a girl, standing in for the author, having a romance with Spock (the so-called Mary Sue strand of fiction). In 1973, D. C. Fontana shared that Paramount and NBC were disinterested in a film or TV series, but she did announce the forthcoming animated show.

*Spockanalia* faded away, ceding its legacy to a new zine, *Masiform D*, which arrived in January 1971 and became the

# STAR TREK CONCORDANCE

Star Date:
Unknown

Call Letters:
MM

Title:
Mirror, Mirror

Page:
55

TO LOCATE ANY STAR TREK EPISODE IN THIS CONCORDANCE, TURN THE WHEEL OF THE ENTERPRISE INDEX TRICORDER TO REACH THE NAME OF THE EPISODE YOU WANT. THE EPISODE, STARDATE AND CALL LETTERS WILL APPEAR IN THEIR RESPECTIVE WINDOWS, ALONG WITH THE NUMBER OF THE PAGE IN THE CONCORDANCE WHERE THE COMPLETE ENTRY CAN BE FOUND.

A FULLY ILLUSTRATED, COMPREHENSIVE, DIRECTORY TO THE TV SERIES, INCLUDING CASTS, PLOT SYNOPSES, FAN ART, GLOSSARY, INDEX, ETC.

Ballantine $3.97 $8.95

Bjo Trimble's fanzine labor of love made the leap to professional publication from Ballantine Books in 1977 and was a must-read item for fans.

longest-running *Star Trek* zine, with eighteen issues spread between then and 1998. Meantime, fan writers were letting their libidos get the better of them and, to avoid problems with younger readers, separate zines, starting with Carrie Peak's *Grup*, became home to such "adult" fare. In the third issue, the first Kirk/Spock story appeared, "A Fragment Out of Time" by Diane Marchant. Some fans felt that there was more to the Kirk-Spock relationship than simple friendship. Much fan fiction explored their possible romance in what was originally known as "K-S fiction." However when the romance turned graphic, it became "K/S fiction," which has since been shortened to "slash fiction" and can be found across all media-inspired fan fiction. Slash artwork and fiction eventually became an embarrassment to both Shatner and Nimoy.

In 1973, aided by Deborah Jones, Bjo Trimble completed a supplement to her *Concordance* incorporating the third season. Ballantine Books hired Trimble to clean up the book, adding in the animated series, and then published *The Star Trek Concordance* as a trade paperback in 1976. Similarly, Geoffrey Mandel offered up *The Starfleet Handbook* in 1974, and he went on to an illustrious career with technical guides from Ballantine and Pocket Books. Franz Josef's *Star Trek Blueprints* came out in 1975 and was a smash success as people finally got to see details of every deck of the starship (even if much of the information in them derived from the illustrator's imagination).

Jacqueline Lichtenberg, Sondra Marshak, and Joan Winston collaborated on *Star Trek Lives!*, a nonfiction offering from Bantam Books in 1975 that shined a light on fandom and their writings. The book saw five printings in its first year, again a testament to the show's enduring appeal. This was a boon to the fans, although it drove zine editors to distraction trying to keep up with the sudden rush of orders. David Gerrold had previously touched on fanzines in his 1973 book *The World of Star Trek*, but by this point, interest had been stirred to a fever pitch. Danielle E. Dabbs tried to help newcomers with her *Introduction to Star Trek Fanzines*. Librarian-turned–fan writer Roberta Rogow would later list all the known zines in her *Trexindex*, which was revised and reissued over the next few years before she gave it up to become a professional writer and popular filk singer ("filk" being a term to describe songs with fan-generated lyrics, often matched to existing music, based on science fiction or fantasy topics, either straight or humorous).

By this time, Paula Block had become one of the best known writers of poetry and fan fiction, winning polls and getting published with increasing regularity. *Star Trek* was a deep passion, which would also become the focus of her professional career just a decade later.

*Above from left:* Makeup artist Fred Phillips, DeForest Kelley (forehead), Leonard Nimoy, and George Takei assembled to talk with their growing number of fans. *Andrew Scholnick*

*Left:* In 1975, William Shatner finally arrived at two competing *Star Trek* conventions a month apart in Manhattan. *Andrew Scholnick*

*Right:* Always happy to speak, George Takei gives a hallway press conference after appearing on stage. *Andrew Scholnick*

*Below:* George Takei talks about his burgeoning political career in this 1975 appearance in New York. *Andrew Scholnick*

*Star Trek* fandom had clearly eclipsed science fiction fandom, with WorldCon attendance hovering in the low four figures while *Star Trek* shows had many times that amount. Though there was a clear divide between those who saw themselves as literary SF aficionados and looked down their noses at "Trekkies" primarily devoted to a canceled television series, plenty of fans ignored the rift and happily embraced both.

With the advent of *Star Wars* in 1977, many *Trek* zines began to broaden their contents with articles, letters, and fiction devoted to the new universe. Such was the declining interest in *Trek*, thanks to a lack of a film or new series, that almost all the zines fretted that fandom was dying. *Star Trek: The Motion Picture*'s arrival in 1979 changed that, turbo-charging fandom and fanzines regardless of whether or not they liked the film. The debates were vigorous indeed.

Apart from the zines and the conventions, there was also a unique entity, the fan club known as The *Star Trek* Welcommittee, which formed in 1972. Although conceived as an entry point for fans by Jacqueline Lichtenberg, its first chair was Jeanne Haueisen. The Welcommittee became the go-to source for information about the show, fanzines, conventions, and related items. Roddenberry and the cast supported the club's efforts, and by 1973 there were a hundred people from twenty-three different states helping to answer fan inquiries from all over the planet.

Helen Young took over for a time, but Shirley Maiewski's tenure is the one best remembered. She became known as "Grandma Trek" and the Welcommittee newsletter, *A Piece of the Action*, became the best known source of news about the show and efforts to revive it. The club nearly buckled under the weight of inquiries after it was promoted in *Star Trek Lives!* In time, as newsstand magazines such as *Starlog* rose to inform a hungry public, eventually followed by the first online forums, the need for The Welcommittee lessened. First the newsletter ended, then the club itself ceased operations in December 1997.

## MERCHANDISE ABOUNDS

James Blish's popular script adaptations rolled out from Bantam Books with regularity throughout the early 1970s, increasingly written with the aid of his wife, Judith (a.k.a. J. A. Lawrence) as his health failed prior to his death in 1975. Lawrence completed the adaptations in *Star Trek 12* and wrote *Mudd's Angels* in 1978 on her own.

Shortly after the series went off air, Bantam hired Blish to write *Spock Must Die!*, an original adult novel. Published in 1970, the slim book sold well, encouraging them to release a new series of novels following Blish's death. Starting in 1976, veteran writer Fred Pohl was handed a deal to edit six *Star Trek* novels and was told they had to be by well-established science fiction writers. The line started with *Spock, Messiah!* by Theodore R. Cogswell and Charles A. Spano Jr. It was poorly received by fans and it did not sell as expected.

Then in defiance of the preference for seasoned professionals, fan fiction authors Sondra Marshak and Myrna Culbreath wrote *The Price of the Phoenix*. The two had edited the well-received fan fiction collection *Star Trek: The New Voyages*, published six months prior to the release of *Spock, Messiah!* Shatner himself was a fan of the manuscript and the fans responded as well. Marshak and Culbreath would go on to write several more works, which polarized fans who liked or loathed their take on Roddenberry's universe, particularly their fetish about the Kirk/Spock relationship, which walked very close to the realm of slash fiction.

Most of the subsequent authors were fans of the original series, but found writing media tie-in fiction outside their comfort zone and the experience was not as pleasant as expected.

As well as a second volume of *New Voyages*, there were also a dozen photonovels adapting key episodes, produced when the fumetti storytelling style pioneered in Italy was briefly in vogue. These have since become highly desired collectibles.

The Bantam line of novels has not weathered the test of time well, largely because reader tastes changed through the years, and these adventures just didn't offer up the characterization or exploration of the established universe that readers craved. Pohl's editorial indifference to the moneymaking books probably hurt as well. Ballantine's *Star Trek Logs* books that decade were far better received.

In addition to publishing David Gerrold's two books about *Star Trek* (*The Trouble with Tribbles*, recounting the making of his episode, and *The World of Star Trek*, which was a more general history of the show), Ballantine produced a collection of fan mail, curated by Roddenberry's secretary Susan Sackett. Roddenberry hired the former teacher in 1974, and she quickly became an integral part of Roddenberry's world, partaking in pranks such as wearing nothing but a British flag to honor a writer's birthday. She subsequently enjoyed a twenty-year affair with him.

Gold Key continued producing the comic book adaptation, switching from photo covers to very nicely done paintings by the veteran George Wilson. By 1971, Len Wein, at the start of his illustrious career, began writing the series, a stretch of eight issues that showed a marked improvement in the content. "I think I was the first writer on the book who had ever actually been a faithful viewer of the series, so much of my time beyond the actual scripting of each issue was basically educating the folks at Gold Key about the show," Wein told me. The Gold Key title ended with issue No. 60, cover-dated March 1979, and these stories have lived on in various reprint collections.

British *Star Trek* fans were treated to new stories starting in *Joe 90*, a weekly comic book featuring rotating media tie-in adventures, mostly those based on the Supermarionation shows of Gerry Anderson. *Star Trek* joined the roster with a story called "Top Secret" from writer Angus Allen and artist Harry F. Lindfield on January 18, 1969, six months before the show debuted on British television. According to Rich Handley, "*Star Trek* became the most popular strip in the magazine—ironic not only in that few Anderson stories remained in what had begun as an Anderson vehicle, but also because televised *Star Trek* had been canceled that same year." The strip moved between various different titles, and the final story appeared on December 29, 1973.

Handley explained that although the stories were "wildly inaccurate in terms of technical details, much of the artwork created for the series was very well-rendered, a contrast to the silly, non-*Trek*-like plots often presented."

Peter Pan Records obtained the rights to audio stories based on various media properties, including *Star Trek*. They contracted with Neal Adams's Continuity Associates to produce the twenty-page comics that would accompany the eleven albums as well as the cover artwork. Alan Dean Foster wrote several of the stories as did comics veteran Cary Bates. Art was produced by a stellar array of talents, including Adams, John Buscema, Dick Giordano, and Russ Heath. Unfortunately, no one at Paramount's licensing department was looking carefully because characters often had the wrong skin tones, such as Sulu being black and Uhura being Caucasian.

In mid-1976, Sackett suggested to Columbia Records that the producer make a spoken word album, answering frequently raised questions. The recording was made at one of Roddenberry's college lectures in New York, supplemented by a series of shorter sessions. Some of the cast were invited to participate; Shatner, Kelley, and Mark Lenard were happy to join in. The recordings proved to be engineering nightmares to clean up and when Paramount asked for a prohibitive fee

# STRANGE NEW MAGAZINES

*Paul Simpson*

While *Star Trek* undeniably had a major influence on the growth of fanzines, it also made its presence felt in the world of professional journalism.

*Star Trek* attracted its fair share of attention from the newspaper industry, but as a television series, its initial run didn't really trouble movie magazines, even ones dedicated to fantasy such as *Castle of Frankenstein*, that were really primarily interested in B movies and the horror industry.

The renaissance of interest in *Star Trek* during the 1970s attracted the attention of art directors Kerry O'Quinn and Norman Jacobson, who had been hired to produce a one-shot complete episode guide to the series. Although they had Gene Roddenberry's cooperation, Paramount Pictures's royalty request made the project uneconomic so they became publishers themselves, producing the magazine in a way that didn't require such a payment. The focus would still be on *Star Trek*, but it wouldn't be an official publication. The resulting magazine, *Starlog*, prospered through the science fiction boom of the late 1970s and 1980s. It spawned various spinoffs (including *Fangoria*, *Comics Scene*, and *Future Life*) and covered all the various iterations of the *Trek* franchise before finally succumbing to economic pressures in 2009.

In America, imitators came and went, but Fred Clarke's *Cinefantastique* took media journalism to a new level with thick, in-depth issues devoted to the making of science fiction films. It also produced an annual issue devoted to *Star Trek* with Mark A. Altman heading up the examination team. His harsh critiques led to him being considered the anti-Christ by the production offices.

On the other side of the Atlantic, science fiction journalism was equally alive. Publisher Dez Skinn launched *Starburst* magazine in January 1978, just in time to ride the wave of publicity that *Star Wars*' opening in the UK a month earlier would provide. Purchased by Marvel in 1979, *Starburst* covered the *Star Trek* movies during their production and featured numerous retrospectives on the TV series. When the magazine was sold to Visual Imagination in 1985, it became the center of a hub of magazines devoted to film and TV science fiction, including *TV Zone*, *Cult Times*, *Xposé*, and *Shivers*. While the output undeniably decreased in quality over the years, with the material spread too thinly between the various outlets, it gave fans worldwide insight into the creation of the various shows.

Other British SF magazines also gave prominence to *Star Trek*. *SFX*, published by Future since 1995, has taken an often-irreverent stance, while the independently produced *DreamWatch* (later published by Titan Magazines) initially took the Marvel period of *Starburst* as its template, looking more behind-the-scenes at the franchise rather than just interviewing the lead actors.

Of course, there have also been magazines officially licensed by Paramount. Starlog Press produced tie-in magazines to all the later iterations of *Star Trek*, barring *Enterprise* (the company had changed hands by the time the prequel came on air). *Star Trek: The Magazine* and *The Star Trek Fact Files* appeared in various markets, with access to the production teams. Titan Magazines launched *Star Trek Monthly* in 1995 for the UK and Commonwealth markets, and in 2006 took over the U.S. license following the demise of *Star Trek Communicator*. During a period with no new televised *Star Trek*, the now-six-weekly *Star Trek Magazine* widened its remit to cover all aspects of the franchise and provided the only official coverage of the 2009 movie.

In a move that unwittingly brought *Star Trek* magazine publishing full circle, *Star Trek Magazine* celebrated the forty-fifth anniversary of the show with a two-issue *Ultimate Guide* that drew together features on the twenty-nine seasons plus the movies, written by some of the key figures in *Star Trek* fandom. Although reduced in frequency to quarterly in 2012, it continues to fly the flag in the hope of a further renaissance in the wake of J. J. Abrams's sequel.

*Author of numerous books and articles on screen science fiction, Paul Simpson was editor of* Dream Watch *1995–2000, and* Star Trek Magazine *2006–2011. He is currently editor of website SciFiBulletin.com.*

In addition to over a dozen original novels, Bantam published the ambitious *Star Trek Maps* and the fan-favorite *Star Trek Lives!*, which celebrated the *Trek* phenomenon. Ballantine Books helped pioneer nonfiction "making of" *Trek* titles but also published the original *Enterprise* blueprints (page 50), a technical manual (page 92), and a medical reference manual which included extraterrestrial anatomy.

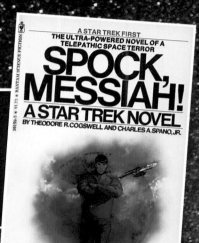

A STAR TREK FIRST
THE ULTRA-POWERED NOVEL OF A TELEPATHIC SPACE TERROR
**SPOCK, MESSIAH!**
A STAR TREK NOVEL
BY THEODORE R. COGSWELL AND CHARLES A. SPANO, JR.

A NEW STAR TREK ADVENTURE
**DEVIL WORLD**
**BY GORDON EKLUND**
BASED ON THE AWARD-WINNING TELEVISION SERIES CREATED BY GENE RODDENBERRY

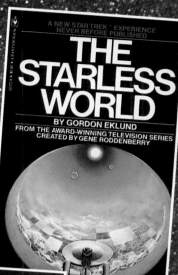

A NEW STAR TREK EXPERIENCE NEVER BEFORE PUBLISHED
**THE STARLESS WORLD**
BY GORDON EKLUND
FROM THE AWARD-WINNING TELEVISION SERIES CREATED BY GENE RODDENBERRY

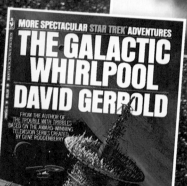

MORE SPECTACULAR STAR TREK ADVENTURES
**THE GALACTIC WHIRLPOOL**
**DAVID GERROLD**
FROM THE AUTHOR OF THE TROUBLE WITH TRIBBLES BASED ON THE AWARD-WINNING TELEVISION SERIES CREATED BY GENE RODDENBERRY

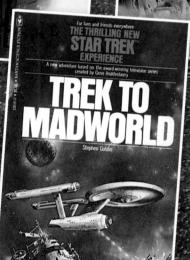

For fans and friends everywhere
THE THRILLING NEW STAR TREK EXPERIENCE
A new adventure based on the award winning television series created by Gene Roddenberry
**TREK TO MADWORLD**
Stephen Goldin

The mind shattering odyssey to an impossible world
A NEW STAR TREK NOVEL
**PLANET OF JUDGMENT**
BY JOE HALDEMAN
WINNER OF THE HUGO AND NEBULA AWARDS
BASED ON THE TELEVISION SERIES CREATED BY GENE RODDENBERRY

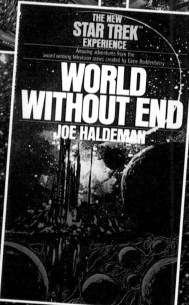

THE NEW STAR TREK EXPERIENCE
Amazing adventures from the award winning television series created by Gene Roddenberry
**WORLD WITHOUT END**
JOE HALDEMAN

THE NEW STAR TREK EXPERIENCE
An astonishing adventure based on the award winning television series created by Gene Roddenberry
**PERRY'S PLANET**
JACK C. HALDEMAN II

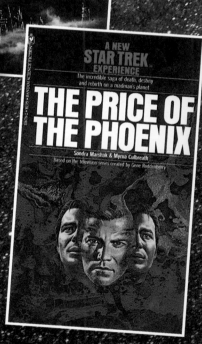

A NEW STAR TREK EXPERIENCE
The incredible saga of death, destiny and rebirth on a madman's planet
**THE PRICE OF THE PHOENIX**
Sondra Marshak & Myrna Culbreath
Based on the television series created by Gene Roddenberry

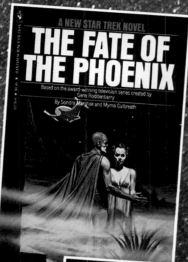

A NEW STAR TREK NOVEL

# THE FATE OF THE PHOENIX

Based on the award-winning television series created by Gene Roddenberry

By Sondra Marshak and Myrna Culbreath

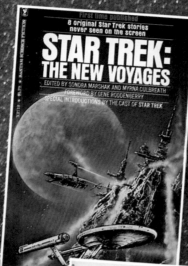

First time published

8 original Star Trek stories never seen on the screen

# STAR TREK: THE NEW VOYAGES

EDITED BY SONDRA MARSHAK AND MYRNA CULBREATH

FOREWORD BY GENE RODDENBERRY

SPECIAL INTRODUCTIONS BY THE CAST OF STAR TREK

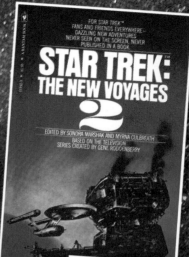

FOR STAR TREK™ FANS AND FRIENDS EVERYWHERE—DAZZLING NEW ADVENTURES NEVER SEEN ON THE SCREEN, NEVER PUBLISHED IN A BOOK.

# STAR TREK: THE NEW VOYAGES 2

EDITED BY SONDRA MARSHAK AND MYRNA CULBREATH

BASED ON THE TELEVISION SERIES CREATED BY GENE RODDENBERRY

THE CHILLING NEW STAR TREK NOVEL

# DEATH'S ANGEL BY KATHLEEN SKY

BASED ON THE AWARD-WINNING TELEVISION SERIES CREATED BY GENE RODDENBERRY

A DAZZLING NEW FULL

NEVER BEFORE PUBLISHED, NE

A NEW STAR TREK™ EXPERIENCE

# VULCAN! BY KATHLEEN SKY

INTRODUCTION BY DAVID GERROLD AUTHOR OF "THE TROUBLE WITH TRIBBLES"

A MIND-DAZZLING ADVENTURE BASED ON THE AWARD-WINNING TELEVISION SERIES CREATED BY GENE RODDENBERRY

Thanks to you, Star Trek fans . . .

Aboard Star Trek's flagship, the U.S.S. Enterprise, the starfaring adventurers are still dreaming the impossible—and making it come true.

# STAR TREK LIVES!

Personal notes and anecdotes

by Jacqueline Lichtenberg, Sondra Marshak and Joan Winston

- What the creators of Star Trek are doing now
- Their goals and achievements since Star Trek
- Their plans for Star Trek's return

# STAR TREK® MAPS

THE NAVIGATIONAL CHARTS OF THE FIVE-YEAR VOYAGE OF THE STARSHIP ENTERPRISE

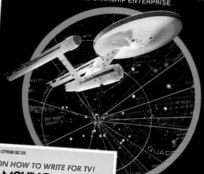

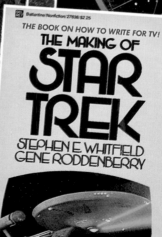

# STAR FLEET MEDICAL REFERENCE MANUAL

ORIGINAL $1.50

The story behind a STAR TREK Show!

# "THE TROUBLE WITH TRIBBLES"

THE BIRTH, SALE, AND FINAL PRODUCTION OF ONE EPISODE

# DAVID GERROLD

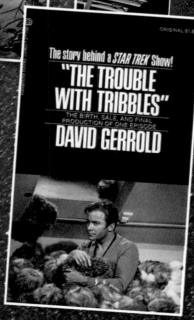

Ballantine/Nonfiction/27636/$2.25

THE BOOK ON HOW TO WRITE FOR TV!

# THE MAKING OF STAR TREK

STEPHEN E WHITFIELD GENE RODDENBERRY

WITH 64 PAGES OF PHOTOGRAPHS

The original model in the Smithsonian showing its age, with many seams clearly visible. *Robert Greenberger*

to use the theme music, producer Ed Naha had an orchestra rerecord it then wrote up the liner notes himself. When finally released, there was no marketing budget and it became a rarity until rereleased years later.

Sturdy action figures as seen in the 1960s were a distant memory when *Star Trek* entered syndication. In 1974, Mego Toys entered the field, producing eight-inch action figures based on a variety of properties. To save money, they created a standard set of male and female figures, only altering heads and costuming to save money. However *Star Trek* was popular enough to encourage the cost-conscious company to invest in specific lower-leg tooling. The first five figures were Kirk, Spock, McCoy, Scott, and a generic Klingon. Each came in a blister pack with a card with profile paintings. Uhura, whose attractive looks were misrepresented on the card, was in the next wave of figures. The company sold thousands of units, made lots of money, and supplemented the offerings with a *U.S.S. Enterprise* playset, Mission to Gamma VI playset, and communicator walkie-talkies.

Over the next few years, the line was slowly expanded to include various aliens. It ended in 1976; Mego passed on licensing the *Star Wars* figures and soon after went out of business.

Also in 1976, Topps Trading Cards released cards and stickers. There was an eighty-eight card set with twenty-two stickers. Each package contained five cards, one sticker, and the usual stick of rock-hard bubble gum. The backs featured Captain's Log entries.

Paramount was getting rich but seemed unwilling to share the wealth with those whose likenesses they were exploiting. This became a sticking point, in 1976—as the studio geared up for a feature film, most of the cast was ready to re-enlist. Nimoy remained a hold out, particularly after he viewed a billboard advertisement in the UK for a beer that "refreshes the parts other lagers cannot reach," which suggested that a pint of their product would return droopy Vulcan ears to their normal erect state. With Shatner's backing, Nimoy involved his lawyers.

## INTO DRY DOCK

On March 1, 1974, when only Roddenberry seriously seemed to be considering a return for the series, Paramount Pictures donated the *Enterprise* model used for the original visual effects to the Smithsonian Institution. Before going on display, it needed a lot of restoration. Sitting in a crate, in the hot California climate, the exterior and interior had deteriorated. Meticulous restoration work was done, completed on July 29 after input from Matt Jeffries and Roddenberry.

The poplar wood, vacu-formed plastic and sheet metal tubes were then packed up and shipped to the National Air and Space Museum. Eleven feet long and weighing 200 pounds, it was initially displayed on the original stand used in the 1960s alongside real life rockets and space capsules, a fitting resting place.

A second restoration was done between August 8 and September 11, 1984, with a third restoration in the winter of 1991. In time, the starship was relocated to the museum store, where it remains to this day, and cannot be missed by the vast majority of the museum's visitors from around the world.

## THE REAL *ENTERPRISE*

Bjo Trimble received a call one day, asking her to help with mounting a campaign to have NASA's first space shuttle named after the *U.S.S. Enterprise*. She started by enlisting the help of the Los Angles Science Fiction and Fantasy Society, resulting in 12,000 letters going out.

Fan clubs and individuals rallied and wrote letters to the White House, with the final tally estimated to be between 400,000 and 500,000 pieces of mail, enough to convince President Gerald R. Ford to acquiesce. A stunned cadre of NASA executives heard the president spurn their plan to call the shuttle the *Constitution* in favor of *Enterprise*.

On September 17, 1976, Edwards Air Force Base played host to a variety of dignitaries, including the majority of the *Star Trek* cast. As Shuttle Orbiter 101 rolled into sight, the Air Force band played the familiar theme as science fiction became science fact.

The rollout of space shuttle *Enterprise*, so named after a letter-writing campaign by *Star Trek* fans, was attended by most of the crew of the starship *Enterprise*. From left: NASA administrator James D. Fletcher, DeForest Kelley, George Takei, James Doohan, Nichelle Nichols, Leonard Nimoy, Gene Roddenberry, an unidentified man, and Walter Koenig. *NASA*

# CHAPTER 8 GOING TO THE

# MOVIES

We appreciate your interest in ''Star Trek'' and are sorry we have to continue to disappoint you. NBC, however, has no plans for the return of the series.

As reported in recent press stories, our Program Department does have under consideration a two—hour science fiction film. Several program concepts have been proposed for this project —— one of which is ''Star Trek.'' While no decision has been made —— nor can we tell you when one will —— we are aware of your own high regard for ''Star Trek.''

NBC AUDIENCE SERVICES

This postcard was sent to fans who wrote NBC about the prospect of *Star Trek* coming back to the screen. *Howard Weinstein*

There has been a lot of speculation as to how serious NBC and/or Paramount were about reviving *Star Trek*. After all, the studio was reaping tremendous profit from the original three seasons, and it could renew interest by providing fresh prints to the syndicated stations so they could advertise the new rerun cycle as having better clarity.

Roddenberry was quoted in the mid-1970s saying that NBC had asked for a new pilot, but since rebuilding the sets would cost upwards of $750,000, Paramount held out for a four-episode order to amortize the costs. The network reportedly refused.

By 1974, though, Roddenberry was happily telling interested parties that Paramount was definitely moving ahead with a feature film with him as the writer. He even told fans that once the film was shot, the sets could be saved for a return to prime time as either an hourly show or, as was the custom of the time, a series of ninety-minute or two-hour telefims. While no formal announcement was forthcoming from any source, Roddenberry continued to develop various projects, anticipating having his *Trek* film script done by May 1975.

In early 1975, Roddenberry told *A Piece of the Action* he was thinking the film might tell how the *Enterprise* was constructed, "how each character became part of the *Enterprise* crew; also something more on the mating cycle of Vulcans . . ." He eventually abandoned that notion in favor of a far larger tapestry.

He finished *The God Thing* by June 30 and loved it. Admiral Kirk would reassemble his crew to confront an enormous entity approaching on a direct course for Earth. The object was to be discovered as a supercomputer constructed by extra-dimensional beings exiled in Kirk's plane of reality. Paramount rejected it in July.

As Roddenberry continued to revise his story, Paramount sought new writers for what was dubbed *Star Trek II*. Theodore Sturgeon, who had written for the original series,

This rare 1977 cloth calendar features a frequent misrepresentation from *Trek*'s early days: the hangar deck at the stern of the lower hull is shown blasting out energy like a rocket, even more than the actual twin engine nacelles above. The careful eyes of a fan will also note a transposition in the numbers on the starboard nacelle and the use of lower instead of uppercase letters.

# WHEN FANS CREATED *TREK*

*Rich Kolker*

I once sat down and divided the entire history of *Star Trek* fandom into five-year missions. The second era (1972–1976) on that list was called "A quest, not an industry." Because, there was a time when the only *Star Trek* that existed was seventy-nine episodes and what we created ourselves in fanzines. Oh, we still tried to convince Paramount (and ourselves) that there was value in putting *Star Trek* back on the air (that was the quest), but if a survey had been taken of organized fandom, I doubt many of us ever expected to see it.

And so the kind of people who were attracted to fandom in those days tended to be the kind of people who wanted to create (or at least read) new *Star Trek*. Everyone wrote, or drew, or filked, or edited, or all of the above. We debated the fine points of the seventy-nine episodes in mimeoed letter zines that crossed in the mail. In many ways, at that point in its history, fandom *controlled* the *Star Trek* franchise, because nobody else was really interested. And if you look at the names of people who write *Star Trek* novels, or edit them, or wrote episodes of *The Next Generation* and beyond, you'll find a lot of those same people. Wander the halls of NASA and you'll find those people (in my case, when I worked at NASA after chairing August Party, they used to find me . . . at the most inopportune times).

Someone once told me one of the things that era did for a lot of writers and artists (and convention organizers for that matter) was it provided us with the opportunity to be bad. After a while, being turned down by editors frustrates many writers and they give up. Being published in fanzines gave a writer the opportunity for others to read their stuff and get the feedback that, if they're serious about writing, can lead to getting better.

It was in 1975 that I started the August Party as a low budget fan (no actors or other high-priced guests) convention at the University of Maryland. How low budget? We didn't use badge holders, we used straight pins. We stayed in dorm rooms for $4 a night.

I don't kid myself, the first one was so disorganized that the only reason there was a second was that in 1975, nobody realized just how bad it was. But we got better. You could do that then.

A lesson from the original series is that when your budget is lower, your creativity has to be higher. We couldn't afford to bring Gene Roddenberry to speak, so we did it by phone. Filk singers were starting to actually rehearse and write their own music as well as words, so we held the first filk concert. *Star Trek* fandom started to have a history, so we added a history room. We can't claim to have invented doing a show at a convention, but we certainly dove in early and used it to anchor our Sunday programming.

August Party was a convention for fans, by fans, and about *Star Trek* fandom more even than it was about *Star Trek*. We believed in free food in the con suite (Carvel ice cream sandwiches were very popular) and lots of small fannish dealers in the dealer's room. And even when we held the last in 1985, we never charged more than $20 at the door for a membership (and if you joined early enough, you could still get a membership for $4, the original price from 1975) because I always thought no *Star Trek* convention was worth more than $20 at the door. Start charging more than that (and even charge that much) and you start losing the casual fan, and the worst thing that can happen to something like *Star Trek* fandom is for it to become insular and elitist.

And when we got tired of running them every year, we stopped. We had built something, and none of us wanted to take the chance the name would continue without the idea behind it.

And, fandom was starting to change. There were movies (as Gene announced at an August Party) and a new TV series (as Gene announced at an August Party) and a new generation of fans who were more consumers of *Star Trek* than creators. Nothing wrong with that, but an era had ended, one that didn't have room for an August Party.

Where are we now? A couple of committee members have written episodes of new *Star Trek*, a couple are representing you overseas in embassies, we've lost a couple. Peter David went from writing and directing our Sundae Shows to writing most everything. We've had book editors and people who wrote software for the space shuttle. Some still help out on other conventions, taking what they learned at August Party to a new generation of fandom.

What did I get out of it? I learned how to organize and lead and manage a team toward a goal. I've gotten to sit in the captain's chair on the Paramount sets and make a small contribution to the mythos of *The Next Generation*. But mostly, I learned living an interesting life is a matter of being in the right place at the right time (with the right skills) and trying. That happened because of what I learned in *Star Trek* fandom back in the days it was a quest, not an industry.

*Rich Kolker is a longtime fan who conceived of the first fan-only (no actor guests) convention. August Party ran annually 1975–1979, once more in 1981, and a final edition was held in 1985. He has since turned his attentions to making the world a safer place.*

was approached. Ray Bradbury, an odd choice given his own lyrical and thoughtful style of writing, was also invited. The only writer to deliver a premise was Harlan Ellison, who must have still liked something about the series to revisit it despite his contentious relationship with Roddenberry.

Ellison's story also involved Kirk rounding up his crew, but the threat was a snake-like race bent on altering Earth history so their race would prove the dominant one. Much of the story was set at the dawn of time, and the volatile writer grew upset when an ignorant executive suggested the Mayan civilization be utilized to tie in with author Erik Von Daniken's *Chariots of the Gods* theory that alien races had visited Earth repeatedly through the millennia. Ellison withdrew his storyline.

Author Robert Silverberg was signed in October 1975 to write a screenplay. John D. F. Black was also recruited to write his own treatment, which proved to be about a black hole threatening all existence.

Roddenberry turned to his recently acquired assistant, Jon Povill, to come up with a new story, this time a universe altered via time travel. Povill was a fan who befriended Roddenberry and, as would many others in the years to come, he began volunteering his time, gaining the producer's trust. They developed the story together but, in the end, Roddenberry recognized it was more appropriate for television than features. As expected, like all the other treatments, this was rejected by Paramount, whose mantra seemed to be "we want it bigger."

On July 1, Povill presented Roddenberry with a list of potential writers who might do right by *Star Trek*. Intriguingly, George Lucas's name was on the list, even as he was shooting *Star Wars*. Lucas had also appeared two weeks earlier on Povill's list of potential directors, which read like a who's who of 1970s filmmaking. None of the writers was approached to pitch to the studio, but the inclusion of one potential director, Robert Wise, proved prophetic.

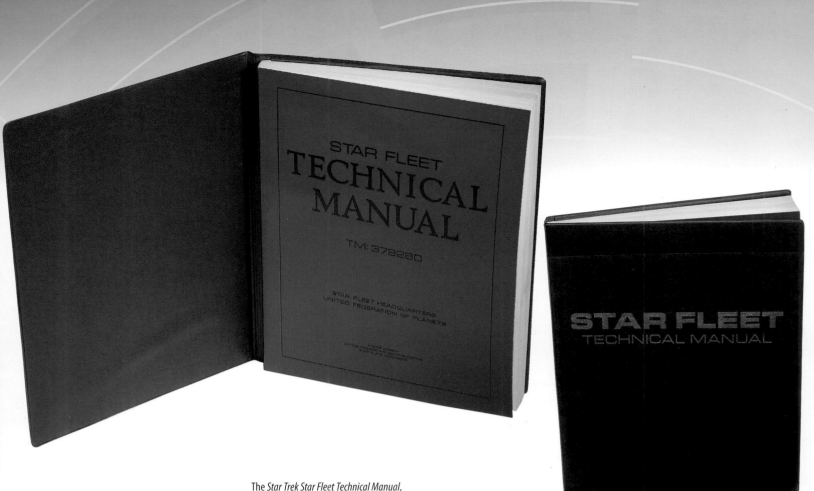

The *Star Trek Star Fleet Technical Manual*, published in 1975, was the first of its kind and set the standard for all that followed. A treasure trove of minutia, it tried to explain the fuzzy science employed by the producers. Its unique packaging included a paperback book slipped into a hard vinyl cover, with a colorful insert in a plastic sleeve on the front cover, a natural for collectors. Later editions were printed as simple paperbacks.

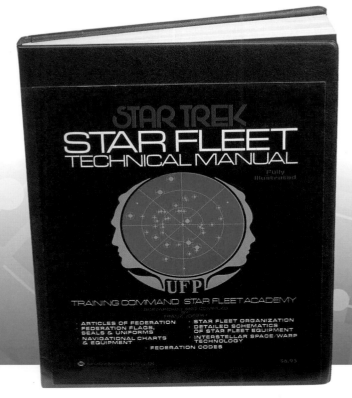

Production on the *Star Trek* feature film was scheduled to begin in July 1976—but didn't. On August 10 David V. Picker, president of Paramount's film division, announced there would be a different *Star Trek* feature film, written by Chris Bryant and Allan Scott for producer Jerry Isenberg and director Philip Kaufman. Gene Roddenberry had been signed to write the film's novelization.

Bryant and Scott were best known for writing the screenplay for Nicolas Roeg's *Don't Look Now* and were a hot commodity. Their ten-page outline would earn the pair $125,000, and the film itself was already budgeted in the $7.5–$9 million dollar range. Ken Adam was tapped to use his James Bond know-how to be the production designer, with *Star Wars*'s Ralph McQuarrie hired to redesign the *Enterprise*.

The writers were delighted when Kaufman was brought aboard. "Phil is a great enthusiast and very knowledgeable about science fiction, and we did a huge amount of reading," Scott recounted years later. "We must have read thirty science fiction books of various kinds. At that time we also had that guy [Jesco von Puttkamer] from NASA, who was one of the advisors on the project. He was at some of the meetings, and Gene was at all of the meetings.

"We were under instructions at the time that they had no deal with William Shatner, so in fact the first story draft we did eliminate Captain Kirk. It was only a month or six weeks later when we were called and told that Kirk was now aboard and should be one of the lead characters.

"Chris and I would sit in a room and talk about story ideas and notions, then talk them through with either Phil or Gene. Without any ill feelings on any part, it became clear to us that there was a divergence of view of how the movie should be made between Gene and Phil. I think Gene was quite right in sticking by not so much the specifics of *Star Trek* but the general ethics of it. I think Phil was more interested in exploring a wider range of science fiction stories, and yet nonetheless staying faithful to *Star Trek*."

Kaufman had been a science fiction fan and was delighted about possibly directing what was then considered to be a quickie film to cash in on the fan following. "I got a call from Jerry [Isenberg], who had been put in charge. I came down and met with him first and then with Gene Roddenberry. In the process of getting involved with the project, I moved it up from being a small project into a $10 million picture," Kaufman recounted.

*Planet of the Titans* was delivered in October, much to the approval of Paramount's two biggest executives, Barry Diller and Michael Eisner. According to the film treatment, three years earlier, a rescue mission had gone wrong. Kirk, provoked into erratic behavior, had seemingly disappeared aboard a shuttlecraft. In the aftermath, Spock resigned in disgrace. Now a refitted *Enterprise*, commanded by Captain Gregory Westlake, is ordered to where Kirk had vanished, bringing along Spock. The starship finds an invisible planet filled with

Leonard Nimoy recorded several *Star Trek*–themed albums, after Gene Roddenberry ensured he'd see a cut of the profits.

technologically superior gear, the creators of which, the Titans, are missing. The world is being threatened by a black hole and the *Enterprise* has to rescue the current inhabitants, the Cygnans, as well as Kirk, before being consumed by the crushing gravitational pull. The climax would reveal that the *Enterprise* had been accidentally slung back through time, with the crew themselves seen by the early inhabitants as the Titans.

While Roddenberry liked the story, despite its Prime Directive implications and characterization, Kaufman wanted changes. A contest of wills began. "With the *Star Trek* script, we have defined personalities and really can't do anything contrary to the behavior patterns we've already established in the past," Roddenberry explained. "We're finding out that it's easier to work from scratch in terms of a storyline, but because all the details of the film are so well known already, it's getting harder and harder to come up with something

new. I don't know what we'll finish with at this point, but I'm sure it will be a film that has a lot of entertainment value—action, adventure, and a little comedy. I want a *2001*."

On February 15, 1977, news broke that production would begin over the summer with an $8 million budget. There remained script issues as winter became spring, so on March 18 the writers left the project with a note stating, "Giving birth takes nine months. We've only been gestating for seven. So there's no baby. But there's an embryo. Look after it." Kaufman declared he would write the new script himself, jettisoning the Scott and Bryant effort.

"My version was really built around Leonard Nimoy as Spock and Toshiro Mifune as his Klingon nemesis," Kaufman said at the time. "My idea was to make it less 'cult-ish,' and more of an adult movie, dealing with sexuality and wonders rather than oddness; a big science fiction movie, filled with all kinds of questions, particularly about the nature of Spock's [duality]—exploring his humanity and what humanness was. To have Spock and Mifune's character tripping out in outer space. I'm sure the fans would have been upset, but I felt it could really open up a new type of science fiction."

*Star Trek* fans display their Klingon costumes during the 2010 Comic-Con International in San Diego Comic-Con. © *Sandy Huffaker/Corbis*

On May 8, 1977, Paramount announced it had changed gears and would shelve the movie in favor of a TV revival, *Star Trek: Phase II*. A mere seventeen days later, *Star Wars* opened, and rewrote the rules for filmmaking and science fiction storytelling.

Kaufman, who would go on to remake *Invasion of the Body Snatchers* with Nimoy, did not take kindly to the film's cancellation. He recounted, "We were dealing a lot with Olaf Stapledon. There were chapters in *Last and First Men* that I was basing *Star Trek* on. That was my key thing. Gene and I disagreed on what the nature of a feature film really is. He was still bound by the things that he had been forced into by lack of money and by the fact that those times were not into science fiction the way they are now. Gene has a very set way of looking at things. My feeling always was that he was anchored in a ten-year-old TV show which would not translate for a feature audience ten years later with all that had been done and could potentially be done in a feature scope."

Word of the cancellation hit the press on June 7, a mere blip in the midst of all the attention being paid to 20th Century Fox's blockbuster surprise. When *The New York Times* reported on the switch from feature to series on June 18, it seemed like a strategic retreat despite the $500,000 spent on a film that would never be made.

In Barry Diller's mind, the property worked better as a television series. "We considered the project for years. We've done a number of treatments, scripts, and every time we'd say, 'This isn't good enough.' If we had just gone forward and done it, we might have done it quite well. In this case, it was the script. We felt, frankly, that it was a little pretentious. We went to Gene Roddenberry and said, 'Look, you're the person who really understands *Star Trek*. We don't. But what we should probably do is return to the original context, a television series.' If you force it as a big 70-millimeter widescreen movie, you go directly against the concept. If you rip *Star Trek* off, you'll fail, because the people who like *Star Trek* don't just like it. They love it."

EFFECTIVE THIS STAR DATE:

is hereby commissioned as    FLIGHT DECK OFFICER    on the

## UNITED SPACE SHIP ENTERPRISE

the above named officer, having given proof of superior judgement and abilities, and having indicated a willingness to engage in hazardous assignment, is ordered to report immediately for STAR TREK duty.

*Gene Roddenberry*
STARFLEET COMMAND

*James T. Kirk*
JAMES KIRK (Commander)
U.S.S. Enterprise

Certificate and membership card from *Star Trek Interstellar*, the official fan club started by Gene Roddenberry while *Star Trek* was still on the air.

To all Starfleet personnel

is a charter member in good standing of

# STAR TREK INTERSTELLAR

and should be given all possible courtesies and co-operation by fellow Federation personnel on behalf of Starfleet command.

THESE PRIVILEGES are non-transferable

*Gene Roddenberry*
Starfleet command

# STAR TREK: PHASE II

Paramount envisioned creating the first new national television network since the Dumont Network failed in the 1950s. The idea was to start with Saturday nights and build slowly across the week. *Star Trek* was seen as a natural lead in at 8 p.m. followed by made-for-television fare. After all, Diller had made a name for himself with ABC's *Movie of the Week* years earlier.

The series would follow the new adventures of the starship *Enterprise*, a second five-year mission exploring strange new worlds.

Roddenberry began work on *Star Trek II* as its producer on June 12, 1977. Bob Goodwin was on board as coproducer with Joe Jennings as production designer, and trusty Matt Jeffries consulting.

For the opening two-hour movie, due for airing by February 1, 1978, Roddenberry plundered various concepts from his rejected pilots. "Robot's Return," one of the stories prepared for *Genesis II* for CBS, seemed suitable for reworking as it was similar to both *The God Thing*, and the second season *Star Trek* episode "The Changeling." The new script was called "In Thy Image."

No one expected the new show would rehire both Shatner and Nimoy, and by then it was clear the series needed the Vulcan more. Roddenberry focused his attention on how to find a new, younger lead. Similarly, he envisioned hiring the remainder of the original cast to contracts guaranteeing them seven out of thirteen episodes, allowing them to be phased out, replaced with a younger (and cheaper) set of performers.

By this time, Nimoy had sued the studio over the merchandising issue, so it was vital the legal issue be settled to allow him to sign on for however large a role could be negotiated. However, Nimoy was not willing to compromise his position. Alternate plans had to be made.

With great enthusiasm, but no scripts, Paramount approved work to begin on refurbishing the *Enterprise* standard sets. Matt Jeffries returned to the starship, replacing and ignoring the McQuarrie sketches. His biggest alteration was making the nacelles thin and tapered, with flat-sided modules. New, distinctive photon torpedo ports on the saucer connector were added. Interior redesign work was conceived by Mike

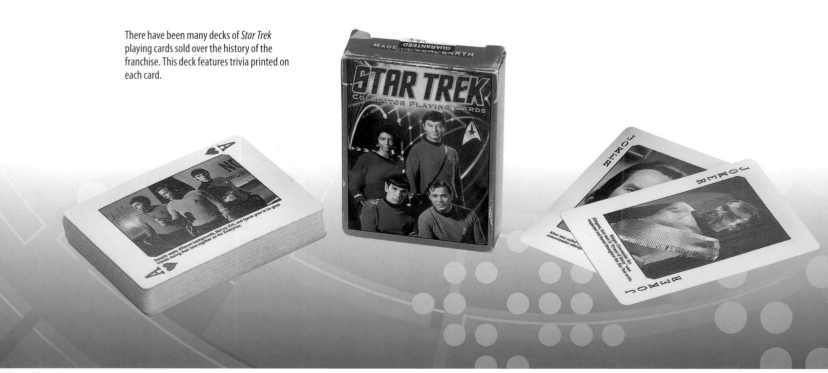

There have been many decks of *Star Trek* playing cards sold over the history of the franchise. This deck features trivia printed on each card.

Minor, who kept Jeffries's original look and feel. His bridge is one of the few television concepts that made it to the first feature virtually intact.

Roddenberry, meanwhile, was creating new characters to prepare for a shift of focus away from the Kirk/Spock/McCoy trio. Willard Decker was going to be the young male lead, struggling with taking the center seat in the wake of the legendary exploits of James Kirk. His life would be further complicated by the arrival of Ilia, a Deltan with whom he had a prior relationship.

The producer knew there was a two-hour telefilm and thirteen episodes to produce, giving him a limited window of time to establish his new characters, and to mix them in with the returning ensemble. He and story editor Jon Povill had to pick the strongest concepts.

Foster, working from a two-page outline by Roddenberry, produced the pilot treatment, which became a script from creative producer Harold Livingston, while many new writers sold stories. Returning to the fold was Theodore Sturgeon who offered up the only light-hearted episode in the first batch; John Meredyth Lucas penned a two-part focus on an alternate Klingon Empire. Shimon Wincelberg and Norman Spinrad were also back with new stories. To Roddenberry's credit, none were sequels and only one brought back a familiar race. However, by the time the plug was pulled on the series, only two full scripts were completed.

David Gautreaux was cast as a new Vulcan, Xon. He had made just one appearance on TV, in the short-lived *The Man from Atlantis*, before joining *Phase II*. Xon's personality was that of a pure Vulcan who struggled to understand his human shipmates. When Nimoy finally signed to return to active duty on *Star Trek: The Motion Picture*, the character of Xon was superfluous and Gautreaux was given a bit part in the first feature as a consolation prize.

Welcome Aboard...
Space Shuttle Enterprise

Paramount Pictures and the thousands of loyal fans of Star Trek are happy that the United States of America's new space shuttle has been named after Start Trek's starship, The Enterprise. (It's nice to know that sometimes science fiction becomes science fact).

Starship Enterprise will be joining the Space Shuttle Enterprise in its space travels very soon. Early next year, Paramount Pictures begins filming an extraordinary motion picture adventure-STAR TREK.

Now we can look forward to two great space adventures.

An ad from the *New York Times* hinting that *Star Trek* was coming back, but it took Paramount a while to make up their minds. *Howard Weinstein*

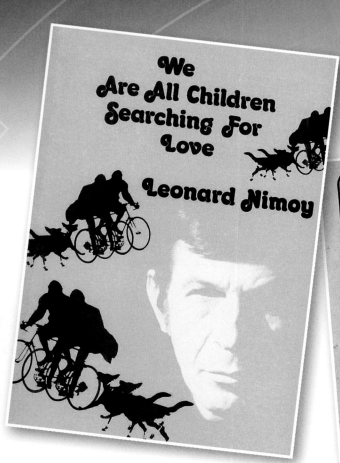

After his recording career ended, Nimoy shifted his creative interests to poetry, including this rare collection published by Blue Mountain Arts in 1977.

An ad for the official *Star Trek* fan club in the seventies, renamed to celebrate the tenth anniversary of the show. *Steve Roby collection*

As for the remainder of the crew, Dr. McCoy, Montgomery Scott, Uhura, and Sulu all received minor promotions, but their backgrounds remained fairly static. The most dramatic changes were Chekov's promotion to commander of the *Enterprise*'s security division and Christine Chapel's graduation from medical school, making her a peer to McCoy.

Robert L. Collins, who was known for his work on police primetime series, was hired to direct the pilot film.

In October 1977, as preproduction continued, Roddenberry declared alcohol was no longer acceptable on the *Enterprise*. While the bad guys like the Klingons could consume the stuff, no member of Starfleet could (an odd decision considering Roddenberry's devotion to the stuff). By month's end, he also had to write to the fans to address the controversy in the press over Nimoy's refusal to appear in the new show.

Paramount eventually concluded there was little interest in a fourth network. The studio was looking for better than 80 percent coverage of the top markets, but they weren't achieving it. In fact, Paramount had realized their concept wasn't going to work in the summer of 1977, but didn't formally cancel *Phase II*. And during an August meeting with Eisner, it had become clear the scope of "In Thy Image" was good enough for a feature.

As *Star Wars* fever ignited a new round of science fiction filmmaking, Paramount watched the box office receipts with a careful eye. When Columbia released Steven Spielberg's *Close Encounters of the Third Kind* in November 1977, it raised the stakes among rival studios. Talk turned openly to taking the still gestating television movie and changing its direction, back to a feature.

The studio decided to pull the plug on *Phase II* and instead prepare for a *Star Trek* feature film. All work on a TV version stopped on November 11, just before filming was to begin. Many of the character concepts worked their way not only into *The Motion Picture*, but true to Roddenberry's history, they would be recycled in *The Next Generation*.

THE
STAR TREK CONVENTION
1976

This is the program cover to the final convention thrown by the original Committee which had no idea what they were getting themselves into when it all began in 1972.
*Howard Weinstein*

# CHAPTER 9
# THE MOTION PICTURE

On March 28, 1978, amidst much fanfare, *Star Trek: The Motion Picture* was announced, complete with the return of Leonard Nimoy and William Shatner. Joining them was former Miss India and model Persis Khambatta. *Associated Press*

# THE TRILOGY

Paramount Pictures hosted the largest press conference in its history on March 28, 1978, packed with countless journalists from outlets around the world. They were on hand to watch chairman Bluhdorn, executives Eisner and Diller, and others reintroduce the world to *Star Trek*.

The entire original cast, complete with Grace Lee Whitney, was on hand, along with newcomer Persis Khambatta. Director Robert Wise, a legend dating back to his editing work on Orson Welles's *Citizen Kane*, stood beside Roddenberry as the studio announced a $15-million *Star Trek* motion picture. Wise, who by then was known for the classic musicals *West Side Story and The Sound of Music*, had established his approach to serious science fiction nearly three decades earlier with the classic *The Day the Earth Stood Still*. The fans rejoiced at the choice.

The *Phase II* pilot script "In Thy Image" was a sufficiently big enough story concept but needed retooling into a motion picture shooting script. Dennis Clark was brought on to revise the script, but he left after clashing with Roddenberry, who insisted on sole authorship. Livingston had his reserve activation clause invoked and he returned to the typewriter. Harlan Ellison revealed in 1980 that Livingston took Roddenberry to arbitration over credits until they were told to share credit. Finally, Foster had to file a grievance before his contributions were acknowledged.

Barely twenty-four hours before the press conference, Nimoy and Paramount had buried the hatchet. Wise knew he didn't have a movie without Nimoy, but the actor was unhappy with the script, feeling it wasn't very good. He met with Roddenberry, Wise, and Paramount executive Jeffrey Katzenberg to talk about the story. Nimoy and Roddenberry, by then, had a very estranged relationship so a sense of tension was in the air. When Roddenberry explained that he envisioned Spock back on Vulcan going through the equivalent of a mental breakdown, Nimoy shot back he didn't think fans would want to see Spock as mentally impaired. That was the cue Katzenberg had been waiting for, and he ushered Roddenberry out of the house. Wise and Nimoy spoke in private for a time and the results of that conversation led to Nimoy signing up. The story amendments were given to Livingston for incorporation into the script.

Roddenberry was back to producing a motion picture, and after the failure of *Pretty Maids*, and his various pilots, he saw *Star Trek* as both his personal savior and an albatross. On television, the producer was in control; on a movie, he was forced to cede much decision-making to Wise. Fortunately, he and Wise shared the same opinion over man's evolution and the nature of God, letting them work in harmony.

Interestingly, the notion of sentient robotic lifeforms continued to irk some at Paramount, all the way from *Phase II* through preproduction of *The Motion Picture*. It wasn't until the subject was positively broached by NASA director Robert Jastrow during an interview in *Penthouse*, of all places, that they finally conceded the point, much to Roddenberry's

Robert Wise, backed by Gene Roddenberry, directs Leonard Nimoy, DeForest Kelley, and William Shatner in *Star Trek: The Motion Picture*. It had started shooting in August 1978; this photo from November 1978 was nearing the end of its long first-unit shooting schedule. *Associated Press*

The cast of *Star Trek: The Motion Picture*, a mixed blessing for fans. They got the series resurrected, but were left divided over the quality of the finished product. From left, Takei, Stephen Collins, Persis Khambatta, Barrett, Shatner, Whitney, Doohan, Nimoy, Kelley, Koenig, and Nichols. © *Steve Schapiro/Corbis*

pleasure since the theme had been one he had wanted to thoroughly explore, going back to the Nomad probe in "The Changeling."

Shatner and Nimoy continued to read drafts, and, even at this point in their careers, they were still counting lines as opposed to figuring out if their part made sense.

Wise brought on Harold Michelson to modify the *Phase II* sets for feature film work. One notable alteration to the bridge was the shape and positioning of Chekov's new security post. Michelson also added the bridge's unique ceiling, and incorporated the subtle new graphics interface, designed by Lee Cole, who had created a forty-four page manual explaining every console and symbol used aboard this new starship.

In the rec room, you could see wall-mounted models of vessels that carried the *Enterprise* name, including an eighteenth-century frigate, the World War II carrier, the space shuttle prototype, a previously unseen ship (in fact, an early Matt Jefferies design for the TV series), and the original series model. This became a running visual in later versions of the starship *Enterprise*.

Robert Fletcher was hired to redesign the costumes. He went for more subdued tones and put everyone in pants, with the shoes sewn into the legs for a futuristic look. The only way you could tell which division people worked was to check the color of the field behind the starship emblem:

white was command, red was engineering, green was medical. Povill figured out the dashes and bars that denoted the various ranks, as seen on sleeves and epaulets.

Fourteen different alien races were seen throughout the film, from familiar Vulcans to redesigned Klingons, plus many newcomers. The returning Fred Phillips used the new film budget to work with Fletcher in extending the look of the United Federation of Planets.

On July 24, Roddenberry admitted the current state of special effects was beyond his and Wise's comfort level and asked Michael Eisner for help. The studio executive assigned Richard Yuricich, who had just worked on *Close Encounters of the Third Kind*, who in turn hired Robert Abel & Associates for the job. Syd Mead, who would go on to fame for his work on *Blade Runner*, was selected to reimagine V'Ger, after initial designs failed to excite Wise and Roddenberry.

Interestingly, even though the character of Willard Decker had been in the script for months, the part was not cast until just before filming began. Some sixty actors were said to have auditioned before Stephen Collins appeared before Wise on July 25.

On August 7, shooting finally was underway, but the script's final act remained elusive. Model designer Andrew Probert went so far as to storyboard his own suggestion, which would have featured the first time audiences saw a saucer separation.

# AUGUST PARTY 79

than twelve hours on set, feeling he lost his edge afterwards. Shooting the scenes for the wormhole sequence proved problematic, and the lights on the transporter pads actually melted the costumed footwear. Chekov's arm injury required ten takes and Koenig wound up slightly singed for real. Persis Khambatta was also mildly scorched, when playing the Ilia simulacrum, by the 12-volt light at the base of her throat.

Roddenberry invited fans and associates to gather for a special sequence, playing the crew addressed by Admiral Kirk in the hangar deck. Dozens of family, friends, and fans got to live out a dream, attired in Starfleet uniforms and standing mixed in with the familiar crewmen. Bjo Trimble helped fill the ranks with 170 or so people who met the height and costume size restrictions.

Shooting was long and laborious, with principal photography wrapping on January 26, 1979. During post-production Roddenberry suggested the scenes set on Vulcan have the characters speak the previously unheard language. Since the lines were spoken in English, the production team first needed to create the language then loop the dialogue, as actors attempted to mimic the lip motions while speaking the new dialogue.

Among the many sound effects in the film were the distinctive sounds for V'Ger, which were generated by a device known as the blaster beam, a musical instrument developed by former child actor and original series two-time guest star Craig Huxley. The blaster beam uses strings attached to an eighteen-foot aluminum body, amplified by motorized guitar pickups.

The special effects caused major problems. After months of fruitless work, Robert Abel & Associates had to be replaced. As luck would have it, Douglas Trumbull, known for

To commemorate the beginning of filming, Wise received an *Enterprise*-emblazoned baseball cap, which came from the nuclear carrier of that name. Producer and director ceremonially smashed a bottle of champagne on the bridge set. Fifteen takes later, the first scene was in the can. From that moment on, production slowed to a crawl. Wise fell immediately behind and remained that way.

## PRODUCTION WOES

By August 9, the production was already a full day behind schedule. Despite the delays, Wise refused to shoot more

his effects work on *2001: A Space Odyssey*, was now free and was hired. He had to begin almost from scratch with the December 7, 1979, release date fixed and immutable. Trumbull and Yuricich had both worked on *Close Encounters*, and Trumbull confidently predicted he could deliver on schedule. Yuricich also completed some hundred matte paintings for the production. The special effects teams took over five soundstages, while Trumbull subcontracted the V'Ger cloud effect and Epsilon IX to effects master John Dysktra and his company, Apogee Inc. Both the *Enterprise* and Klingon battle cruiser models needed to be rewired for better lighting and then were repeatedly filmed, creating enough footage needed for their scenes.

Trumbull provided story input as well, reconceiving Spock's spacewalk through V'Ger to omit Kirk coming after his friend. By the time the effects were completed, the team was working double shifts, and the $10 million outlay neared one-quarter of the film's total budget.

Roddenberry brought Jerry Goldsmith on to score the film. Goldsmith had been on his wish list dating back to "The Cage" and Wise was in favor of the choice, considering him one of

*Top:* A CHP officer arrests a *Star Trek* Mugato at the 14th Annual Hollywood Charity Horse Show on May 1, 2004, at the Los Angeles Equestrian Center in Burbank, California. The event, hosted by actor William Shatner, raises money for three local charities dedicated to improving the lives of special needs children. *Amanda Edwards/Getty Images*

*Above:* Even Star Trek can't escape the zombie craze. *ThinkGeek, Inc.*

HE'S UNDEAD, JIM.

William Shatner starred in ABC's cop show *T.J. Hooker*, which guest-starred Leonard Nimoy, who also directed an episode.
*Bettinan/Corbis*

the greats. His first attempt at the score was too close to John Williams's instantly recognizable *Star Wars* soundtrack, so Wise rejected it and Goldsmith went in an entirely different direction.

Goldsmith needed help to complete the lengthy score, with both original series composers Alexander Courage and Fred Steiner assisting. The final scoring session was completed at 2:00 a.m. on December 1, a mere five days before the film opened! Goldsmith's feverish efforts earned him Oscar and Golden Globe nominations the following spring.

The film cost Paramount a record setting $46 million ($130.4 million at 2012 rates, a modest budget for an SF blockbuster today), thanks to costs from the aborted television development along with the expensive optical effects and rush charges for sound effects, film editing, and scoring.

Wise had wanted to test the film in front of an audience, but everything ran so late he never got his chance, something he came to regret. As it was, he had to personally carry the final print to the world premiere in Washington, D.C. This was held at the Smithsonian Institute on December 6 as a fund-raising event for the National Space Club. Everyone who had anything to do with the film was on hand, including Roddenberry, beaming for the cameras, accompanied by his entourage that included Sackett and her date, fan Richard Arnold.

Fans around the country clamored to buy tickets in advance and camped out days ahead of time to secure best seats for the first showing. Personally, I had collected cash and purchased thirty-four tickets for campus pals the night before and then was among those braving the chill Binghamton air for five hours on December 7, 1979, before the Crest Theater let us in.

While the opening weekend gross of $11,926,421 was then a record, the film's final take of $139 million was deemed by Paramount and film analysts to be a major disappointment, although not the bomb of legend. The rule of thumb at the time was that a film had to earn three times its budget to be profitable (excluding ancillary rights, merchandising, and the like). While successful television series had spawned movies before (*Batman*, for example), this was the first time a canceled show led to a feature film, and it was carefully watched by studios and networks alike. The holiday opening seemed like a wise move, eclipsing the box office record set only a year earlier by *Superman The Movie*. Still, given the decade-long anticipation and the gossip regarding its production woes, Paramount was looking for a home run and got, at best, a double. The studio, which remained more at odds than in tandem with Roddenberry, blamed the producer for the mediocre story, script, and the film's pacing, the latter blame actually belonging to Wise.

After waiting all this time, it was great to have the gang back in action, but the things fans loved most about the series were markedly absent from what felt like a slow, ponderous story. The theme was appropriate, but the lack of characterization, especially the absence of byplay between Kirk, Spock, and McCoy, was a problem. The fan letters to the dozens of fanzines showed the divide among the audience: those who loved the more adult approach to the series, and those who felt Roddenberry let everyone down.

Professional reviewers found much to pan, starting with the

*Below:* Sulu and Uhura, in the oft-reviled *Star Trek: The Motion Picture* uniforms, stand beside the android probe that V'Ger created from Lieutenant Ilia, one of the new crewmembers of *Star Trek*'s silver screen debut. The franchise provided myriad opportunities for Playmates Toys to issue new versions of beloved characters alongside first-time figures.

*Above:* After the sales success of blueprints based on the television *Enterise,* a revised set of drawings for the modified movie starship seemed to be in order.

thin story (big theme, not enough meat to explore it), and all faulted the pacing and overly serious tone. Many also criticized the film for not having a clear antagonist to pit against the courageous Admiral Kirk. Spock was the one character with an emotionally involving story arc, with Nimoy receiving good notices. Many criticized the film for neglecting to properly introduce the familiar crew to those new to the premise.

Despite underwhelming the fan base, it did get recognized by the Motion Picture Academy with three nominations for Best Art Direction, Best Visual Effects, and Best Original Score.

In 2001, Wise finally was given permission to go back and tweak the film. His *Director's Cut* was released on DVD, complete with film restoration and plenty of fascinating commentary. Money was provided to allow for remastered audio, and a complete re-edit along with brand new visual effects, although shortsightedly these were done on video, not film, meaning that they cannot be reincorporated into higher-resolution versions of the movie released subsequently.

Marketing exec Dawn Steel had nothing to work with but created a razzle-dazzle presentation that got licensees salivating to beam aboard, leading to the very first Happy Meal and scads of related merchandise.

Despite raking in considerable licensing cash, Paramount was quite lax with quality control during the 1970s, as seen by the flopped image of Kirk from this movie-era Peter Pan release: the insignia belongs on the other side. *Voyageur Press collection*

## REINVENTING LICENSING

"I was a desperate person. There was no product because there was no movie to show anyone," Dawn Steel recounted of her assignment. She had been hired in 1978 by Jeffrey Katzenberg to work in the Paramount merchandising and licensing department and was told in the spring of 1979 to get higher advances from people eager to create merchandise based on the *Star Trek* feature film. "So I had to do this razzmatazz bit onstage so I could convince the people making pajamas and toys and Coca-Cola and McDonald's to do the tie-ins. I figured out how to do this laser thing. I beamed myself onto the stage."

No sooner had the audience gasped, than Shatner, Nimoy, and other members of the cast were similarly beamed on stage. Steel then ran into the audience posing *Trek* trivia questions to the people she was hoping to secure deals from. They ate it up, committing millions of dollars with no clue what they were supporting. "Coca-Cola bought all this network time to advertise our movie," Steel recounted. "It hadn't been done before." Her successful marketing campaign propelled

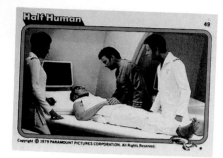

A complete set of Topps *Star Trek: The Motion Picture* collector cards.

her into a wildly successful production career before her death in 1997.

The promotions included the very first Happy Meal from McDonald's, providing the sight of Klingons eating hamburgers or sucking down Cokes. With crudely drawn comic strips, trivia, and riddles, six boxes were available that came with *Star Trek* gear such as a bracelet, puzzle, board-game, ring, or "video communicator."

A daily comic strip based on *Star Trek* began running in newspapers four days before the premiere. The low-budget *Los Angeles Times* syndicate hired writer/artist Thomas Warkentin to execute the strip. Editor David Seidman has speculated the reason the *Trek* strip failed to find a home in many papers was that newspapers around the country already committed space months before to their *Star Wars* strip, and few would carry both.

Months after Gold Key ended their comic adaptation, Marvel took over the license and issued a magazine-sized adaptation of *The Motion Picture*. This was followed by a creatively uneven comic book that lasted just under two years.

Writer Mike Barr explained, "Marvel thought they were doing *Trek* a favor by publishing it as a Marvel comic, and didn't care what the stories were about, as long as the covers said *Star Trek* on them, and someone between the covers had pointed ears. They made no attempt to keep the stories consistent with filmed *Trek*, and any stories that

 **"HE'S DEAD, JIM!"** ***STAR TREK***®

 **BEAM ME UP, SCOTTY**™ ***STAR TREK***®

**" HAILING FREQUENCIES OPEN "** ***STAR TREK***®

**UNITED FEDERATION OF PLANETS**™ **DELEGATE**

**USS NTERPRISE**™ **NCC-1701**

**FEDERATION SHUTTLECRAFT NCC-1701/7** *Galileo*™ ***STAR TREK***®

USS ENTERPRISE™
NCC-1701-A

TM ℗ & ©1993 PARAMOUNT PICTURES. ALL RIGHTS RESERVED. CREATION CONVENTION AUTHORIZED USER.

STAR TREK®

STARFLEET ACADEMY

STARFLEET ACADEMY
EX ASTRA, SCIENTIA
SAN FRANCISCO · MMCLXI

STAR TREK
THE NEXT GENERATION

...TION AUTHORIZED USER.

I AM A TREKKIE

© 1979 Paramount Pic...

BEAM ME UP MR. SPOCK

©1979 Paramount Pictures Corpor
AVNA ENTERPRISES INC. SAN FRANCISCO C...

STAR TREK
THE MOTION PICTURE™

AVNA ENTERPRISES, INC., SAN FRANCISCO, CA. 94103

©1979 Paramount Pictures Corporation
TM designates a Trademark of
Paramount Pictures Corporation

DR. McCOY DOESN'T MAKE HOUSE CALLS

NCC-1701

AVNA ENTERPRISES, INC., SAN FRANCISCO, CA. 94103    ©1979 Paramount Pictures Co...

No 8

$2.50

TREK

The Magazine For Star Trek Fans

*Trek* was a long-running fanzine. Favorite articles from the magazine were collected in eighteen *The Best of Trek* paperbacks, edited by the magazine's editors, Walter Irwin and G. B. Love, and published by Roc. *Voyageur Press collection*

did, did so due to the efforts of the writer and/or artist. They also used lots of writers who knew nothing about *Trek*. One issue in the original run of Marvel's *Trek* was originally entitled 'Tomorrow Is Yesterday.' Neither office nor writer knew that had been the title of an episode of the original series until I informed them of same."

Martin Pasko got to write for the Marvel series and noted, "Writers were asked to think in self-contained story terms, rather than multi-issue arcs, because the approval process was slow, so no one writer was encouraged to think of himself as the 'regular' assignee. I was told that, in order to make ship-dates each month, Marvel had to have a number of stories by different teams in the works at all times, and each job was published on a first-come, first-scheduled basis. That's probably why the book didn't do too well in the direct market: the solicitations were sometimes a bit vague because Marvel couldn't always be sure which story was going to be in which issue.

Fortunately, Pocket Books was more successful as they took over the original fiction license from Bantam. Under editor David Hartwell, the line was launched with Roddenberry's own novelization of the feature (and despite rumors to the contrary, Alan Dean Foster did not ghostwrite it). Fans delighted in learning additional details not found in the finished film from Kirk having been married, to Decker being the son of Matt Decker from "The Doomsday Machine" (a detail intended to be explored during *Phase II*).

Clearly, the movie launched a new era for the franchise, its characters, its fans, and the product produced supporting the *Enterprise* and its crew. As 1980 wore on, though, with no news of a sequel or fresh television series, fans began to ask one another, "Is *Star Trek* dead?"

A Peter Pan reissue comic and record set. The original series story was given a *Star Trek: The Motion Picture* cover. In another example of illustrators working withcut photo references, the art portrayed Sulu as African American and Uhura as a blonde Caucasian.

# CHAPTER 10

# THE *SPOCK*

## TRILOGY

SORTIE LE 13 FEVRIER

Après le sacrifice de Spock et la création de la planète Génésis, une guerre interstellaire éclate...

STAR TREK III
A LA RECHERCHE DE SPOCK

Paramount présente une production HARVE BENNETT "STAR TREK III-A LA RECHERCHE DE SPOCK" · WILLIAM SHATNER · DeFOREST KELLY
avec JAMES DOOHAN · GEORGE TAKEI · WALTER KOENIG · NICHELLE NICHOLS · MERRITT BUTRICK et CHRISTOPHER LLOYD
Conseiller Exécutif GENE RODDENBERRY · Musique de JAMES HORNER · Producteur Exécutif GARY NARDINO · Effets visuels spéciaux par INDUSTRIAL LIGHT & MAGIC
D'après STAR TREK créé par GEN RODDENBERRY · Ecrit et Produit par HARVE BENNETT · Réalisé par LEONARD NIMOY
DOLBY STEREO · PANAVISION · Bande originale du film sur le label PATHÉ MARCONI EMI distribué par Original

Collectible postcard featuring the French one-sheet for the third feature film. *Star Trek* may not have performed as well internationally as it has domestically, but there remains a strong interest abroad.

Bjo Trimble helped shape *Star Trek* fandom and can easily be considered its godmother. She was one of dozens who have memorialized the amazing experience in print, in *On the Good Ship Enterprise* from Starblaze Editions in 1983.

Between 1964, when Gene Roddenberry threw him off the production of one of his pilots, and 1980, when he walked into a meeting at Paramount Pictures, Harve Bennett had become one of the most successful producers of television series. His credits included genre fare such as *The Six Million Dollar Man* and miniseries including *Rich Man, Poor Man*, which led to his being put under contract to the studio's television division.

At the meeting were television chief Gary Nardino, studio execs Diller and Eisner, and, most surprisingly, chairman Bluhdorn. Their first question was Bennett's opinion of *The Motion Picture*. Instantly, the veteran producer knew he was there to audition for the inevitable sequel. Bennett admitted he was bored by it, and Bluhdorn asked if he could not only do it better, but for less than the $46 million Roddenberry cost the studio. When Bennett said he could make several movies for that price, he secured the assignment.

Roddenberry suspected there would be a sequel. He wrote an outline featuring the Klingons locating the Guardian of Forever, as seen in the time-travel episode "The City on the Edge of Forever." Their plan was to alter Earth's past, preventing the assassination of President John F. Kennedy. Kirk would also have to travel in time to undo their meddling, even if it meant ensuring Kennedy's death, an echo of "City." Paramount rejected the story and furthermore decided that Roddenberry would be no longer be trusted with feature film work. Instead, he would be named Executive Consultant, paid a producer's fee, and given a percentage of the net profits. In exchange, he would consult with the new production team and give a public thumb's up, keeping the fans loyal to the franchise.

Bennett signed on and steeped himself in a series he had never watched. He screened most of the original episodes to learn the world and characters. He kept thinking back to Ricardo Montalban's magnetic performance as Khan Noonian Singh in the first season story "Space Seed," and began constructing a story featuring his return.

When Bennett sent material to his predecessor for consultation, Roddenberry sent back negative memos objecting to just about everything save the characters' names. This would be their habit for the next few years.

On November 13, 1980, an outline for *Star Trek: War of the Generations* was presented to Nardino for approval. This involved a former lover of Kirk's and a son from that union, as well as Khan, but every other element wound up being changed or dropped. Receiving a green light, Bennett hired writer and *Star Trek* fan Jack B. Sowards to expand the outline. It was Sowards who suggested that killing Spock might be interesting enough to entice a reluctant Nimoy back into the fold. By December 18, a nineteen-page outline was delivered, focusing on Kirk's midlife crisis, with the death of Spock added to provide Nimoy a dramatic exit from the franchise.

Every member of the original main cast has received a star on Hollywood's famous Walk of Fame. On January 16, 1985, it was Leonard Nimoy's turn with Gene Roddenberry on hand.
*Associated Press*

Sometime afterward, a new six-page outline was generated that substantially shifted away from the proposed story and added in Captain Terrell commanding a ship that young rebels, led by David Kirk, had commandeered. This story now had a male character named Savik (sic), the mind-controlling Ceti eels, and the rebellion ignited by the revenge-seeking Khan and his wife Marla McGivers on Ceti Alpha V.

Sowards delivered the first draft of *Star Trek: The Omega System* on February 20, 1981, which ended with Kirk and son together on the *Enterprise*, with his final draft, *Star Trek: The Genesis Project*, arriving on April 10.

Bennett had hired Robert Sallin as his line producer with Mike Minor back on board as production designer. However, Sallin and Bennett lacked faith in the storyline's sweep. Bennett called upon veteran *Trek* writer Samuel Peeples for a new draft. With a June 1982 release date looming, there was pressure to get production underway, and they had yet to sign a director.

Bennett invited Nimoy to lunch, asking the actor about the franchise, its fans, and whether he was really ready to call it quits. Nimoy admitted that the door was not entirely closed to him reprising Spock. Around this time, Bennett also met with novelist-turned-director Nicholas Meyer, who was urged to make contact by his longtime friend, Paramount executive Karen Moore. The two men got to know one another over beers and screening several *Star Trek* episodes. Meyer was only vaguely familiar with the series and had admitted he'd never seen any of Bennett's own shows. But when he watched "Space Seed," he too felt that there was something to Khan. Meyer agreed to read the expected new draft in two weeks and went home.

Peeples's version dropped Khan and McGivers in favor of two new antagonists, Sojin and Moray, exiled from another dimension, and he added layers of complexity to the story rather than give it an epic feel. Bennett refused to show Meyer this draft of the script.

Meyer thought his involvement was over by this point, but over the next few days he considered what he liked about the premise. He concluded that Kirk reminded him of Horatio Hornblower, inadvertently connecting with Roddenberry's inspiration. Meyer called Bennett and suggested both men mark up the existing drafts, noting the pieces they liked, and he would compile an entirely brand new script.

Bennett and Sallin were aghast at the notion. Industrial Light and Magic (ILM) needed a final screenplay within twelve days to have their special effects work done in time for the agreed release. It was only then that Meyer realized the film was due out on a fixed schedule. He told Bennett to forget about everything for the next twelve days while he wrote.

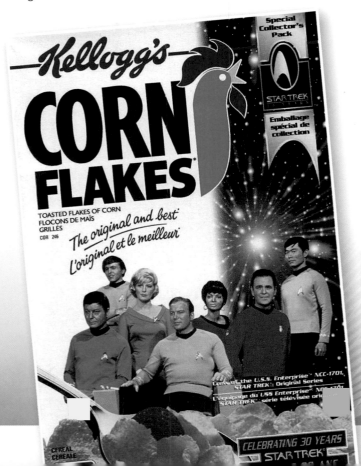

KDLH·TV 3
DULUTH

KDLH • TV BROADCASTING COMPANY, A DIVISION OF PALMER COMMUNICATIONS, INC.
5 WEST SUPERIOR STREET ■ DULUTH, MINNESOTA 55802 ■ TELEPHONE (218) 727-8911

April 3, 1985

Scott Pearson

Dear Scott,

Thank you for your intelligent comments about Star Trek. Your letter and many others have caused us to increase our schedule of Star Trek episodes. In the very near future, you will see additional episodes each week.

This Sunday, April 7, 1985 will be our last preemption until the NFL football double-headers. We should be airing 2 or 3 episodes per week when football starts, so the occasional preemption shouldn't be as severe.

Sincerely,

Jim Cuzzo
Program Manager

JC/jg

Meyer cobbled together a new script from the bits and pieces they identified. Meantime, Bennett and Katzenberg pitched Nimoy the storyline, starting with "How'd you like a great death scene?" Nimoy was intrigued and said he would be open to the role if the script was strong.

Meyer delivered *Star Trek: The Undiscovered Country* on schedule and a deal was made for him to direct the story. While he visited ILM to discuss the effects, the script went out to the production staff as well as Shatner, who hated it. While the star didn't mind a script about Kirk growing older, he didn't like the specific age being spelled out. A minor tweak to the dialogue solved the problem, and Shatner declared Meyer a "genius."

Bennett's first outline to contain the death of Spock was circulated to only eight people but within three weeks fans were already decrying the news. Word spread at warp speed. In October 1981, a quarter-page ad in *Variety* threatened a boycott of Paramount that could cost them $28 million. This was big enough news to merit a page one story in the *Wall Street Journal*. Two months later, the venerable *New York Times* weighed in with an editorial suggesting killing the Vulcan was a mistake.

Strongly suspecting that Roddenberry was behind the leak, Bennett continued to fume over the creator's passive/aggressive nature, noting that he had some valuable ideas, with about 20 percent of his suggestions being used in the final film. Still, it rankled Bennett to see Lincoln Enterprises selling copies of his first outline when he attended his first convention in 1982.

Meyer was dealing with an $11.2 million budget, about one-quarter of the previous film, but he insisted on redressing the starship's sets and outfitting the crew in more interesting uniforms. Joe Jennings took care of making the ship sparkle and feel busy, with more lights, dials, and read-outs, and Robert Fletcher handled the costuming. For Khan, Fletcher said, "We wanted to show Ricardo Montalban's physique. He was rather proud of it, as he should have been. That was a theatrical gesture." And yes, those pecs were real.

Meyer met with the regular cast before casting the new roles. Fortunately, he was warmly welcomed by the veterans, all of whom were delighted to be back to work. Kirstie Alley, a newcomer from Wichita, Kansas, was cast as Spock's protégée, Lieutenant Saavik. Merritt Buttrick, just beginning his career, played the pivotal role of Kirk's son, David Marcus, paired with veteran actress Bibi Besch as his mother. Paul Winfield lent some gravitas to the pivotal role of Captain Terrell.

Montalban had been looking for something different than the elegant, enigmatic Mr. Roarke he had been playing on *Fantasy Island* so the offer to reprise Khan intrigued him. He

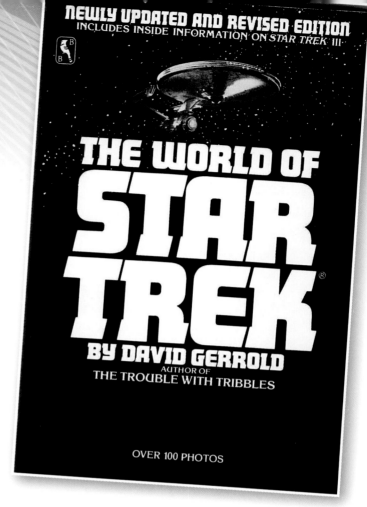

THE WORLD OF
STAR TREK

BY DAVID GERROLD
AUTHOR OF
THE TROUBLE WITH TRIBBLES

OVER 100 PHOTOS

David Gerrold went from college student to screenwriter to novelist to social observer. His nonfiction explorations on the series' phenomenon also contained seeds for what became *The Next Generation*. This updated edition of *The World of Star Trek* was published by Bluejay in 1984. The 1974 edition was from Ballantine.

screened "Space Seed" and thought back to how he had attacked the part. Slowly, he recaptured Khan's personality, then added the pain of years gone by, turning him into the vengeful character required by the script.

To score the film, Meyer hired the young (and affordable) James Horner. The director asked for a nautical sound and Paramount insisted the familiar Courage theme be a part of the fanfare. In the end, Horner's score became one of the highlights of the finished film.

Meyer insisted on schedules allowing a few days for the cast to work together before the twelve-week shoot began on November 11, 1981. Unlike the first film, this was a fast, efficient production without much in the way of drama. Montalban responded well to being directed, and he and Meyer formed a tight bond. Shatner, the director learned, needed repeated takes before he relaxed enough to let Kirk just come through. A strong performance was shaped as a result.

Writing about the key day when he put his alter ego to bed for the last time or (so it seemed), Leonard Nimoy said, "By the time I headed back to the set, I was an emotional wreck, in deep pain, and the deference everyone displayed toward me only added to my inner turmoil."

The studio liked what they saw, and Frank Mancuso, then a marketing exec in Paramount's New York offices, took it upon himself to rename the movie *Star Trek: The Vengeance of Khan*. Meyer called the exec and suggested it might be helpful if Mancuso actually spoke to the director before changing the title. He pointed out George Lucas had named the third *Star Wars* film *Revenge of the Jedi* and suspected the director might object to the two titles being similar. Mancuso scoffed, but months later, the title was altered to *The Wrath of Khan*. Ironically, Lucas changed his mind and called his film *Return of the Jedi*.

Unlike the first film, there was time for an audience screening,

and the reaction was incredibly positive. After the comments were analyzed, it was decided to open the door to Spock's possible resurrection. Meyer argued against it as a creative cheat and thought he could sway people by suggesting Nimoy, not Shatner, record the iconic narration to be used at the film's conclusion. With Meyer refusing to play along, Sallin was sent to San Francisco to shoot the coffin torpedo in the woods scene that ends the film.

When Diller finally saw the movie, he complained that no one told him Spock was being killed. As a fixture in the franchise, that was not acceptable. He also found the final scene between Kirk and David flat, but Meyer drew the line at further reshoots. Diller said, "It's your movie," and left him alone.

The budget meant the film needed about $34 million in domestic box office to be considered profitable. With $14,347,221 earned in the opening weekend alone, Paramount's concerns were assuaged. The movie wound up the sixth-highest grossing film in 1982, earning $78,912,963. Adding in worldwide grosses, the film did a whopping $97 million.

The major critics from the *New York Times*, the *Washington Post*, and *Variety* all noted it felt more like the television series than its predecessor, words that no doubt stung Roddenberry. Some criticized the film for not having Kirk and Khan meet *mano y mano* or complained Spock's death was an unnecessary touch, but generally they all found something to like about it.

## DEATH OF THE *ENTERPRISE*

Unsurprisingly, Paramount wanted a sequel. Roddenberry, now distanced from his creation, took the attitude with friends and fans that *Star Trek* would always be a part of his life, but not the sum total of his accomplishments. Meyer was asked to write and direct the sequel, but rejected the offer, still smarting over being overruled on key elements in the second film.

While Roddenberry felt distance growing between him and his creation, Nimoy felt a stronger attraction. Sensing *Star Trek II* was going to be a hit, he began considering what demand he would make to remain involved in the inevitable sequel. He decided it was time to ask for a chance to direct.

Bennett went on to produce the TV series *The Powers of Matthew Starr*, and he hired Nimoy that summer to direct an episode, which may well have acted as an audition. Also around this time, Gary Nardino brought Nimoy to meet with Michael Eisner, who was initially skeptical of Nimoy making his debut on a big budget feature where he would also act. Nimoy briefly considered caving in, but Nicholas Meyer told him to hold firm. Eisner came to recognize that Nimoy directing the resurrection of Spock was marketing gold.

Once Nimoy signed his contract, he began discussing the story with Bennett in earnest. There were enough

threads hanging from the last film that assembling a logical continuation was fairly easy. Nimoy's reminder to Bennett of Vulcan spirituality led to the notion of the *katra*—the Vulcan soul—which they decided Spock had given McCoy at the end of the previous film. The producer was inspired by a piece of fan poetry about Kirk deciding to revisit Genesis because he had left a key part of himself behind, and Susan Sackett had the notion that Spock's rebirth and accelerated growth was tied to the Genesis device. For Nimoy, the driving theme of the film was a discussion of scientific ethics, as opposed to the more religious overtones inherent in Spock rising from the dead on a planet called Genesis.

Bennett hammered out a first draft screenplay for *Star Trek: Return to Genesis* in six weeks, starting with the final scene with the crew reunited, and working backward. He realized that so much of the film was predictable that he needed something surprising and dramatic, which led to the concept of sacrificing the noble starship.

Paramount increased the budget to $16 million, and, since many sets and costumes were being reused, the added cash

Playmates Toys version of Christopher Lloyd's *Star Trek III* character, Commander Kruge.

Linguist Marc Okrand was hired to turn gibberish uttered in the first film into a formal Klingon language for the third. He continued to consult with Paramount as the language gained thousands of adherents.
*Time & Life Pictures/Getty Images*

went toward special effects. Still, they filmed most of the Vulcan and Genesis scenes in the studio, robbing the film of the scope provided by location shooting. Nimoy, never happy with Spock's quarters, got to redecorate the set to his liking, and the bridge deck was repainted gray to photograph better.

Robert Fletcher was back to dress the crew in civilian garb, not realizing they'd be stuck in those threads for the next film as well. He was also involved in designing the Klingon and Vulcan makeup, which was subsequently handled by Thomas R. Burman.

Linguist Marc Okrand, who had been hired to provide the snippets of the Vulcan spoken between Spock and Saavik in the last film, was asked to give the Klingons their own tongue. James Doohan had provided the few words required for the opening Klingon scene in *The Motion Picture*, but far more was needed for this movie. Since the scenes had been shot in English, Okrand studied the actors' lip movements and began to craft a new language from scratch. From these humble

beginnings, a brand new language began which was adopted and learned by scores of fans, leading to language tapes and dictionaries from Pocket Books.

Kirstie Alley's agent demanded a larger salary for her client since Saavik had such a significant role. Nimoy objected and Alley left the franchise after one film. Robin Curtis, who had arrived in California in 1982, was screen-tested on the bridge that summer and was offered the part. Christopher Lloyd, at the time a beloved figure on NBC's *Taxi*, played the lead Klingon, Kruge, while John Larroquette, a deft performer, signed on as Maltz a year before making an indelible mark in the sitcom *Night Court*.

Nimoy decided he needed someone as impressive as Celia Lovsky had been playing Vulcan elder T'Pau in "Amok Time" to portray T'Lar the Vulcan priestess. He settled on Dame Judith Anderson, only to learn the eighty-five-year-old had never heard of *Star Trek*. The novice director managed to convince her to join the production, ending her fourteen-year retirement.

*Star Trek III* collectible card set.

As things ramped up towards an August 1983 start date, Shatner expressed his displeasure with the script for *The Search for Spock*. Agent and lawyer in tow, he met with Bennett and Nimoy, and went through the script line by line. Nimoy recalled that once the star saw his concerns were being taken seriously, he relaxed, and the changes proved to be minor.

Bennett couldn't make up his mind over who should die on the Genesis planet—David or Saavik. Eventually, it was deemed more dramatic to make it David. Nimoy cleared the bridge set so he and Shatner could discuss the pivotal moment when the captain learns of his son's death. Given their long-standing friendship, the conversation didn't require much time and Shatner's physical reaction to the news impressed his director.

Nimoy the actor was nervous given his double-duty on the film. If he was acting, he came into makeup earlier than usual so he could be prepared as Spock, then worked as a director until he stepped in front of the camera. It was concerning, especially during scenes when Spock was unconscious so he could not watch his actors at work. Nimoy had to rely on their instincts to know if the scene worked. "It drove DeForest Kelley crazy. He swears that I was trying to direct him with the movement and flutter of my eyelids," he recalled.

As part of the hyper-vigilant security to protect the secret of Spock's return (despite everyone on Earth anticipating as much), any time Nimoy the actor was needed, the call sheets referred to the character as Nacluv. There's an extra beat or two during the credits where Nimoy's name was expected to be but the space was blank.

Despite everyone's best efforts at keeping plot points a secret, word got out about the *Enterprise*'s destruction. By fall, fanzines were filled with fan comments. Later, fans were at least pleased to see a nod to the original series with the self-destruction sequence repeated from "Let That Be Your Last Battlefield."

Bennett couldn't understand how fans already knew this vital plot point long before shooting was to begin. Thankfully, he had coded each script, and when a fan sent him a copy, Bennett matched the code to Roddenberry. Once more, the creator was using his audience to push his private agenda.

By this time, Bennett and Roddenberry were each holding tight to their respective beliefs about the future of mankind. Roddenberry was an optimist, and with every passing year, he came to believe that mankind will become enlightened by the twenty-third century. Bennett argued that while the technology might get more sophisticated, basic human nature had yet to substantially change in millennia and was not likely to in a few hundred years. As a result, the creator kept arguing the producer was revising his characters beyond recognition.

Post-production ran smoothly. Paramount's executive team was pleased with the final result, and, before the new film had even opened, they asked Nimoy to begin thinking about another installment, but this time taking the characters wherever he wanted.

The film felt like a genuine sequel considering the subject matter, cast, and crew. James Horner's score also went a long way to maintain that feeling of continuity as familiar cues appeared once more. This time, he focused on the emotional content of the scenes as opposed to the grandiloquent battle of wills between Khan and Kirk.

The movie opened June 1, 1984, to largely positive reviews from the critics and enthusiastic reactions from the fans, despite the loss of the *Enterprise*. Nimoy generally got good reviews as a director, feeling he recaptured the special essence of the original series. *The Search for Spock* had a contained feel, akin to the original series' reliance on sets to represent alien worlds. As a result, more than a few critics and fans felt this offering felt more like a telefilm than a feature film.

Paramount wanted to make a splash and opened on a then-record 1,996 domestic screens. The film went on to earn $76.5 million in North America, totaling $87 million worldwide.

The *Enterprise* in mid-self-destruct in *Star Trek III*, from the Johnny Lightning "Legends of Star Trek" series.

## LET'S DO THE TIME WARP AGAIN

While shooting the third movie, Bennett and Nimoy recognized the films to date had been heavy on the drama and metaphysics, and not as much fun as some of the best-loved episodes. The fourth outing needed to lighten things up.

However, Shatner announced that without a substantial pay increase, he would be unavailable to make the fourth movie. Eight months were spent trying to conceive of a new feature without Captain Kirk, with producer Ralph Winter, who had replaced Robert Sallin after the second film, suggesting a prequel set at Starfleet Academy.

The studio finally came to terms with Shatner, and Nimoy and Bennett did not waste time, spending the fall of 1984 working up ideas for the next film. Nimoy explored many contemporary themes that would lend themselves to the *Star Trek* treatment. Bennett concluded that the new film had to involve time travel, a notion Nimoy accepted. By December Nimoy had met with several scientists involved in the Search for Extraterrestrial Intelligence program (SETI).

Early in 1985, Nimoy received a call from Katzenberg with the news that Eddie Murphy, the studio's most bankable star at the time, was a fan and wanted in on the next film. At a meeting with Murphy, Nimoy avoided making an offer since the storyline was still evolving. By this time he was focused on the notion of species becoming extinct, after reading *Biophilia*, a book on the subject. Nimoy credits his friend Roy Danchik with first mentioning the humpback whale, but he was not alone, as novelist Howard Weinstein also mentioned whales as an endangered species when Nimoy and the writer met at the *Starlog* offices (Weinstein's contributions merited a special thanks in the end credits).

Bennett and Nimoy hired Steve Meerson and Peter Kirkes to flesh their ideas out into a script. At this point, the biggest challenge was finding a role for Murphy. Since the story would have Spock walking around the twentieth century, a contemporary role was devised for Murphy: a psychic investigator with his own radio show, exploring *Weekly World News* concepts.

The writers went through several drafts, but when none were considered strong enough, they were replaced by Nick Meyer, who Dawn Steel called just four weeks before shooting was scheduled to begin. Liking the basic concepts, Meyer agreed to sign on, writing the twentieth-century sequences since he understood the inherent comedy in a time-displaced person, after writing the wonderful *Time After Time*. Bennett handled all the twenty-third century aspects that bookended the story, focusing on wrapping up the loose ends.

It became clear to Paramount that Murphy and *Star Trek* were both major assets for the studio and they were wasting box office potential by combining the two into one project. Additionally, Murphy reportedly didn't like the part suggested for him, wanting to play an alien or Starfleet officer. Nimoy admitted to being relieved when Murphy went off to shoot *The Golden Child*.

Ned Tanen, then president of Paramount, loved the story and draft script, so a green light was happily given. Whereas the last film felt confined on the studio sound stages, this one was going on location. Specifically, it made sense to set the twentieth-century scenes in San Francisco where Starfleet would one day reside.

Michael Okuda was hired to work on this film designing graphics that would become known as Okudagrams. His first efforts focused on computer displays, marking the first touchscreen consoles, and he redesigned the worker bee pod interior first seen in *The Motion Picture*.

Nimoy was determined to honor the series and its fans by adding in some familiar faces, so Starfleet Command was populated by the likes of Majel Barrett and Grace Lee Whitney. Since Spock was spending quality time with his parents Amanda and Sarek, Jane Wyatt returned to the franchise alongside screen husband Mark Lenard. Robin Curtis was briefly back as Saavik, although early drafts of the script revealed a potentially more significant part: she was to be carrying Spock's child, hence her decision to remain on Vulcan.

New to the movie was Catherine Hicks as Gillian Taylor, the scientist responsible for the whales. Her audition gave Taylor a naiveté that charmed Nimoy. Soon after, he arranged a lunch meeting with Shatner to gauge the pair's chemistry. By the time the meal ended, Hicks was welcomed to the *Star Trek* family.

Once production began on February 24, 1986, working in a crowded city posed its logistical issues, especially when the general population learned a *Star Trek* film was shooting nearby.

*Left:* Collector glass commemorating the new *Enterprise*, NCC-1701-A, introduced at the end of *Star Trek IV: The Voyage Home*.

*Below:* A variety of collectable *Star Trek III* erasers.

Not everything worked smoothly. A nice moment was scripted for Sulu when he encountered a young boy on the street and it became clear he was speaking with his great-great-great grandfather. The local youth hired rehearsed with Takei, who had initially suggested the scene to Bennett, but when the cameras started rolling, the boy froze. The production ran out of time, deeply disappointing Takei.

The only real clash between director and producer occurred after filming. Nimoy was deeply influenced by one of the SETI scientists, so much so that a line from Spock to McCoy was included about human arrogance with regard to alien intelligence. Bennett felt the exchange between the rescued whales and the alien probe needed to be expressed in human terms, but Nimoy thought it worked better if it were unintelligible. The producer wrote out draft dialogue and sent it along in a memo to Tanen, Steel, and Katzenberg, effectively going over Nimoy's head. Steel sought Meyer's advice, and the writer backed the director, as did Katzenberg, ending the discussion.

In the weeks prior to the film's November 26, 1986, release, it had its thunder stolen by Rodenberry and Paramount when news of a brand new television series was confirmed on October 8. Still, it only made interest all the keener in *Star Trek*, as the series was now celebrating its twentieth anniversary.

James Horner declined an invitation to complete a hat trick of scores, so Nimoy's friend Leonard Rosenman was hired. At first, he wrote a theme that heavily incorporated Alexander Courage's fanfare, but Nimoy asked for something brand new.

The movie opened to uniformly positive reviews and huge box office receipts. Bringing the crew "home" to NCC-1701-A brought a rousing cheer from coast to coast. It was dedicated to the crew of the space shuttle *Challenger*, which had exploded on January 28 of that year.

Being Thanksgiving weekend, the five day total was a whopping $39.6 million, concluding its run with $109.7 million, while winding up with an astonishing global total of

$133 million. Given the previous films' weak international performance, the marketing team de-emphasized the *Star Trek* elements and played up the whales and the threat to Earth. Some trailers also recapped the previous films.

After being ignored the last two times by the Motion Picture Academy, *The Voyage Home* was nominated for Best Cinematography, Music, Sound, and Sound Effects Editing, the most nominations earned by a *Trek* film.

## THE NEW FANS

After years of little new material, fans were suddenly given four films to rejoice over and debate. As a result, a wave of new fanzines appeared, while the discussion in the existing titles was increasingly given over to the films and their worth.

The new decade opened with some 301 fan clubs and 430 fanzines, according to the *Star Trek* Welcommittee. Fanzines continued to feature correspondence from the professional side, as Susan Sackett and NASA's Jesco Von Puttkamer shared news and information about the first film. Roddenberry also contributed pieces, including the affirmation that if fans saw his name on a film, then it had his seal of approval. After *Star Trek II* was warmly received, Bennett sent letters of thanks to various zines.

In 1981, Dan Madsen formed the *Star Trek: The Motion Picture* Fan Club after falling in love with the movie. At twenty, he was beginning what turned out to be a thirty-year relationship as his club evolved into the first official *Star Trek* Fan Club, blessed by Paramount. By the time of the second film, he had a deal with Paramount, and his newsletter became *Star Trek: The Official Fan Club Magazine*, eventually evolving into *Star Trek: Communicator*. He was successful enough to be hired by Lucasfilm to help launch and execute the *Star Wars* Fan Club.

With *Starlog* and competitor professional magazines now spreading the news, the Welcommittee's *A Piece of the*

William Shatner gets a kiss from Yaka, an orca at Marine World in Vallejo, California, in March 1987. The appearance tied into *Star Trek IV: The Voyage Home* and promoted contributions to the California Rare and Endangered Species Preservation Program. *Associated Press*

Fanzines would get a little more colorful and attractively bound in the eighties. *Voyageur Press collection*

*Action* dropped from a monthly newsletter to barely appearing bimonthly, before publishing its final issue in 1982.

This was the period when chain conventions spread beyond the Creation Conventions, which had gone nationwide a few years before. Regional operators ran shows around the country, booking performers as guests to multiple shows. This led to an evolution in contracts with specified geographic exclusivity. Smaller regional shows were beginning to fade away. In their wake, though, came many other conventions attempting to capitalize on the renewed interest in the series. Few lasted more than few years, with one exception being Maryland's Shore Leave. The convention started small in 1979, grew smartly, and continues to thrive in its fourth decade.

Some people got in way over their heads, such as the promoters of the disastrous Ultimate Fantasy, held in June 1982. Fans flocked to Houston for what was promised to be a star-studded extravaganza. After the organizers ran out of cash, Bennett had to take charge, urging the actor-guests to make their promised appearances for fans who paid their fees in good faith. Merritt Buttrick paid the light and sound crews out of his own pocket. While the show did go on, and those in attendance had a great time, it has lingered long in the memory of fans.

Another major factor that changed fandom was the introduction of the personal computer, followed soon after by online newsgroups. In June 1984, Alice Green first wrote in a zine about USENET, heralding a massive change in how fans would interact with one another.

Pocket Books also received a lot of fan attention for their original novels. Vonda McIntyre's *The Entropy Effect* kicked off the line in 1981 and garnered headlines with a sequence featuring the death of James T. Kirk. The acclaim led to McIntyre being hired to write the next three movie novelizations.

The first few years of Pocket's program were haphazard, resulting in alternating elation and frustration from the fans. It got so bad in 1983 that fans, including future professional authors Julia Ecklar and Lisa Wahl, began talking about boycotting the books coming out at the end of the year, to send then-editor Mimi Panitch a message. Howard Weinstein, whose novel *The Covenant of the Crown* was well-liked, argued against such a move, prompting Wahl to call off the boycott. The books slowly improved in quality as stronger editors and a slew of fans-turned-professionals made their first sales.

Meantime, after Marvel's lackluster run, the comic book license lay fallow until Marv Wolfman convinced the management at DC Comics to pick it up. The series arrived in the fall of 1983 with Wolfman editing and Mike Barr writing. Fortunately, DC cut a smarter deal than Marvel, giving them access to the entire *Star Trek* canon, not just what was seen in the feature films.

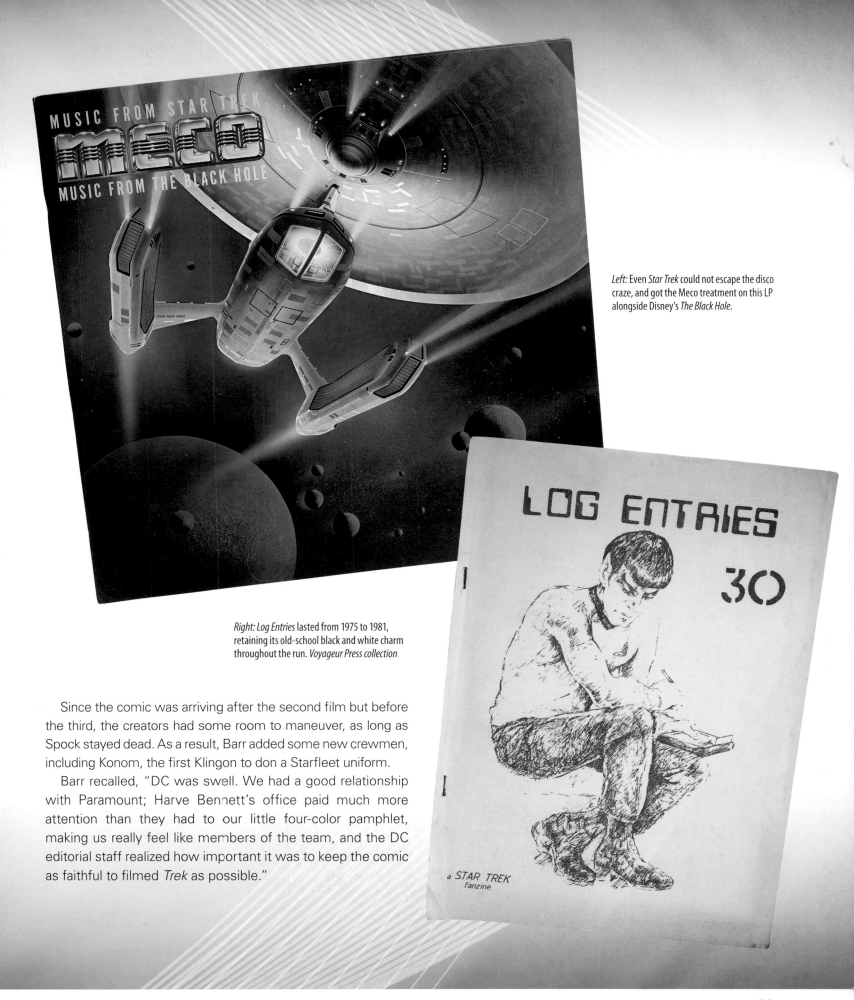

MUSIC FROM STAR TREK
meco
MUSIC FROM THE BLACK HOLE

LOG ENTRIES 30

a STAR TREK
fanzine

Since the comic was arriving after the second film but before the third, the creators had some room to maneuver, as long as Spock stayed dead. As a result, Barr added some new crewmen, including Konom, the first Klingon to don a Starfleet uniform.

Barr recalled, "DC was swell. We had a good relationship with Paramount; Harve Bennett's office paid much more attention than they had to our little four-color pamphlet, making us really feel like members of the team, and the DC editorial staff realized how important it was to keep the comic as faithful to filmed *Trek* as possible."

# CHAPTER 11

# IN SEARCH OF

# *GOD*

The cast assembles for a celebratory toast during a news conference in December 1988 announcing *Star Trek V: The Final Frontier*. William Shatner's directorial debut was much reviled by fans and critics. *Associated Press*

The original cast continued to own the silver screen, even after *Star Trek: The Next Generation (TNG)* claimed the television frontier from the fall of 1987. Paramount was delighted to have two flavors of the concept to offer fans and merchandisers, anticipating double the revenue. After the smash success of the fourth film, there was never any question about a fifth.

However, the trilogy had wrapped up nicely with Spock not only no longer dead, but reunited with his friends aboard a brand new *Constitution*-class vessel, the NCC-1701-A. What would the next story be about? Paramount turned the question over to the director, William Shatner. Part of his favored nations' clause meant he and Nimoy were offered similar deals, and part of the agreement to get him back for the last film was a promise that it was his turn to direct.

Shatner had been giving the subject matter a great deal of thought and finally drew his inspiration from television evangelists. The way they mesmerized the faithful and convinced them they were speaking on behalf of God struck him as ripe for exploration on a grander scale. That led him to develop Zar, a Vulcan, who would challenge the beliefs of the crew.

His verbal pitch to marketing exec Frank Mancuso was enthusiastically received and Shatner targeted novelist Eric van Lustbader to be his screenwriter. After negotiations broke down, Shatner dictated the basics of the story and delivered his first written outline, *An Act of Love*, to Paramount president Ned Tanen. The story contained many elements that survived to the final film.

Shatner then turned to Harve Bennett, feeling he needed the steady hand of the producer to guide him through his maiden voyage as a feature film director. Bennett, though, had tired of the grind and also felt an unwanted member of the *Trek* family after he and Nimoy found themselves drifting apart during the last film. Shatner convinced the producer to give it one more try. However, he felt the outline needed work, lacking an adventure storyline. He also questioned the search

Klingon battle cruisers from the original series and *Star Trek: The Motion Picture* on display at the Smithsonian Institute. *Howard Weinstein*

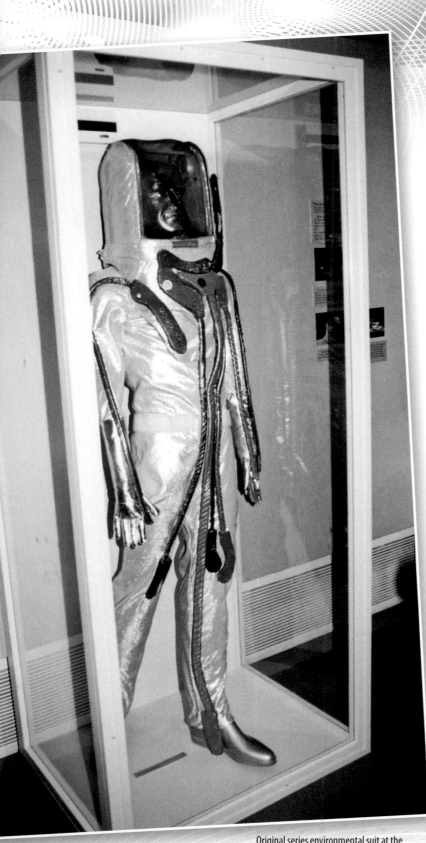

Original series environmental suit at the Smithsonian. *Howard Weinstein*

for God; since so many people saw the subject in different ways, it could prove unsatisfactory.

News about Shatner's new role as director broke on December 18, 1986, while *The Voyage Home* was still raking in big box office bucks. It also hinted at troubles between Shatner, Paramount, and Roddenberry over who had control of the franchise at this point.

The issue of faith had largely been ignored by Roddenberry. He spent so much time exploring other worlds he largely eschewed such developments on Earth in the twenty-third and now the twenty-fourth century, a reflection of Roddenberry's own distaste for it in real life. This search for God, then, would be jarring to the fans and potential new audiences.

Paramount agreed with Bennett, and work on the story began anew. It was the producer who turned the object of the *Enterprise* crew's search into an evil being who masqueraded as God in order to escape confinement. The studio approved the changes, authorizing the hire of a screenwriter. Their first choice, Nick Meyer, was unavailable so Bennett suggested David Loughery, who made a splash in 1984 with *Dreamscape*.

Loughery worked with Shatner to expand the outline before writing a script during the early months of 1987. A final story outline was delivered on May 18. Roddenberry was incensed and implored Shatner and Bennett to reconsider. He felt the religious overtones were not what *Star Trek* was about, nor did he imagine such experienced explorers as Kirk, Spock, and McCoy would be taken in by Zar.

On the earlier movies Roddenberry had quibbles about the story, but this one went too far afield. He went so far as to write his lawyer and explore the complaint, following up with an early June letter to Mancuso expressing his anger. Roddenberry feared the film would ruin his creation. "From the mass audience point of view, it would be hard to imagine a more inappropriate time to do a story with religious and cultish overtones," he wrote, citing then-current headlines featuring fallen televangelists.

On June 8, Roddenberry wrote to Shatner with his voluminous concerns about the script, concluding, "Finally, Bill, I ask you especially to rethink Kirk's position as a sole hero, an implied insult to the other cast members (who were an important factor in *Star Trek IV*) and which is certain to become a sensitive matter with audience and critics given your triple capacity as star-director-writer."

Roddenberry shared the outline with Isaac Asimov, who wholeheartedly took the Great Bird's side. The veteran author went so far as to write a letter, to be shared with concerned parties, warning the Zar character would be laughed at while others would wince at the terrible science. Arthur C. Clarke agreed with them.

Loughery continued to write until a six-month writers' strike halted all work on the screenplay. Once there was a settlement in August 1988, work resumed and finally a script was completed. Paramount was cautious with their comments, but Roddenberry and others were unhappy. While he was happy to see Shatner get his own chance behind the camera, Nimoy had long cautioned that the story was weak and its religious overtones would not be well received. Shatner's mantra was: "Trust me, it's going to work."

Nimoy also pointed out the Vulcan served no story function in the script. Many conversations ensued before Nimoy felt comfortable resuming his role. He did object to many other elements, such as the flashback to his personal pain, but Shatner remained fixed with his "vision."

The writing hiatus did allow Shatner to rethink his antagonist. He softened the character, renaming him Sybok, and making him a half-brother to Spock (a continuity implant that never sat well with fans or the production staff, hence it never being mentioned again). Loughery named the planet they sought Sha Ka Ree since Shatner had high hopes of landing Sean Connery as Sybok. The draft Shatner finally read bothered him greatly, feeling Loughery took too many liberties from the outline they discussed. Revisions began immediately.

The Smithsonian display was a year-long salute to *Star Trek* in 1991–1992 and put many props and costumes on display.

One wonders how many fans sully this solid metal pizza cutter by actually using it on gooey cheese? *ThinkGeek, Inc.*

Rather than casting someone as high profile as Connery, Shatner settled on the almost unknown actor Laurence Luckinbill as Sybok. The other small roles were filled with newcomers and character actors, with David Warner the best known of the bunch. The additions to the cast certainly lacked the impressive credentials the last few films boasted. (Bennett cameoed as a Starfleet admiral in a nice touch.)

When Paramount finally spoke up, it was regarding money. They felt the climax, which called for angels, demons, and a rock monster, would prove prohibitively expensive. Additionally, the delay from the writers' strike made them nervous that the goodwill and momentum from the last

film had dissipated. They penciled *Trek V* in for a June 1989 release and rushed the crew into production.

Loughery's script continued to be refined, but the core story, weak as it was, remained fixed. Nilo Rodis came aboard as art director to help Shatner add some grit to the *Star Trek* universe, notably the civilian garb and sets on Nimbus III. Budget constraints meant Shatner couldn't remake the Starfleet uniforms once more, but Rodis did add field uniforms, which helped liven the look. The director invited Herman Zimmerman, impressed with his work on *TNG*, to join the team as production designer. Also on the crew was Michael Okuda who gave the Klingon bird-of-prey interior new control panels.

Roddenberry's prophetic warnings remained ignored right up to his final note on the matter, written in September 1988. Production began the following month and went smoothly enough. As a director, Shatner earned praise for his preparedness and professionalism. He was absolutely focused on delivering the film according to the schedule and budget.

The production wrapped in December with the campfire scenes with the Big Three. As the movie shifted to post-production, the loss of ILM for special effects (they were booked with other films) meant Executive Producer Ralph Winter turned to Associates and Ferren for the visuals. They worked quickly, trying to finish in three months. Shatner, however, asked for numerous changes, so the overall budget crept up, pushing $33 million. Paramount stepped in and began ordering effects trimmed back or removed. Shatner's hoped-for battle with the rock creature was eliminated.

Shatner was further disappointed when Paramount refused Bennett's request for money to redo the weakest effects. Editor Peter E. Berger and Shatner worked for weeks salvaging the ending to make it as spectacular as originally envisioned. Shatner's delivered cut to Paramount weighed in at over two hours, at least twenty minutes longer than the studio wanted.

Bennett re-edited the film down to the required length, a version that Shatner hated. The two haggled over the final version.

Jerry Goldsmith was hired for a new score, and he used themes from *The Motion Picture*, which further tied the film to the legacy of the original series. Fans of *TNG*, though, were confused to hear what they considered to be their theme being used, unaware it came from the first movie.

The derisive laughter Roddenberry warned about long months before was heard at a disastrous screening in April 1989. Worse, the news reached the *Los Angeles Times* and word spread quickly among the fans. Paramount ordered the film re-edited with countless notes for the rookie director. As Nimoy noted in his second autobiography *I Am Spock*, Shatner was still shooting a bad story. If the story doesn't work, the movie won't work. Five minutes were trimmed, and a sequence on the Klingon vessel was added to help clarify the storytelling. A second test screening earned the film higher, though unspectacular, marks.

Maybe Paramount finally realized they had put their faith in a weak story, or they were preoccupied with their other summer 1989 movies, which included *Indiana Jones and the Last Crusade*, but their marketing for the fifth movie was lackluster at best. They even saved money by using a rejected one-sheet poster concept from *Indiana Jones* for *Trek*. The studio may have put too much faith in the analysts' prediction the movie would earn $200 million domestically, great numbers for the fifth film in a series.

There was initial encouragement when it earned $17.4 million during its opening weekend, beating *The Voyage Home*. However, the critics were savage. *Variety* led off by saying, "William Shatner's inauspicious feature directing debut is a double letdown." *TV Guide* noted, "Although the film's ontological approach may be intriguing, this rather dull entry fails to generate the kind of thoughtful, exciting adventure that made the Gene Roddenberry TV series so

*Top:* Kirk, Kor, Uhura, and Spock turned into Potato Heads by a terrible transporter accident. *Ian McLean*

*Above:* Fan Ian McLean, dressed as Maltz from *Star Trek III*, introduces Guest of Honor Bjo Trimble at Eccentricon, in Richmond, New South Wales, Australia, in 1987. *Ian McLean*

# PERMISSION TO COME ABOARD: FROM FANS TO PROS

*Dayton Ward*

Among the production crews of the various *Star Trek* spinoff series and films are a host of people who were fans before getting into show business. Prominent contributors to the ever-evolving *Star Trek* tapestry, such as *Star Trek Nemesis* screenwriter John Logan and graphic artist Michael Okuda, cite their love of the original *Star Trek* in particular as a prime inspiration for their choice of career.

Before traveling to Hollywood to work as a makeup artist, eventually ending up on staff with *Star Trek: The Next Generation*, Doug Drexler was a fan. He cowrote two issues of the Gold Key *Star Trek* comic book, and coedited the series of *Star Trek* Giant Poster Books in the 1970s. During this period, he also collaborated with Geoffrey Mandel on reference works such as the *U.S.S. Enterprise Officer's Manual* and the *Star Fleet Medical Reference Manual*. More than twenty years after creating the fan-favorite *Star Trek Maps* in 1980, and while working as a scenic artist on *Star Trek: Enterprise*, Mandel revisited the mammoth effort of documenting and illustrating the worlds of the final frontier with *Star Trek: Star Charts*.

While providing opportunities for established industry professionals who also happened to be devout fans, *Star Trek* has also opened doors and launched careers. Many young or unknown actors got their "big break" on a *Star Trek* set, and the same holds true behind the camera. Noted screenwriter and science fiction author David Gerrold scored his first professional writing credit in 1967 with the script for the classic episode "The Trouble With Tribbles." He later wrote for the animated *Star Trek* series before assisting Gene Roddenberry in developing *The Next Generation*. Likewise, nineteen-year old Howard Weinstein, still in college in 1974, sold his script for the animated episode "The Pirates of Orion." Weinstein went on to author several *Star Trek* novels and enjoyed a lengthy run as a writer of *Star Trek* comics.

Such good fortune continued into "the next generation," when Ronald D. Moore, then a writer struggling to make a career in Hollywood, sold his first teleplay in 1989 to *TNG* executive producer Michael Piller. "The Bonding" was the beginning of Moore's decade-long association with *Star Trek*, during which he became one of its most influential voices. Moore subsequently developed the acclaimed "re-imagining" of the cult-classic TV series *Battlestar Galactica*.

*Star Trek* has also welcomed contributions from fans in other arenas. Between 1998 and 2007, Pocket Books, the licensed publisher of *Star Trek* novels and reference works, held an annual contest seeking *Star Trek* fiction from unpublished writers. Each year, thousands of entries were received by hopeful contestants, from which fewer than twenty stories were selected and published in an anthology, *Star Trek: Strange New Worlds*. Ten such collections were produced, serving as launching pads for numerous authors who have since established writing careers in a variety of genres and mediums.

My initial professional sales were to the first three *Strange New Worlds* anthologies, which in turn led to me writing *Star Trek* novels. As a reader of such stories since childhood, adding my own stamp to a line of books that stretches back nearly as far as the original series itself is an unparalleled opportunity. I've had tremendous fun creating my own stories in the *Star Trek* "universe," and many of the same writers whose books I was reading as much as thirty years ago are people I now call my friends and colleagues. I've even had the great privilege of collaborating with a few of them on all new *Star Trek* projects. After getting over my initial hesitation about attending a *Star Trek* convention as an actual guest, I've since learned that there is very little that offers the same satisfaction as talking to a fan who traveled all day by bus, or who flew stand-by, just so they could shake your hand, get their copy of your book signed, and tell you how much they enjoy reading your work.

Hey, I can relate. After all, I'm a fan, too.

*Dayton Ward went from a career in the military to becoming a software developer by day and* Star Trek *author by night. He has written original science fiction and blogs more often than is good for him.*

compelling." Caryn James at the *New York Times* wrote, "Captain Kirk and his crew go where too many film makers have too often gone before."

The film remained in first run theaters for a mere ten weeks, the shortest run of any *Trek* film so far. In the end, it earned $49,566,330, a quarter of the estimates. It was deemed one of the year's biggest disappointments, and rather than earn any Oscar nominations, the film won numerous Golden Raspberry Awards—Worst Actor and Worst Director (both Shatner) as well as Worst Picture. It was also in contention for Worst Screenplay, Worst Supporting Actor (DeForest Kelley), and a year later, Worst Picture of the Decade.

Why did the movie disappoint all concerned? The story was clearly a departure from what people had come to expect of *Star Trek* and was never fully realized. As director, Shatner also misused the ensemble cast, deriving humor at the characters' expense. Bennett said the summer competition was more than the aging franchise could handle. Paramount accepted an inferior story and then slashed the budget and rushed it into production, never letting Shatner and Bennett really polish it.

The fans were unhappy with many elements from the mundane (misnumbering the decks) to the major (Spock has a half-brother?). They felt the hint at a Scotty/Uhura romance came out of left field, and joined Nichelle Nichols's outrage to learn that her vocals were dubbed by another singer without her knowledge.

At a time when movie merchandise was not faring well for any property, Paramount was delighted at how well *The Final Frontier* product sold. J. M. Dillard's novelization even spent four weeks on the bestseller lists. On the other hand, the film was so poorly received, some countries declined to run it in theaters, so international fans had to wait for the home video release a year later. Similarly, the film's performance led Bandai Nintendo Entertainment System to cancel a planned tie-in video game.

*Above:* Sometimes *Star Trek* fans need to wear a tie. *ThinkGeek, Inc.*

*Below:* No one should beam down without an official *Enterprise* church key. *ThinkGeek, Inc.*

*Voyageur Press collection except for "Beam Me Up Scotty" and "Don't Mess with Sulu," Ella Pearson*

*Voyageur Press collection*

More Missions   More Myths

Rumor has it that Kim Cattrall had photos taken on the bridge while wearing nothing but her pointed ears. Nimoy learned of it and, incensed, had the prints and negatives destroyed.

Fan writing showed no signs of leaving, as demonstrated by this fanzine from 1987.
*Voyageur Press collection*

Only the best dressed cadets can be found sporting these stylish cufflinks. *ThinkGeek, Inc.*

Playmates Toys' General Chang, as played by Christopher Plummer in *Star Trek VI: The Undiscovered Country.*

## CURTAIN CALL

Despite the poor performance of *Star Trek V* compared with the previous three films, *Star Trek* was still the closest thing to a cash cow Paramount had. Initially, they acceded to Bennett's desire to look backward, approving work be done on a script focusing on Kirk, Spock, and McCoy at Starfleet Academy, with a plan to use a fresh cast. Loughery was hired to work on the concept, but by the time a draft script was completed, President Ned Tanen had resigned. Frank Mancuso wanted one last film with the same cast, dangling the academy notion as a possible seventh film, leading Bennett to bitterly leave the franchise for good.

Walter Koenig pitched Mancuso his own take on a swan song, *In Flanders Fields*, that saw the Romulans and Federation partner to wage war on the Klingons. This would have resulted in the original crew dying to save Spock and McCoy. His idea wasn't taken any further forward.

Mancuso told Nimoy he wanted the final film to come out in time for the series' twenty-fifth anniversary in 1991. The actor agreed, but he wasn't sure he wanted to direct and suggested they invite Nick Meyer back. Nimoy, now executive producer, met with Meyer in Cape Cod and Meyer seized on Nimoy's simmering notion of using the fall of the Berlin Wall as a way to examine Federation/Klingon relations.

Once Paramount approved the premise, they abruptly assigned the writing to Lawrence Konner and Mark Rosenthal, the team responsible for the poorly received *Superman IV.* The pair was already under studio contract and in need of work. When they proved stumped and exited the production, Meyer cut a deal for the script, cowriting it with his production partner Denny Martin Flinn. Working via e-mail, the two put together a script that grew stronger with input from Nimoy, who sought stronger drama for the characters.

For the first time since *Star Trek II*, there would be a real villain for Captain Kirk to face: General Chang, written with Christopher Plummer in mind. He headed an interracial conspiracy that was designed to maintain the status quo in a changing galaxy.

The script was well-received, but at a meeting with studio executives, the $30 million budget Mancuso promised was

The Continuum Edition covered the franchise from series to movies. *ThinkGeek, Inc.*

*Star Trek VI*'s banquet scene was intended to be longer but proved problematic to write and shoot. The cast was also reluctant to eat the blue-dyed food (mostly lobster and squid) until Meyer bribed them at $20 per mouthful, with Shatner being first to accept.

reduced to $25 million. Meyer walked everyone through the history of *Trek* movie budgets, noting the film had to be $30 million based on reality. They offered $27 million. Meyer took his budget analysis to Mancuso, hoping to get the remaining $3 million. Instead, Mancuso canceled the film. Days later, Mancuso found himself out of work and new presidents Stanley Jaffe and Sherry Lansing approved the needed funds.

Casting director Mary Jo Slater secured Plummer, then found Kim Cattrall to play Valeris, another protégée of Spock. Initially, Meyer wanted Kirstie Alley back as Saavik and have her betray her mentor, but the actress rejected the offer. The character of Saavik was rewritten as Valeris and given an eerily similar background. David Warner, misused in the previous film, played Klingon Chancellor Gorkon, while Brock Peters returned as Starfleet Admiral Cartwright, demonstrating how deep the conspiracy ran on both sides. Future *Deep Space Nine* star René Auberjonois was cast as coconspirator Colonel West, only to have his scenes cut to appease Roddenberry. Michael Dorn came over from *TNG* to play Worf's grandfather. Slater also found a cameo for her son, Christian, who was a major fan of the series.

Roddenberry was angered by the blatant bigotry exhibited by Starfleet's finest. He railed against the script and Meyer later admitted he badly mishandled their meeting. Nichelle Nichols and Brock Peters also had issues with some of the dialogue. Lines were transferred from Uhura to Chekov, and Peters needed multiple takes to get through one particularly racist speech.

Nimoy, meantime, agreed with Roddenberry the movie should have more thoroughly explored Klingon culture, but the evolving story structure never allowed for that. As it was, Roddenberry saw the film mere days before his death and was satisfied with how the subject matter was handled. Word was, he had a change of heart and instructed lawyer Maizlish to order fifteen minutes trimmed, but the series creator died before the order was delivered.

The tight budget meant all ship models were refurbished from other productions while the *Enterprise* sets were made darker, more claustrophobic, and worn in appearance. Many standing sets from *TNG* were redressed to save money.

Production was uneventful as Nimoy and Meyer, who felt tensions between them during development, fell into a natural rhythm. Author Peter David was visiting the production one day when George Takei was filming a scene, and he suggested now might be a good time to have Sulu utter the first name "Hikaru," which had been first mentioned in Vonda McIntyre's novel *The Entropy Effect* and used in the spinoff literature ever since. Meyer agreed, leaving Uhura the only main character not to have an onscreen first name. Sulu also received his long overdue promotion to captain and command of his own vessel, *U.S.S. Excelsior*.

The filming ran from April 16 through September 27, 1991. Early on, Cliff Eidelman joined the production to score the film, taking his cue from Meyer, who was seeking sounds similar to Holst's *The Planets* and Stravinsky's *The Firebird*.

The movie opened on December 6, earning $96,888,996 worldwide. The reviews all lauded it as a proper farewell to the original crew in addition to noting it being a vast improvement on its predecessor.

Just before the final credits rolled, the cast's signatures appeared against the stars, a fitting farewell and paving the way for the film franchise to be passed from one generation to another.

CHAPTER 12

# CREATING *THE NEXT GENERATION*

Adm. William Crowe visiting the set of the TV series, *Star Trek: The Next Generation*, flanked by actors Jonathan Frakes (left) and Patrick Stewart. *Time Life Pictures/Getty Images*

During Gene Roddenberry's annual phone interview with the fans at August Party in 1981, he was asked: "If there were a series again, would you be interested in doing it?" He said, "No, I won't line produce it again. TV is not as it used to be. There are too many people who will try to change what you are doing. I realize now that I had an easier time before. Now everybody has become an expert on science fiction."

Five years later, Paramount celebrated *Star Trek*'s twentieth anniversary with a new wave of marketing and merchandising. The fourth film was scheduled to come out at year's end, and the studio hosted a bash on September 8, the show's birthday. To veterans experienced with Paramount's ways, everything felt a tad too big and lavish. Robert Justman and David Gerrold sensed something was in the air.

Sure enough, a month after the party, the studio gave the fans a present. On October 10, 1986, Paramount formally announced a brand new television series, to debut a year later. Set some time after the Kirk era, it would feature a new crew and starship. Some were surprised to hear that Roddenberry himself would come back from the wilderness to produce the show.

Paramount had not originally planned it that way. Months earlier they had taken it on themselves to develop a brand new version of *Star Trek* without reference to Roddenberry. Gregory Strangis, the producer of *Eight is Enough* and *Falcon Crest*, was hired to create a new show under the direction of Paramount Television president John Pike. Strangis toiled in anonymity for months, envisioning a future where a Klingon was a member of Starfleet, a century or so after Kirk's time.

Paramount's idea was to sell the series to Fox, which just then was preparing to launch the fourth network Paramount failed to achieve a decade before. Fox very much wanted *Star Trek* for their new network, but demanded it be ready to air in March 1987 and would only give a thirteen-episode commitment, something Paramount rejected. After the other networks refused their demands, Paramount decided to launch the new series into first-run syndication, bypassing the

Ian McLean

primetime networks. This would allow them to control the creativity and costs, while reaping all the profits.

Fans first heard of this possible new series in mid-summer 1986 as unconfirmed rumors that Paramount was up to something surfaced in the press. On September 12, Roddenberry read Strangis's take for the new series and was displeased. The notion was that the starship would be crewed by new cadets, under the guidance of some older figures. He insisted in a memo issued a week later that Strangis missed the point of *Star Trek* and only he knew what to do. By this time, Frank Mancuso had already approached Leonard Nimoy about executive producing the new series to keep it within the "*Star Trek* family," and allow the studio to avoid dealing with Roddenberry beyond his advisory role. The actor passed, seeking a career beyond the franchise.

Paramount feared that a new crew was already going to make the diehard fans they needed to watch the show nervous, so they recognized that angering Roddenberry

Above: Ian McLean

was not in their best interests. Roddenberry held fast to a fat pay day in addition to total creative control. For years he felt betrayed by Paramount for their handing his creation to Bennett and then ignoring him for the next three films. In his mind, it was payback time.

Once more the hand of Gene could be seen manipulating events. *Electronic News*, a technical trade publication, somehow found out about the negotiations and ran a story forcing Paramount's hand. It was believed leaked to them by Roddenberry, his secretary Susan Sackett, or their aide de camp Richard Arnold.

But Roddenberry also needed to sort out his own problems. The producer had always liked a good stiff drink, but as the years rolled by, he became a borderline alcoholic who added cocaine, the "in" drug of the 1970s. Both ravaged his large frame. Once the basics of an agreement to produce the new *Star Trek* series were in place, Sackett convinced him to go into rehab for fourteen days.

*Below:* The original cast assembles to celebrate the silver anniversary of their series at the entrance of the *Star Trek* exhibit at the Smithsonian's National Air and Space Museum in Washington, February 1992. *Associated Press*

The new crew was not left out of the anniversary celebration. *Steve Roby collection*

Strangis was informed that he was no longer required, although he was retained as Creative Consultant for a handful of first season episodes. After completing the program, Roddenberry attended a few speaking engagements, then flew to attend the October press conference.

With a guarantee of twenty-four episodes budgeted at $1.2 million apiece, Roddenberry felt confident in moving forward quickly. The first person he met with was D. C. Fontana, making a verbal agreement to have her read and consult on everything written until a place could be found for her on staff.

Four days after the formal announcement, Roddenberry took David Gerrold to lunch and they talked about what the new series could be. Roddenberry listened as Gerrold expounded on the ideas he had been harboring since the first series ended, which he wrote about in his 1973 book *The World of Star Trek*. These included an older, less impetuous captain, who didn't beam down to the planet *du jour* very often, but let his first officer do the exploring. By October 20, Gerrold was invited onto the new staff, being paid a mere thousand dollars a week but promised the higher paying role of Executive Story Consultant. Roddenberry's lawyer Leonard Maizlish craftily wrote a contract dated to the time of that first lunch, thereby making those cherished ideas the property of the new series. Gerrold also came to realize that his former mentor had hit a creative dry patch, unable to finish an original science fiction novel after years of effort, and not having written any filmable scripts for over a decade.

A joyful Roddenberry returned to the Paramount lot on October 17. Soon after settling in, he also invited Justman and one-time producer Edward Milkis back into the fold. Justman returned as much out of loyalty to Roddenberry as to the show. Milkis would not remain with the production for long, replaced by Rick Berman, a coproducer brought over from the Paramount ranks.

Roddenberry held a series of screenings of current science fiction films to get ideas and see what was popular, much as he raided Samuel Peeples's pulp magazines years before. One inspiration, derived from James Cameron's recent

*Above:* Unlike the first cast, the crew of the *Enterprise*-D enjoyed a reputation for having a happy set as seen in this candid moment between Gates McFadden and Jonathan Frakes. © *Neal Preston/Corbis*

*Left:* Denise Crosby and Wil Wheaton on the Paramount lot during production of *Star Trek: The Next Generation*'s first season. © *Neal Preston/Corbis*

*Below:* Marina Sirtis mugs for the camera, pleased with how well Pablo Marcos enhanced her physique in the first mini-series based on *Star Trek: The Next Generation*. © *Neal Preston/Corbis*

Several characters from the original series made guest appearances on *The Next Generation*. From left, Scotty, McCoy, Spock, and Sarek, Spock's father, are captured by Playmates Toys in their older incarnations.

*Aliens*, was the idea of an Hispanic security chief, named Macha Hernandez when the first eight-page bible was finally written. Other characters in that first bible included Lieutenant Commander Troi, described as "a four-breasted, oversexed hermaphrodite," and Wesley Crusher, "a Yodaish midget."

Clearly, Roddenberry needed help.

Gerrold and Justman dove in, extrapolating from everything written about the twenty-third century setting of the original series forward by nearly a century. At first Roddenberry was thinking of leaping as many as one hundred fifty years into the future, then scaled it back to a century, before finally settling on the seventy-eight year mark. Justman suggested the notion of having families aboard a far larger starship, and using a holodeck for recreation and training. He even came up with an android with Spock-like qualities, which no doubt appealed to Roddenberry since that closely resembled the character of Questor, a concept that had made it to pilot in the mid-1970s. Gerrold came up with the notion of this android having golden skin. On October 27, he also suggested giving some of the crew members handicaps, including blindness, an idea Roddenberry accepted two days later.

Justman, like Strangis (and indeed comic book writer Mike Barr before him), suggested it was time for a Klingon on board the *Enterprise*. While Roddenberry proved surprisingly resistant to the notion, he finally gave in—then took credit for the innovation.

The ship's captain was going to be the older, wiser "Julien" Picard although Fontana rejected the name and offered up variations, including Jean-Luc. She also objected to Troi's mammary count, berating Roddenberry with a "Don't be silly!"

While Gerrold continued to wait for Roddenberry to keep his promises, he agreed to begin screening potential writers. He was devastated when he realized that the promises were hollow. There would be no promotion, just a staff writer's contract for twenty weeks' work.

Roddenberry and Paramount agreed on a series name in November, just before *The Voyage Home* opened. The November 26 bible called the show *Star Trek: The Next Generation*, echoing a fan's suggestion during Roddenberry's appearance at the Museum of Broadcasting that August.

In December, Roddenberry asked Fontana to take on the pilot script, trusting her approach with characters and deft way of introducing backstory. She agreed, but still was waiting for the promised staff job.

Roddenberry clearly wasn't up to steering a modern-day television production and needed to surround himself with people he felt comfortable with, so in January 1987, he invited Robert Lewin, who worked on *Mission: Impossible* back in the 1960s, aboard as Creative Producer.

Lewin formally began on staff in February, and he was told to hire Fontana as the series story editor, finally honoring at least

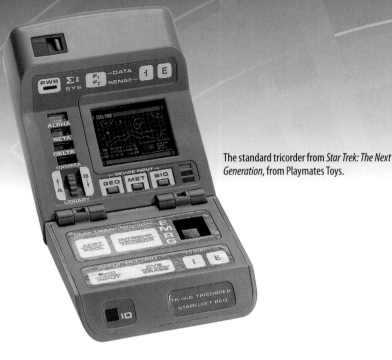

The standard tricorder from *Star Trek: The Next Generation*, from Playmates Toys.

one promise. It was then things began to turn ugly, well before a single foot of film was shot. Roddenberry continued to make offers to Gerrold and Fontana that were below the standard Writers Guild guidelines, and when they complained, he brought Maizlish onto the lot. The lawyer soon became a daily presence and was seen as doing Roddenberry's dirty work.

Maurice Hurley was added to the staff as a coexecutive producer, taking the role of lead writer in the months to come. He, Herb Wright (hired as a writer/producer, joining the staff on March 30), and Lewin never had clearly defined roles, leading to clashes and miscommunications that only further plagued the nascent show.

Despite being one of the series' creators, Gerrold found himself denied script assignments until he more or less shamed Roddenberry into green lighting "Blood and Fire," an AIDS allegory right in the old *Star Trek*'s wheelhouse. Unfortunately, he was pulled off that to revise and expand the bible, with a threat of being fired if he insisted on the Guild-approved additional compensation. Roddenberry then spiked "Blood and Fire," sundering his relationship with Gerrold once and for all.

John D. F. Black was invited by Justman to pitch some stories. One got the producer so excited, he grabbed Black and dragged him to Roddenberry's office. As expected, the Great Bird liked the notion and sent Black off to write. However, after two rounds of changes, Black learned his script "Justice" was reassigned to Worley Thorne.

Fontana, meantime, was busily writing and rewriting. Part of the problem was that Roddenberry and Paramount disagreed over the pilot's length. While the studio wanted an hour plus some special features, Roddenberry wanted the story to run two hours. However, he instructed Fontana to write a ninety-minute script to which Roddenberry himself would add the remaining thirty minutes. After she delivered a draft in March, he asked her to take his notes and ten script pages of "The Naked Now" and complete his work on that. Fontana read the material and found it wanting, so she suggested she'd start from scratch. Roddenberry objected, insisting the studio wanted a Roddenberry-penned script, even though he had no time to do so, given the thirty-minute script he also needed to write. Fontana refused to do all the work but only receive half the pay, residuals, and credit. She suggested letting the Writers Guild determine credit. In the end, the teleplay was credited solely to Fontana, while she shared story credit with Black on whose original series episode "The Naked Time" the script was based.

By this point, Roddenberry's sobriety had quietly ended, and he was mixing alcohol with a pharmacopeia of medications that no doubt contributed to both his inability to write and his behavior issues. Maizlish began acting as Roddenberry's proxy, going so far as to rewrite scripts and deliver notes to Roddenberry, which the producer then copied almost verbatim and delivered to writers as if they were his own thoughts. Staff writers were hired and then fired with no explanation, which did not help the show's morale.

In Roddenberry's posthumous defense, Lewin said that while the producer couldn't handle life in the twentieth century all that well, he was plainly thinking about the future quite often, clearly writing the rules of the twenty-fourth century, rules that would guide—and hamper—writers for the next decade. Roddenberry was so optimistic about how man would evolve in the next few hundred years that he decreed humans were above interpersonal conflicts. This robbed the series of the dramatic tension that had been a staple in good fiction dating back to Plato. Trying to write within these confines, which became known as "the Box," would sink experienced writers time and again.

Folded shut, this miniplayset looked like a *Star Trek: The Next Generation* combadge. Opened up, it featured a "working" transporter—with the spin of a dial, Data and Riker beam away.

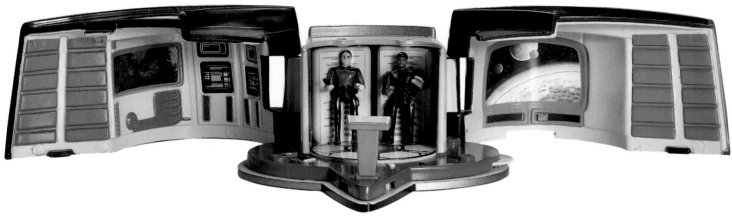

*Above:* Still in the box! The *Enterprise*, NCC-1701-D, of *Star Trek: The Next Generation*, from Playmates Toys. *Becky Pagel*

*Below:* The standard tricorder packaging. *Becky Pagel*

In time, word of what a toxic production the new series had become spread across Hollywood, and few agents called seeking work for their clients. This, Roddenberry insisted, was everyone else's fault, despite the fact that his habits and work ethic pretty much matched his behavior on the Paramount lot two decades earlier. When Paramount realized the depth of the problem, they gently suggested to Roddenberry that he elevate Wright to total control over the series and take the title Creative Consultant. He adamantly refused, then distrusted

Wright, forcing him from the series. After Wright fell out of favor, Tracy Tormé became the next favorite.

As the production began in earnest and the fall air date began to loom on the horizon, Gerrold filed a grievance with the Writers Guild over compensation and credit over the bible. Soon after, Roddenberry turned his ire on Fontana, seeking her support against Gerrold, but she held firm that she didn't want to be involved. She was punished by being relocated to a horrible office and then denied permission to work from home. Majel called to apologetically disinvite her from a birthday party for Gene. Eventually, in February 1988, she filed her own grievance against her former boss, settling for cash compensation a year later. Gerrold's case actually began before Roddenberry decided he had had enough fighting and he also settled with his former friend.

*I*nitially, the new *Enterprise* was designated the NCC-1701-7 but taking a cue from the lettering used in the fourth feature, it was renamed the 1701-D. Said to be eight times the size of the original *Constitution*-class vessel, it was large enough to support a veritable city in space, including civilians in support roles, such as teachers to the crew's children.

Roddenberry rehired Andrew Probert, who helped redesign the *Enterprise* for *Phase II* and the first film, to create a new class of ship. The first sketches were attached to a December draft of the bible, but were not publically seen until May 1987 when they appeared in *Starlog*. By the time of the February 4, 1987, writers' guide, the crew complement was set at 907, swelling to 1012 by the March 23 draft. In between, the entire production team met for the first time on February 18 and worked their way through "Encounter at Farpoint," Fontana's pilot script, discussing what needed to be created, determined, and executed.

Miniatures were commissioned for filming from ILM, and for a time, the producers considered going for all computer-generated effects. However, they deemed the new technology was not stable enough to rely on for a weekly television series so they sought traditional effects houses. Peter Lauritson

Klingon disruptor from Playmates Toys, used in various movies and series.

This television remote is cleverly disguised as a *Star Trek: The Next Generation* Type 2 phaser.

was hired to handle the in-house video effects, working under Justman's direction.

Also climbing aboard was designer Rick Sternbach, who heard the news of *TNG* on the radio, found the first payphone, and called Sackett, asking for a job interview. Okuda, who impressed everyone on the fourth film, was brought on to the team as a scenic artist.

Roddenberry turned once more to Bill Theiss for new Starfleet uniforms, and Justman and Milkis hired Herman Zimmerman to be the show's art director. One of Zimmerman's tasks was taking Justman's notion of a captain's ready room, adjacent to the bridge and figuring out what it would look like. Probert was already updating the original bridge design, although Roddenberry's notion of a massive viewscreen proved impractical.

## CASTING THE FUTURE

On December 10, 1986, while the bible continued to be refined and revised, agents were given the first crew descriptions. The other producers convinced a reluctant Roddenberry the cast needed more women, so as a result, in this version, Wesley Crusher became Leslie.

Roddenberry took aspects of his earlier self and applied them to the crew. Picard was how he saw himself at the time: wiser, experienced, and prone to choose diplomacy over fisticuffs. Riker was the young fighter pilot and a ladies' man. Wesley/Leslie represented the younger Roddenberry, a teen with unlimited potential. The avaricious and libidinous aspects of his personality were reserved for the Ferengi.

The second in command, called Number One—an echo back to "The Cage"—was William T. Riker. Also aboard were android Data; half-alien counselor Deanna Troi; security chief Macha Hernandez; blind bridge officer Geordi La Forge (named after handicapped fan George La Forge, who died back in 1975); and doctor Beverly Crusher, mother to Wesley/Leslie.

Worf, the Klingon officer, was not part of the bible as casting got underway, and he wouldn't be added until Fontana wrote him into the April 13 draft of the pilot script.

Finding the right man to play Picard proved elusive. Watching a reading of "The Changing Face of Comedy" at UCLA with his wife, Justman was mesmerized by a Royal Shakespeare company actor named Patrick Stewart. He turned to his wife and announced, "I think we have just found our captain." The problem then became convincing

*Above:* The light-up *Enterprise*-D holiday ornament from Hallmark.

*Below:* The box is well worn, but this limited-edition *Star Trek* game from 1992 has never been played. *Voyageur Press collection*

Roddenberry, who was determined to cast a Frenchman in the part. Justman brought Stewart in for a meeting with Roddenberry, who liked the performer and even briefly considered him for Data.

Meantime, television actor Jonathan Frakes became Roddenberry's favorite for Riker, and during the six weeks before the role was formally offered, the two became close.

British-born Marina Sirtis read for Tasha Yar, the renamed security chief, as Bing Crosby's granddaughter Denise Crosby tried out for Deanna Troi. Each actress thought she did well, but both were stunned to learn they had been given the other's part.

Brent Spiner had gone from a solid Broadway career to Hollywood, where he gained attention in a recurring role on *Night Court* before landing the part of Data. Joining him was LeVar Burton, certainly the biggest name among the cast at the time, thanks to his memorable work years before in the landmark miniseries *Roots*. Soap opera veteran Cheryl McFadden earned the role of Dr. Crusher. After being cast, she decided her name was too pedestrian, so altered it from Cheryl to Gates, a move that made Paramount's publicity team hastily revise their press materials.

By the time casting was well underway, Roddenberry insisted that the younger Crusher be male. Juvenile actor Wil Wheaton, who gave a moving performance in *Stand by Me*, won the role.

Worf was finally considered a recurring player, envisioned to be used in maybe half the episodes when they cast *CHiPS* veteran Michael Dorn. After he filmed the pilot, his presence convinced the production team that he needed to be a regular.

The new cast was introduced during a major press conference in May 1987, garnering international headlines and leaving the diehard fans wary. This wasn't the *Enterprise* crew they knew, or the performers they had come to consider family after fifteen years of conventions. There was a cautious undercurrent to the fanzine conversations and the growing online community.

Michael Westmore began working on the actors' makeup, notably that for Dorn and Spiner. Some two dozen makeup combinations were tried out on Spiner, with Roddenberry leaning towards a grayish hue and Westmore preferring golden tones. As for the Klingon look, a nose and forehead appliance helped simplify the process, and Roddenberry insisted Dorn have a short haircut to match Starfleet regulations. The makeup design evolved over the first few seasons.

Westmore struggled to find a prop to use for Geordi's visual-enhancing VISOR, until Okuda walked in with a banana clip, which was quickly adopted for use.

Sirtis's original outfit of a skant (a combination of skirt and pants) and boots left the producers unconvinced she was serious or sexy enough. The poor actress was repeatedly photographed with varying cuts of fabric and hairstyles. She was miserable, feeling like meat on display, never quite happy with the final designs. Thankfully, they changed to something better suiting the actress and the role she played by the third season.

*Voyageur Press collection*

There was concern that the pilot script was running short so extra scenes were added. One of these saw an unnamed elderly "admiral" arriving for a brief inspection. Roddenberry wanted something to tie the original series to the new show, beyond a ship with the same name. He took DeForest Kelley to lunch and made the pitch, expecting to be politely turned down. Instead, Kelley happily agreed, taking only the Actors' Guild minimum for his work, and pleasantly surprised fans with a touching scene.

Filming began on May 29 and wrapped a month later. Paramount was pleased with the footage, and in early August showed clips to 170 stations that had signed up to air the series, covering 94 percent of the United States. Over fifty network affiliates pre-empted network shows in favor of the syndicated series.

While fans cautiously awaited the September 28 premiere, two fans, including T. Alan Chafin, produced the first *TNG* fanzine. According to Chafin, "It saw print before actors were cast in the parts, but we used all of the correct characters."

CHAPTER 13 THE NEW

# FRONTIER

Beverly Crusher, William Riker, Tasha Yar,
Jean-Luc Picard, Data, and Deanna Troi from
Playmates Toys.

A light-up Romulan *D'deridex*-class Warbird ornament from Hallmark.

Newspaper critics were kind to the pilot, opinions ranging from mediocre to enthusiastic. The fans were at first equally divided, but clearly one episode was not going to be enough to make a judgment. They did respond well to John de Lancie's performance as the omnipotent Q and all the dialogue references indicating this was clearly the same world they knew. They were curious enough to come back week after week.

As the season progressed, fans groused that Roddenberry's stand-in Wesley was growing exceedingly annoying. He had been identified in an early episode as being "special" and was getting favorable treatment as a result. The revolving carousel of writers and inelegant rewriting of their scripts left much to be desired. Bad enough that the second episode to air was "The Naked Now," making fans wonder if the new show would simply rewrite the old episodes. Another early episode saw the crew visit a planet populated solely by black people, and no one could figure out if the story was a message about racial equality, racism, or something else.

There were elements that the fans enjoyed. The Riker/Troi relationship was nicely explored, and Worf finally got in touch with his heritage in "Heart of Glory," the first of many strong episodes at long last spotlighting the Klingon culture.

The Romulans made a token appearance in a late season episode, "The Neutral Zone," and the final episode of the season, "Conspiracy," introduced a scheme by alien parasites to infiltrate Starfleet Command, a storyline the series chose to drop.

Despite putting families and children aboard the ship, the series never really explored life aboard the *Enterprise* from the civilian perspective. By not making any of the regulars a civilian, they missed a real storytelling possibility.

Character bits, introduced to deepen the crewmembers, became fixtures going forward. Data's playful version of Sherlock Holmes and Picard's shamus Dixon Hill were seen in holodeck-based storylines while Riker became known as a jazz aficionado. We got some insight into Data's mysterious background when his flawed predecessor, Lore, was introduced in "Datalore."

Characters and actors arrived who would become part of the ongoing ensemble. Colm Meaney was cast as an officer on the starship's battle bridge for the pilot, and he would become a recurring character, O'Brien, in the second season and a regular later on. Majel Barrett finally found the role of a lifetime: the ebullient Lwaxana Troi, mother to Deanna. Her

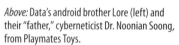
*Above:* Data's android brother Lore (left) and their "father," cyberneticist Dr. Noonian Soong, from Playmates Toys.

*Below:* Fans were quick to adopt *Star Trek: The Next Generation* as their new favorite, adding new costumes to their convention wardrobe.
© *Mark Peterson/Corbis*

Auntie Mame approach brightened the screen each time she appeared. Armin Shimerman joined the *Star Trek* universe as a Ferengi in "The Last Outpost" before returning as a vastly different Ferengi in sequel series *Deep Space Nine (DS9)*.

The cast was largely uneasy going through the season. On the one hand, they were working and getting paid, and excited to be a part of the *Star Trek* mythos, but they were less than thrilled with the spandex costumes and the chaos behind the scenes. Denise Crosby felt so underutilized she asked to be written off the show, so, late in the first season, Tasha Yar was killed in "Skin of Evil," a seemingly casual and meaningless death. Gates McFadden was also unhappy, choosing to leave when Paramount refused to investigate complaints she made about a member of staff.

Given all the shifting roles behind the camera, it is a bit of a miracle that the season was as good as it was. Worn down by the grind, Bob Justman asked that his second-year option not be picked up, while also negotiating a reduced role for the final eight first-season episodes. With Fontana and Gerrold no longer involved, the story editor role fell to others, including Johnny Dawkins and Greg Strangis early in the first season, to be followed by Richard Manning and Hans Beimler, Hannah Louise Shearer, and Tracy Tormé.

Rob Legato was struggling to make the hundred-plus optical effects required by each show come in on time and on budget, so was running roughly $100,000 over per episode. He clearly needed help and Dan Curry was hired, letting the two men split episodes going forward.

Just as the staff writers struggled to be consistent with the original series and the films, Okuda and Sternbach were trying to devise a visual language to the designs. Their efforts so impressed everyone that they were credited as Technical Advisors and

Professor Stephen Hawking was a big fan of *Star Trek: The Next Generation* and asked for a cameo appearance, which was easily done thanks to the holodeck where Data played cards with Einstein, Hawking, and Isaac Newton in the 1993 sixth-season episode "Descent." *Associated Press*

were given access to the scripts early. In time, Okuda became the premier expert on figuring out the technology of the twenty-fourth century, and he would become the chronicler of the United Federation of Planets' fictional history.

Financially, the plan worked beyond Paramount's hopes, earning them something around $1 million per episode during the first season. As the series progressed, Paramount was bringing in upwards of $90 million for the first-run episodes. They saw a 40 percent return on their investment before counting the revenue from rerun syndication. Ratings showed the series was being watched by an average of twenty million people per week, exceeding the most successful syndicated series at the time.

Production wrapped in spring 1988 and the final first-season episode ran in late May. Roddenberry had solidified his production team, and the various bugs and glitches were being ironed out so the second season promised to run more smoothly.

## THE SECOND SEASON

What nobody anticipated was a writers' strike, which crippled all television and movie production from March to August.

As work began on the second season, there appeared to be no resolution forthcoming. One casualty was the episode order, which was trimmed to twenty-two. One solution was

to delve into the written and unproduced *Phase II* scripts, with "The Child" dusted off and rewritten for Troi.

After McFadden announced that she was leaving the cast, the production team needed a new chief medical officer. Deciding to go with someone older and crustier, but still female, they created Kate Pulaski. They gave her an edge by having her treat Data more as a machine than a crewman. Diana Muldaur was cast, having previously appeared in two different roles on the original series. She eschewed her credit appearing with the cast, preferring to be listed as a Special Guest Star.

When Crosby left the cast in the first year, comedienne/actress Whoopi Goldberg had called LeVar Burton and asked him to tell the producers she'd love to beam aboard the starship. When they were initially skeptical, Goldberg convinced them she was serious, so they created a new character: Guinan, a civilian who ran the Ten Forward lounge, a new permanent set.

It had become clear the ship needed a chief engineer so Geordi La Forge was promoted and Worf formally named Security Chief. This solidified the crew roles going forward.

Frakes made a change of his own, growing a beard during hiatus. When the producers saw it, they decided to adopt it for Riker. The production staff also underwent some changes

Worf, Guinan, Geordi La Forge, Ro Laren, and Miles O'Brien from Playmates Toys.

as Lewin and Shearer left the team, and Tormé went from coexecutive story editor to creative consultant. Beimler and Manning were named executive script consultants, and Melinda Snodgrass joined the team after wowing the staff with her script "The Measure of a Man."

When the strike ended and production resumed, they started off with "The Child," airing in late November 1988, and barreled ahead.

Data was becoming a breakout character, as Spock had been before, and was heavily featured early in the second season, culminating in "The Measure of a Man," which saw him put on trial to determine if he was sentient or mechanical. It was a strong script, anchored by dynamite performances from Frakes and Spiner. "Measure" was also the first time the weekly poker game was seen, which became a fixture right up to the final episode of the series.

"Contagion," cowritten by Beth Woods, an IT consultant

working on the staff's computers, gave us Picard's interest in both archaeology and "Tea. Earl Grey. Hot." Worf and the Klingons proved so popular they became the focus of recurring stories in the years to come.

Late in the season Q returned and we learned he and Guinan did not like one another. More importantly he introduced Picard, and the viewers, to the threat of the Borg, which would loom large over the franchise for the next decade.

The second season ended with a whimper with "Shades of Gray," a hastily written bottle show that heavily relied on clips from previous episodes, and is largely considered the weakest script in any *Star Trek* series.

Fans recognized the generally improved quality of the show and rallied around it as fandom found themselves dividing over which *Star Trek* they preferred. It certainly made for interesting debates at conventions, which saw a resurgence thanks to a new set of potential guest speakers.

# THE THIRD SEASON

The behind-the-scenes turmoil that led to the first two seasons feeling incredibly inconsistent began to fade with the arrival of a new set of writers and producers. As Roddenberry grew frailer, and ceded more day-to-day control to Rick Berman, the show also bid farewell to the exhausted head writer Maurice Hurley. He was briefly replaced by Michael Wagner, but illness forced him to leave after just four episodes. However, his recommended replacement, Michael Piller, proved to be the turning point in the show's fortunes.

As Berman focused on the physical aspects, Piller, no stranger to dramatic television, took control of the writing staff, incorporating input from the actors, especially Stewart who not only wanted to see Picard off the bridge more often, but running, shooting, fighting, and kissing babes.

Piller noted that the series and its successors were the only television shows that accepted submissions of amateur teleplays as long as a legal release form was signed. He said thousands were submitted and each one read. Of the thousands submitted, 1 percent was deemed interesting enough to make the process worthwhile.

The problem was the same one that had troubled writers since the pilot—the Box. Roddenberry's adamant view that humanity had evolved beyond petty emotional turmoil was both curse and blessing. In his unpublished book *FadeIn*, Piller admitted to liking the Box. Almost every other writer hated the restrictions and looked forward to their contracts expiring so they could leave the "suffocating" Box behind them. How on earth could a show find drama when Earth's inhabitants lived in a utopia?

Piller came to recognize the show and its predecessor worked, so there had to be something to The Box. Acknowledging Roddenberry was still the boss, Piller accepted his place in The Box and told the staff they would make do. Sure enough, they found ways to think outside the Box for seven straight seasons.

It's DeForest Kelley's turn to receive his star on the Walk of Fame, honoring a career that spanned radio, movies, and television. Appearing with him on December 18, 1991, were Grace Lee Whitney, Leonard Nimoy, George Takei, Nichelle Nichols, and Walter Koenig. *Associated Press*

Ambassador produced stickers for *The Next Generation* as well as the original series.

The cast had been complaining about the physical discomfort caused by the spandex they were wearing. For the third season, the uniforms were retooled by newly arrived costumer Bob Blackman and made looser with the addition of a high collar. However, complaints continued, so during the season, the regulars received near-wool gabardine outfits. The men welcomed the jackets while the women continued to wear one-piece outfits.

The most significant alteration to the writing staff this year was the arrival of Ronald D. Moore, who submitted "The Bonding" as a spec script and was promptly hired on staff, joining the team of Beimler and Manning (now credited as coproducers), and Snodgrass (now executive script consultant). Moore's familiarity with the original series helped him tremendously. He quickly grew to be the writer to focus most on the Klingon culture, which resulted in significant developments for Worf and the Federation's allies. Future *DS9* showrunner Ira Steven Behr also joined the staff during the season and got acclimated.

Berman recognized the valued contributions made by designers Rick Sternbach and Michael Okuda, elevating them to technical consultants, ensuring greater internal consistency. Meantime, Greg Jein built a more detailed four-foot *Enterprise* miniature for filming, which allowed the audience to see into Ten Forward, when the model debuted in the tenth episode, "The Defector."

Another significant change was the return of Gates McFadden as Beverly Crusher. Muldaur's Pulaski had not gelled for the producers, and with the various changes in production personnel, there was no reason not to bring McFadden back. Following a year-long letter writing campaign and Stewart's own support, Berman personally invited McFadden back. Other character alterations saw Wesley Crusher receive a field promotion to ensign.

The stories contained greater impact and consequence for the crew as we learned more about them. We got a greater sense of cosmic politics through shows like "The Defector" and "Sins of the Father." Frakes began his directing career this season with the moving Data tale "The Offspring."

Old friends returned. Mark Lenard gave a moving turn

as Spock's father in "Sarek," and the emotional "Yesterday's Enterprise," a strong story featuring a "what if?" scenario, allowed Denise Crosby to visit. Featuring some very strong writing, this was one of the best of the run.

New additions to the crew included Reg Barclay (Dwight Schultz), who became a favorite and was brought back in subsequent seasons and series.

The third season's most significant impact, perhaps, came in the final episode. It was the series' first cliffhanger and marked a ratcheting up of the threat level. The Borg finally arrived in force, wanting to add the Federation's "biological and technological distinctiveness" to their own. Seeing Picard assimilated as Locutus, followed by Riker's order to fire on the Borg cube from where the captain was speaking, meant fans had a very long summer of anticipation ahead of them. It was the first time a threat was introduced with lasting repercussions.

Ever since the introduction of the Borg the previous season, the staff had wanted to bring the alien menace back, but Piller struggled to find a way. It had been suggested to him to add a "queen bee" who spoke for the collective, but he rejected the concept. "To me, there was something special and frightening about the Borg that their lack of character brought," Piller said in *Captains' Logs: The Unauthorized Complete Trek Voyages*. "For a show that dwells and specializes in character to be challenged and possibly destroyed by a characterless villain seemed, to me, to be a special kind of threat. But when we started talking about the cliffhanger and the Borg, we really did talk about who was going to be the queen bee. It all just fell into place. I said, 'I've got it. Picard will be the queen bee.'"

The producers' peers seemed to acknowledge the improvement with six episodes receiving eight Emmy nominations. "Yesterday's Enterprise" received an award for Outstanding Sound Editing while "Sins of the Father" won for Best Art Direction.

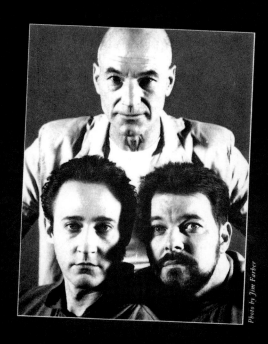

# EVERY GOOD BOY DESERVES FAVOUR
## A PLAY FOR ACTORS & ORCHESTRA

by Tom Stoppard & Andre Previn

Photo by Jim Farber

**NORTHROP AUDITORIUM
MARCH 27, 1993**

The cast had so much fun working together that they went on to appear together in other works, including Brent Spiner's solo CD, *Old Yellow Eyes Is Back*, and this Tom Stoppard play.

MN6327  1          19   7  A   45.50
45.50 MAIN  FLOOR
4.14
1                  SPACE AGENCY PRESENTS:
2HP  5x            "EVERY GOOD BOY
                   * * * * * * *
19   7             DESERVES FAVOUR"
4311033            NORTHROP AUD.  U OF MN
A20JAN3            SAT MAR 27 1993  8:00 PM

*Above:* Micromachines' shuttlecraft from the *Enterprise*-D, named for writer and producer Rick Berman.

*Below:* The crew of *The Next Generation* had plenty of enemies for Playmates Toys to cover, from Commander Sela—the daughter of Tasha Yar (from an alternate timeline) and a Romulan general—to the ruthless cyborgs known simply as the Borg.

## THE FOURTH SEASON

Watching the third season cliffhanger was Brannon Braga, who was hired for the crew as the show aired in spring 1990. Piller had struggled with whether or not to come back for a second year and much of Riker's soul-searching in the cliffhanger was Piller putting his feelings into words. In the end, he signed on for another season.

Rick Berman was upped to Executive Producer, as Roddenberry's health continued to fail. By then, the machine was running just fine without him, although his driver, Ernie Over, continued to bring him to the lot every day. Roddenberry was consulted and he visited the set now and then, but he was reduced to using a wheelchair. His memory was rapidly failing, and a series of small strokes robbed him of his vitality.

Ron Moore was named Executive Story Editor, splitting responsibilities with newly hired Joe Menosky. A handful of others came to work on the show for brief periods, but the ones to make lasting impressions were Braga and Jeri Taylor, who joined as a supervising producer, replacing Beimler and Manning. The solid writing staff began exploring running themes in this season, building off what had been established.

Wil Wheaton moved from regular to guest star, with Wesley Crusher finally being accepted into Starfleet Academy. Crosby was back, but not as Yar. Instead she played Sela, Yar's daughter, the result of the character traveling back in the time rift created in "Yesterday's Enterprise." Spiner got to play Data's creator, Dr. Noonian Soong, in "Brothers," one of many family-oriented stories that season and the first script by Berman.

Colm Meaney's O'Brien not only was given a first and middle name, Miles Edward, but also got married, and we learned something of his background in

Deanna Troi's mother Lwaxana from Playmates Toys.

"The Wounded." We were introduced to Picard's brother in "Family," the charming aftermath episode from the season opener. Worf met his son Alexander, and Tasha Yar's sister visited the starship.

The show also took storytelling chances, with "Data's Day" showing a day in the life of the ship from the android's point of view, and "First Contact," recounting the story from an alien race's perspective. The latter also featured *Cheers* star, and longtime fan, Bebe Neuwirth in a cameo written just for her. De Lancie was back as Q in the amusing "Qpid," which also featured Jennifer Hetrick's Vash, a romantic foil for Picard introduced the previous season.

Behind the camera, Stewart finally got to make his directorial debut as did cinematographer Marvin Rush and producer David Livingston. Rush's episode, "The Host," introduced the Trill race, an important part of *DS9*, and gave McFadden her strongest role of the season.

The Klingon civil strife took viewers into the offseason as "Redemption" saw Worf leaving the service to rejoin his brother Kurn (Tony Todd) and Gowron (Robert O'Reilly) in opposing the Duras sisters, aided by Sela.

The season was noteworthy for breaking the seventy-nine episode mark of the original series with the aptly titled "Legacy." The series pressed ahead and also filmed their one hundredth episode this season.

## THE FIFTH SEASON

The fifth season took shape in relative quiet. Paramount was delighted with the improved quality, high Nielsen ratings, and merchandise profits. Berman was running a smooth operation that saw Moore and Menosky promoted to coproducers. Herb Wright came back for a six-episode stint and was then replaced by Peter Allan Fields.

As production began over the summer of 1991, changes were minor. Picard, for example, received a "captain's

jacket" to differentiate his uniform from the other crewmen. Creatively, the season opened with the resolution to the Duras/Romulan alliance in "Redemption, Part II."

Paul Winfield, last seen as Captain Terrell in *Star Trek II*, guest-starred as the alien Dathon in "Darmok," which was all about communication. While wonderfully written by Menosky, Piller recalled it being the story that took the longest to go from concept to final script. The episode also introduced Ashley Judd as Robin Lefler.

Michelle Forbes so impressed the producers with a guest appearance the previous season, she was invited back, this time as the recurring character of Ro, a Bajoran member of Starfleet who had been court-martialed for disobeying orders. Picard learns of her true reason of being aboard his ship, a plot hatched by Admiral Kennelly (Cliff Potts) as part of the brewing hostility between the Bajorans and the Cardassians, a nasty race introduced back in the fourth season.

With 1991 marking *Star Trek*'s twenty-fifth anniversary, the creators wanted to do something special and struck on finally introducing Spock to the twenty-fourth century. Nimoy agreed to appearing in the two-part "Unification" as part of the

*Left:* While the real U.S.S. *Enterprise* was in drydock, its captain, Daniel C. Roper, was a guest at Shore Leave 14. He was given a handmade Starfleet uniform with measurements provided by his wife. *Constantine Hannaher*

*Right:* Malcolm McDowell, killer of Kirk, auctions a plush "Clockwork Orange" while a guest at Shore Leave 30. *Regina DeSimone*

*Above and right:* George Takei belts out a country tune as authors Robert Greenberger, Keith R. A. DeCandido, and Peter David work as backup dancers. *Stephen Lesnik*

*Left:* George Takei and James Cawley, the Captain Kirk of fan show *Star Trek: Phase II*, at Shore Leave 30. *Regina DeSimone*

*Below:* Robert Picardo and Ethan Phillips of *Voyager* share the stage at Shore Leave 31, sharing stories and working the crowd into a frenzy. *Donna Davis*

*Above:* Dominic Keating, *Enterprise's* Malcolm Reed, smiles for the camera while autographing at a table at Shore Leave 32. *Jen Snyder*

*Right:* John de Lancie, aka Q, no stranger to convention audiences, regales fans with tales of his storied career at Shore Leave 33. *Jen Snyder*

*Above:* The original series continues to draw in fans born decades after its cancellation. *Jen Snyder*

*Left:* The masquerade has become a staple at conventions, with as much attention paid to the presentation as with the costumes. Just ask this victorious Klingon. *Jen Snyder*

*Above:* Fans show their generous spirit at the annual blood drive at Shore Leave 33. *Jen Snyder*

*Below:* Fans in uniform can be found promoting their fan clubs or wearing hall costumes to demonstrate their affection for specific series or characters, such as Guinan. *Jen Snyder*

*Above:* Sally Kellerman made a rare convention appearance at Shore Leave 33 to talk about "Where No Man Has Gone Before," *M*A*S*H*, and other work in a long career. *Jen Snyder*

*Above:* Gary Lockwood, Gene Roddenberry's *Lieutenant* and good luck charm for the second pilot, meets with fans at Shore Leave 33. *Jen Snyder*

*Right:* Another great cause supported by fans at Shore Leave 33. *Jen Snyder*

*Left:* Yeoman Rand costume at Shore Leave 33. *Jen Snyder*

Micromachines versions of the Borg cube and a Klingon Bird of Prey.

marketing push for *Star Trek VI: The Undiscovered Country*, the last feature film to use the original cast, which was opening around the same time. He and Paramount initially negotiated for him to make an appearance in the season two opener, to be written by Tracy Tormé, but the writers' strike and negotiations combined to derail the plan. When Paramount marketing chief Frank Mancuso suggested tying that fall's film to the series during the invaluable November sweeps period, things began to gel. Nick Meyer, who cowrote and directed the film, came in to brainstorm ways to connect the two time periods.

Piller was to write both parts, but time constraints prevented that, so he offered the job to Jeri Taylor. At the same time, Pocket Books wanted to mark the event with a novel and Taylor, hoping to break into prose, requested the assignment. She spent a hectic September writing the script and novel simultaneously. Production schedules were adjusted to accommodate Nimoy's own schedule, so part two filmed first.

Unfortunately, on October 21, while visiting his doctor, Roddenberry had a fatal heart attack. At age seventy, the towering figure in science fiction was suddenly gone. Production was halted as the news spread, and huge throngs gathered later for his memorial service. Both "Unification" and *The Undiscovered Country* were dedicated to the Great Bird of the Galaxy's memory.

Truly, the torch had been passed to a new generation.

Whereas Walt Disney Studios was paralyzed for a decade or more in the wake of Walt Disney's death, *Star Trek* had been operating more or less without Roddenberry's close input for several years. As a result, Berman took full control of the franchise with Paramount's support. While writers thought they were finally freed from The Box, Berman honored Roddenberry's legacy by keeping people in line.

The remainder of the season was adequate, if not as memorable as the fourth season. "The First Duty" took the crew back to Earth to help Wesley, who was up on charges of misconduct. The episode was the first visit to the academy and introduced fans to Boothby, the aged and wizened gardener so wonderfully portrayed by Ray Walston, who years before was *My Favorite Martian*.

The penultimate episode was "The Inner Light," a brilliant spotlight for Stewart, who wound up playing Picard and Kamen, a Kataan who died centuries before and sought

someone to remember his race as they perished. Picard experienced thirty years of Kamen's life in thirty minutes in what proved a touching tale.

"Time's Arrow" wrapped the season with the seemingly bizarre cliffhanger of Data's disembodied head being found on Earth five centuries in the past. The story featured Mark Twain and revealed Guinan had been on Earth in the nineteenth century.

During season five, word was released about a new spinoff, *Star Trek: Deep Space Nine*, scheduled to debut in January 1993. Fans began speculating *TNG* might be wrapping up during its sixth season or actually end after the fifth season. As a result, the production team changed their initial plans and ended season five with the outrageous cliffhanger. Paramount in fact had laid their plans carefully, with Berman's input. With *DS9* debuting in 1993, they could double-up on *Star Trek* television to get the new show firmly established, then spin the *TNG* cast into the feature film slot now left clear by the original series cast.

# THE SIXTH SEASON

As work began on the sixth season, Maurice Hurley and the team of Moore and Braga were at work on separate screenplays for the first TNG film. Even then, there was talk of the original cast in some way being a part of the story.

The ratings continued to build, so much so that when *TNG* actually beat the World Series, carried on a major network, Paramount took out a trade ad to do some well-deserved boasting. The sixth season saw its ratings jump an astonishing 22 percent. Merchandisers were practically printing money during this period and the interest was strong enough to prompt the *New York Times* Syndicate to hire journalist Ian Spelling to write a regular column, *Inside Trek*. Pocket Books, which had hit the hundred book mark in their program, crowed about having sixty-four of them hit the bestseller lists.

At the production offices, script coordinator Eric Stillwell left to work for Creation Conventions and was replaced by Lolita Fatjo, who registered over 3,000 unsolicited script submissions during her first nine months.

The Playmates Toys line was filled out with many alternate versions of characters. From left, Data in period costume for the holodeck episode "The Big Goodbye," a future Picard from the finale "All Good Things...," Picard assimilated into Locutus of Borg, and Worf in Klingon uniform.

# ALONG FOR THE RIDE: WORKING AT WARP SPEED

*Michael and Denise Okuda*

To say that *Star Trek* was tough work is an understatement. During the years that we were lucky enough to be employed at Paramount, there was never enough time, never enough money, and there was always too much pressure. It was stressful, exhausting, and unrelenting. And it was totally worth it.

It's not just that *Star Trek* is cool. (Which it is.) It's not just that we got to work with great people and play with amazing toys. (Which we did.) What made everything worthwhile was the knowledge that *Star Trek*'s version of the future has been—and continues to be—a powerful force to inspire young people all around the world.

When we started working at Paramount, we really didn't know what this meant. Sure, we knew that a lot of people loved *Star Trek*. Including us. But being associated with the show opened a lot of doors for us and gave us the opportunity to meet a lot of fascinating people. And nearly everywhere we went, we discovered people who love *Star Trek*.

We are constantly amazed that so many people from so many different walks of life have been inspired by Gene Roddenberry's vision of a better tomorrow. We've met doctors, teachers, nurses, engineers, artists, and scientists, whose career and life choices were inspired by the adventures of the *Enterprise* crew. (And the *DS9* crew. And the *Voyager* crew. You get the idea.)

Even astronauts. One day Mike got an e-mail from astronaut John Grunsfeld, asking him to design the crew mission patch for STS-125, the final space shuttle servicing mission to the Hubble Space Telescope. John, who had also served as NASA's chief scientist, explained that one of the reasons he became a scientist and an astronaut was because he had loved *Star Trek* as a child and he wanted to be "like Mr. Spock." So it seemed natural to him to reach out to one of *Star Trek*'s designers to help create a symbol for their mission to Hubble, that great instrument of deep space exploration.

Several months later, we were proud to be NASA guests at the Kennedy Space Center to witness John and six of his colleagues as they rocketed into the final frontier aboard Space Shuttle *Atlantis*, each wearing Mike's patch on their pressure suits.

As much as working on *Star Trek* was fun, there were also many, many days of stress and anxiety. Television and film productions are relentless machines (kinda like the Borg), and the greatest sin is to hold up the production schedule. So everyone on the production team is always running as fast as they can, trying desperately to stay just a little bit ahead of the next deadline.

That's why we always tried to think of the young people whose imaginations might be uplifted by *Star Trek*'s tales of future adventure. They are the real reason why we worked so hard to contribute to Roddenberry's world, even when the pressures of the job got to us. *Star Trek* is, at the end of the day, just a bunch of television shows and movies. Fun stuff, but it's really just entertainment. But people like John have gone on to make a very real difference in so many different aspects of the real world, each working toward that better tomorrow.

Gene himself so often said that he was proud that *Star Trek* had inspired so many young people. And we're delighted that he allowed us to go along for the ride.

*Michael and Denise Okuda have worked in various capacities on* Star Trek *dating back to the fourth feature film and have maintained its internal continuity for the benefit of mankind.*

Next Gen Type 1 (left) and Type 2 phasers from Playmates Toys. They no longer had the modular design from the original series.

The new series meant some people, including David Livingston Michael Westmore, Bob Blackman, Rick Sternbach, and Mike Okuda, had to split their focus between the two shows. As a result, Peter Lauritson was promoted to *TNG* producer; Unit Production Manager Merri D. Howard became a line producer; and associate Wendy Neuss became a coproducer. Rob Legato moved to *DS9* so Dan Curry took over the effects work for *TNG*, assigning half the work to Ron B. Moore and David Stipes.

With Piller and Berman attending to the gestating new series, Jeri Taylor, now coexecutive producer, was in charge of *TNG*. She ran the writers' room where stories were discussed, taken apart, and put back together again until ready to be turned a scripts. Taylor was joined by Frank Abatemarco while Joe Menosky took an extended creative sabbatical. And when Peter Allen Fields moved over to *DS9*, it allowed the team to hire René Echevarria, whose freelance work had been much admired. The final writing spot went to former intern Naren Shankar.

Collectively, the writers determined to move away from the serialized character arcs and develop high concept ideas worthy of *Star Trek*. As a result, the characters were tested in new ways, such as Picard being captured and tortured by a Cardassian (David Warner) in the two-part "Chain of Command." Later, Picard's artificial heart was damaged and he hung near death in "Tapestry." Q arrived to take him on a tour of potential life paths in what proved a captivating story.

By now, the show had such a rich fabric of threads to pluck at that it was easy to infuse every episode to references dating back to the pilot or even the original series. "The Chase" finally revealed that genetically the Cardassians, Klingons, Romulans, humans, Yridians and other races all shared common traits, left behind by a long dead race.

Such was the show's appeal that real-life astronaut Mae Jemison and physicist Stephen Hawking both made cameo appearances. Michelle Forbes, Whoopi Goldberg, and Brian Bonsall, who played Worf's son Alexander, all had busy schedules elsewhere so only appeared briefly.

Their absence, though, was compensated for by "Relics" when Montgomery Scott was rescued from a transporter loop after eight decades. Ron Moore, a diehard original *Trek* fan, rose to the occasion and wrote a brilliant story about a man truly in the wrong era.

The script called for the holodeck to recreate the bridge of the original *Enterprise*, or as the time-displaced Scotty called it, "NCC-1701. No bloody A, B, C, or D." Only a section of the bridge was built with digital trickery used to complete the rest. Dan Curry recalled the clean footage of the bridge from "This Side of Paradise." Curry, designer Richard James, and cameraman Jonathan West painstakingly researched the

Specialialized medical tricorder from Playmates Toys. The hand scanner, an homage to McCoy's in the original series, tucked into a space at the top of the tricorder when not in use.

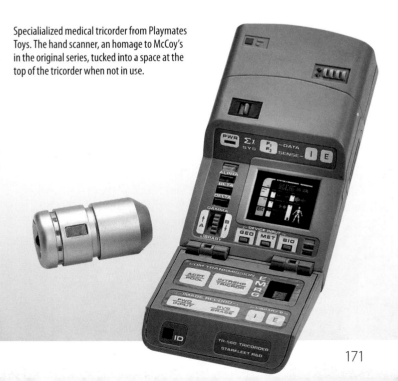

Promotional hat for fan-favorite author Peter David's latest book at the time, 1992's *Imzadi*. Bookazine is a book wholesaler and distributor.

original camera angles and lighting to exactly match the original series. To save on the budget, Okuda tracked down fan Steve Horch who had built his own bridge replica. The production rented his center console and captain's chair, spruced them up, and rolled the cameras. Everyone was convinced, save Bob Justman, who noticed the carpet color was wrong.

The crew lost another of their founders as William Ware Theiss died of complications from AIDS in December 1992. Roddenberry was posthumously awarded NASA's Public Service Medal when the *Star Trek* exhibit at the Smithsonian closed. Some 3,000 visitors a day had crowded the Air and Space Museum for a look at the exhibit.

## THE FINAL SEASON

Cast contracts were up after six seasons, but Paramount had a plan. They renegotiated with everyone for one final season and then intended to move the *Enterprise*-D crew over to feature films, replacing them on television with yet another spinoff. In 1995, this became *Star Trek: Voyager*.

There were mixed emotions at the notion the series was coming to an end, even if fans were already promised movies. After all, fans, new and old, had come to embrace these characters with the same fervor that the original *Enterprise* crew enjoyed. Waiting two years for new adventures seemed impossible.

What felt impossible for cast and crew was getting started on the seventh season so soon after wrapping the sixth. With *Star Trek Generations* now penciled in to open in November

1994, production had to begin a month earlier than normal. Worse, Moore and Braga took the month of May to go to Hawaii and write the movie screenplay. This left the rest of the writing team—Taylor, Echevarria, Shankar, and newly hired André Bormanis—to get to work, knowing they had twenty-six episodes in which to find something new for each member of the crew to do, bring back old favorites for curtain calls, and seed threads for *Voyager*. Some of the crew would also be splitting their attention between multiple projects, including the feature, which officially moved into preproduction mode.

The first order of business was resolving the Lore story from the sixth season cliffhanger. Soon after came "Gambit" a two-parter that violated one of Roddenberry's rules. He swore there would never be space pirates shown, but Taylor really liked the story. When Berman called her in to discuss it, on his desk was a bust of the Great Bird. He put a blindfold over Roddenberry's visage and heard her out. He finally gave her his blessing and the blindfold became a running gag, going on and off as needed forever after.

Data explored his dreams in "Phantasms," but it was Lwaxana's nightmares that made "Dark Page" a harrowing experience. There we learned that Deanna had an older sister (Kirsten Dunst) who died in a holiday accident. Riker experienced his own repressed memories in "The Pegasus," which dealt with his pre-*Enterprise* career.

"Parallels" took the notion of multiple universes to the *n*th degree in a fine tale from Braga that showed variations of the crew and the *Enterprise*. That also ignited the

*Star Trek: The Next Generation* collectible two-deck card tin.

Worf/Troi romance in earnest, much as Picard and Crusher finally admitted their feelings in "Attached."

"Journey's End" allowed Wesley Crusher to return and find his destiny, foretold back in season one, as he left Starfleet to explore other realities. The remainder of the episode dealt with a Native American–populated colony world being turned over to the Cardassians, setting up threads to be used by *Voyager*.

The two-hour finale, "All Good Things…," was designed to bookend the first episode and was a creative tour de force for the cast and the crew as Q, at his most dangerous, showed Picard past, present, and future. He dipped his hand into the primordial ooze and taunted Picard, noting a swish of his fingers would deny humanity from ever existing. Colm Meaney was back as O'Brien, and Denise Crosby returned for a final bow as Tasha Yar in the past sequences, which led up to the beginning of the pilot, while the future scenes showed Dr. Crusher captaining a medical starship and Worf as an ambassador.

In December 1993, Paramount asked for the finale to be a two-hour episode, and by early February the producers finally had a story that satisfied all concerned. As a result, Moore and Braga had six days to write the script and director Winrich Kolbe had just five days to prep the ambitious story. The finale aired in mid-May 1994 amidst much hoopla. In Toronto, fans crowded the SkyDome to watch it on the JumboTron.

At the Emmy Awards in September, the series was honored with Outstanding Individual Achievement in Special Visual Effects for the finale, and Outstanding Individual Achievement in Sound Mixing for a Drama Series for "Genesis," directed by McFadden. The finale also won the Hugo Award for Best Dramatic Presentation.

Looking back, Ron Moore felt, "*Next Generation*, I think, overstayed its welcome. The last season of that show is kind of rough. To be honest, there are chunks of it I haven't watched myself. The show just didn't know what it was trying to do in the last year."

Still, ten days after wrapping the series, a new chapter began as filming on *Generations* began.

Hallmark 1995 Picard ornament.

CHAPTER 14

# THE NEXT GENERATION GOES TO THE *MOVIES*

Micromachines versions of the *Enterprise*-B and -D.

From the first *TNG* film, Playmates Toys gave us the desperate Dr. Soran and a Worf dressed for nineteenth-century sailing courtesy of the holodeck.

*First Contact*'s Zefram Cochrane and Lily Sloane from Playmates Toys. Their six-inch series of figures featured more realistic likenesses.

# GENERATIONS

### "Who am I to argue with the captain of the *Enterprise*?"

Paramount scheduled the new film series featuring the *TNG* cast to open on November 18, 1994, three years after the original crew took their final bows. The studio handed the order to Berman in late 1992. He recruited Hurley and the team of Moore and Braga to pitch stories, with Piller declining to participate in a bake off.

Berman offered the director's chair to Nimoy, who passed, allowing *TNG* veteran David Carson to get his shot. Returning to the crew was Herman Zimmerman, who took a break from *DS9* to ready the *Enterprise* for its close-up.

The story slowly took shape before Braga and Moore left for the Pacific in May, knowing that Paramount wanted the movie accessible to those unfamiliar with the television series. The writers met with Shatner, who was game for an appearance and didn't flinch when the possibility of killing Kirk was raised. By then, it was also decided the *Enterprise*-D was also scheduled for demolition. It seemed obvious to have the long-lived Guinan appear as a connection between eras, allowing her El-Aurian race to be explored.

Despite writing roles for the original cast so they could all appear in the opening sequence, one by one they refused. Nimoy once more complained there was nothing meaningful for Spock to do, and Kelley felt he made his farewell in the previous film. In the end, Spock and McCoy's lines were rewritten and given to Scotty and Chekov, while Sulu's lines went to his daughter, the newly created Demora Sulu (although she was originally conceived as Chekov's child). The *Enterprise*-B scenes were shot while the *TNG* finale was still in production.

The *TNG* cast signed aboard for the $25 million film and principal photography began just ten days after the seventh season wrapped. Draft after draft jettisoned character moments and tightened the focus on Picard and the desperate Dr. Soran, played by Malcolm McDowell.

There was now the luxury to spruce up the sets and go for an entirely different style of lighting. Compare the bridge from the seventh season to *Generations* and you will see the subtle but substantial changes, from the raised

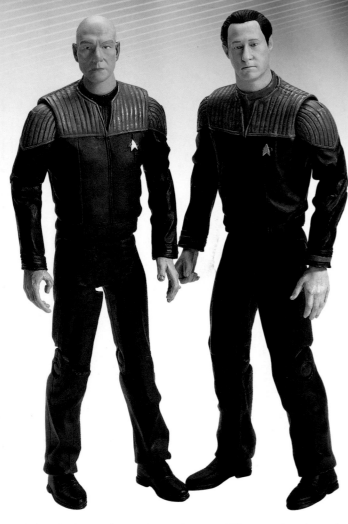

captain's chair to the color scheme. The production also added the massive stellar cartography room.

After production wrapped in the early summer, a test screening was held and it was clear the overall movie was fine, but Kirk's death at Soran's hands lacked the necessary drama. President Sherry Lansing authorized an additional $5 million, and a more heroic end for the captain was reshot in September.

Interestingly, *Generations* was the first film to have its own website, cutting-edge marketing that once more acknowledged the value of *Star Trek*'s following and its happy band of early adopters.

Despite heavy marketing around the meeting of the two legendary captains, the film opened to very mixed reviews, with the *New York Times*'s Janet Maslin succinctly summing it up: "*Generations* is predictably flabby and impenetrable in places, but it has enough pomp, spectacle and high-tech small talk to keep the franchise afloat."

McDowell felt the script was feeble, and Moore and Braga admitted their two-hour finale script was the stronger effort,

and more should have been done to make the first *TNG* feature better.

Still, audiences turned out and the film ultimately took in $118.1 million worldwide confirming to Paramount the new crew could sustain the film series.

# FIRST CONTACT
### "The line must be drawn here!"

Paramount Pictures decided that a two-year gap between features would be fine and provisionally set the next film to debut on November 22, 1996, as part of the franchise's thirtieth anniversary. By the time Berman sat down with Braga and Moore in February 1995, he had already determined the movie would once more be a time-traveling tale. The writers, though, wanted to tackle the Borg. All three immediately concluded both ideas could be mixed together.

The preferred time period was the Italian Renaissance and the first outline called the film *Star Trek: Renaissance*. When the period sets and costumes were deemed prohibitively expensive, the team rethought the notion, until settling on the previously unseen first contact between humans and aliens. Braga seized on the visual of Vulcans emerging from their craft, which everyone agreed had merit.

Paramount chairman Jonathan Dolgen liked the story for *Star Trek: First Contact* but felt the Borg were too faceless to be a credible film threat, so the writers conceived the Borg Queen. Stewart also had issues with the story. Moore took the various notes and decided that making warp pioneer Zefram Cochrane integral to the tale would show the best humanity had to offer at the time. Berman added the notion of a holodeck party sequence, and the story was substantially revised.

As the script moved into preproduction, Berman offered the director's job to Frakes, continuing a tradition of the *Enterprise* first officer being in charge behind the camera.

Michael Westmore was tapped for the makeup and worked with costume designer Deborah Everton to upgrade the Borg's appearance. After Alice Krige was cast as the Borg Queen, she was given a one piece bodysuit made from hard rubber. When she complained of blisters, a soft foam version was created overnight to make her ten-day shoot more comfortable. Her silver contact lenses caused her so much pain she could only wear them four minutes at a time.

Blackman returned and, with Frakes, came up with new uniforms, reflecting the film's darker tone.

Herman Zimmerman had to create the brand new starship, the *Enterprise*-E. Moore, Braga, and Berman all had their ideas, which illustrator John Eaves incorporated into his early sketches. While exploration remained important, the *Star Trek* universe had grown a shade darker, and the next generation Starfleet flagship had to reflect that by looking more muscular. By January 1996 the final designs were approved, and Rick Sternbach could begin creating the ship's blueprints for ILM.

Berman suggested using a defunct nuclear missile as the basis for Cochrane's pioneering warp-capable ship, the *Phoenix*,

*Top:* Interior designer Tony Alleyne stands in his *Trek*-theme studio apartment in Hinckley, Leicestershire, England. The apartment took nearly ten years to redesign in the style of the *Starship Enterprise* and, in 2003, was put up for sale for approximately $1.7 million (US). *Getty Images*

*Above:* The uniforms may change along with the sophistication of the makeup, but dressing up for conventions is a perfectly natural activity. Fans Lauren McCaslin (left) and Charles Aston, both from Texas, pose at the fifth annual official Star Trek convention at the Las Vegas Hilton, August 19, 2006, in Las Vegas, Nevada. *Getty Images*

Patrick Stewart, a Shakespearean actor turned
international star, receives his star on the
Hollywood Walk of Fame in December 1996.
*Associated Press*

Members of the Lawn Mower Brigade wear *Star Trek* costumes and march in formation in the Mardi Gras parade in Spanish Town, Baton Rouge, Louisiana, circa 1994. © Philip Gould/Corbis

which was also executed by Eaves, using Okuda's designs from *The Star Trek Chronology* as a guide. The military allowed the crew to shoot within the Green Valley, Arizona, silo.

In addition to Krige, *TNG* and *DS9* veteran James Cromwell was signed as the hard-drinking Cochrane, and Alfre Woodard joined as Lily, Picard's guide to life in the twenty-first century. Nods to the television series included cameos from Robert Picardo as a version of the Emergency Medical Hologram from *Voyager*, and Dwight Schultz and Patti Yasutake returning as *TNG*'s Reginald Barclay and Nurse Alyssa Ogawa.

Filming began on April 8, 1996. Location shooting took place in Bozeman, Montana, and Angeles National Forest in the San Gabriel Mountains. Los Angeles's Union Station doubled for the period nightclub seen in the holodeck. The Borg scenes aboard the new starship took May and June to shoot on three sound stages. Apart from Stewart developing breathing difficulties in his tight spacesuit during this time, the shoot proceeded without problem until wrapping on July 2.

Jerry Goldsmith returned to active duty to score the new movie; *TNG* composer Denis McCarthy had provided the music for the transition film.

Opening the day that Sarek's portrayer, Mark Lenard, passed away, *First Contact* was a critical hit, once more invoking the axiom that the even-numbered *Trek* films were the good ones. Internet review site Rotten Tomatoes, for example, currently rates *Generations* at only 48 percent "fresh" while this one has achieved 92 percent. While the film's obvious themes of *Moby Dick*–like obsession—with Picard standing in for Ahab—were commented on, fewer touched on the more personal seduction of Data by the Borg Queen, a subplot that proved powerful to the performers.

The worldwide box office was $150 million, justifying the higher budget and faith in the franchise.

Marvel, which had negotiated the comics license for a second time, released an adaptation of the film, followed by a sort-of sequel, *Second Contact,* that saw the crew meet the superhero team X-Men. This in turn led to the crossover novel *Planet X* by Michael Jan Friedman. Prior to that point, Paramount had refused to allow their franchise to appear with other properties. Years earlier, DC suggested a *Star Trek* Superman pairing, prompting a Paramount licensing exec to reject it because Superman "was not real."

Data and Troi from Playmates Toys' nine-inch series, sporting their civilian attire from *Insurrection*. Voyageur Press collection

# INSURRECTION

### "Can anyone remember when we used to be explorers?"

With Paramount again eager for a sequel, in March 1997 Berman turned to Michael Piller for story ideas. While Berman considered borrowing a classic from the public domain, such as Anthony Hope's tale of mistaken identity, *The Prisoner of Zenda*, Piller's first thoughts turned to society's fascination with retaining youth, and the lengths some people go to appear vigorous.

Piller created a story involving Picard, his old colleague Duffy, and the "one that got away," giving the captain an overdue romance. In *Stardust*, Duffy would go rogue, attacking Romulan vessels to protect the "fountain of youth," located in a dangerous portion of space known as the Briar Patch. After reading the outline in April, Berman had issues with the structure, requiring Piller to revise his outline, jettisoning Duffy in favor of Data.

With Berman and Paramount's Executive Vice President of Production Don Granger happy with the June 23 draft, a script order was almost assured. However, *Star Trek* fan Jonathan Dolgen, who was also chairman of Viacom Entertainment Group, had serious issues with the aliens and antagonist. Then came word that Stewart absolutely hated the new story. To secure his appearance, Stewart had been named an associate producer and promised story approval. He wanted Picard front-and-center in the action, but also felt the overall tone had to be lighter, counterpointing the previous film. He noted how Picard had been "toughened" up in *First Contact*, a trait that needed to be maintained. When Piller and Stewart sat down to talk on July 23, they realized they both liked the core story but differed over its telling. The actor liked the youth theme, which encouraged Piller to use it as the main focus, shifting the "Data run amok" thread to the story's first act.

Piller went back to write about a new race, the Ba'ku, whose world and its unique properties were being threatened by the Son'i (later changed to the Son'a). Picard would defy orders to protect the Ba'ku from forcible relocation, planned by an unconscionable alliance between a rogue Starfleet admiral and the Son'i.

According to Piller, when Spiner was shown the script, the actor was unhappy about Data malfunctioning, after the android had exhibited similar behavior in the last two movies. The performer made the bold suggestion that the android be killed. Piller and Berman rejected the notion, and they set about adjusting the script to address the valid concerns.

Piller spent August revising the script. *DS9* producer Ira Steven Behr was the next critic, forcing Piller to reconceive the Ba'ku from a race of children to adults. This allowed him to add a romantic interest for the captain, in the person of the three-century-old Anij.

By then, Berman had decided Frakes merited a second turn behind the camera and signed him to direct. Frakes joined Berman and Piller for story meetings that helped sharpen the focus. Piller spent October writing the final draft.

When the script was costed by the various departments, the film was many millions over Paramount's approved budget, so a new round of rewrites reduced the action and tightened scenes. One key decision meant totally revising the climax, to heighten the confrontation between Ru'afo, the main Son'a antagonist, and Picard. (It also gave us the absurd sight of an emergency joystick being used to steer the state-of-the-art starship.)

Zimmerman and Eaves were rehired as designers and worked with Blue Sky Studios and Santa Barbara Studios on what turned out to be the first *Star Trek* film to use virtually entirely digital effects. The Son'a ship's ultimate destruction was the only model photography.

Veteran character actor Anthony Zerbe was cast as Admiral Dougherty, paired with Broadway stars F. Murray Abraham—stuck under layers of latex as Ru'afo—and Donna Murphy as Anij.

Frakes was confident behind the camera of the $58 million production, even though he felt the story remained on the fragile side, which may be why this is the shortest of

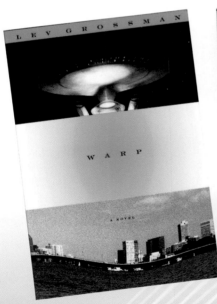

Lev Grossman's first novel, *Warp* (St. Martin's Griffin, 1997), concerns the lyrical misadventures of a Boston slacker who has trouble distinguishing between reality and *Star Trek*.

Some people think it's the best *Star Trek* movie ever made. *Galaxy Quest* (DreamWorks, 1999) is a loving spoof of *Star Trek*, featuring actors of an old TV show making convention appearances.

Bloopers have become a regular feature on television and as DVD extras thanks to Gene Roddenberry revealing their existence by showing the *Star Trek* bloopers at the first convention. This VHS tape includes the original series and *The Next Generation*.

Michael Dorn, Marina Sirtis, and Jonathan Frakes share a light moment during the production of *Star Trek: Nemesis*. © Gail Albert Halaban/Corbis

the *Trek* films to date. It's also the first film to reflect events happening elsewhere in the franchise, such as Picard's consternation they were not involved in the Dominion War, while advancing several character arcs, notably the rekindling of the Riker/Troi romance.

Sets from *Voyager* were redressed during its production hiatus to save time and budget, and the various scout ship and shuttle interiors were reworked versions of *DS9*'s Federation runabout. Even so, Zimmerman oversaw the construction of fifty-five sets, the most for a *Trek* film.

Goldsmith returned to score the new movie, continuing to develop musical themes dating back to *The Motion Picture*.

An October 14 test screening led Dolgen and Lansing to demand a brutal re-edit. Lansing told Berman, "You've got two major problems: pacing, and there's no boom at the end. There's too much romance. Picard and Anij walk and talk forever. I kept saying, come on, already."

Dolgen approved the millions needed to revise the climax, again, adding in the *Enterprise* coming to the rescue as the Son'a station self-destructed. The studio wanted an even bigger moment, but Berman held firm, saying they either used the new ending and kept the release date, or moved the opening.

The movie hit theatres December 11, 1998, and lived down to Frakes's pessimistic expectations. It was harshly reviewed, earning 54 percent at Rotten Tomatoes. Most notices criticized the actual story while approving of the themes.

Audiences still turned out, but just not in sufficient numbers. The worldwide gross dropped slightly to $146 million, but coupled with inflation, in real terms *Insurrection* earned far less than its predecessor, a cause of concern for the studio.

# NEMESIS

**"The Son'a, the Borg, the Romulans. You seem to get all the easy assignments."**

Berman was minded to let the two-year gap between movies go to three after hearing comments from the cast. But, in the end, by the time Paramount ordered a new film, deal-making lengthened the gap to four years. Berman was ready to think about stories when Spiner and his friend, screenwriter John Logan (best known for his work on *Gladiator* and *The Aviator*), approached him with two ideas. Neither excited the producer, but he invited them to come in and brainstorm with him.

As Worf knows, Romulan Ale should be illegal.
*ThinkGeek, Inc.*

Logan grew up a major *Star Trek* fan and knew one moment he had to include: the *Enterprise* actually ramming another vessel. When the decision to use the Romulans was made, Logan suggested introducing the Remans, a new twist on Romulan history. The Star Empire's internal strife would fuel some of the story. Meantime, the theme of family became predominant, leading to the wedding of Riker and Troi; the arrival of yet another Data prototype, B4; and the discovery of Shinzon, a clone of Picard. One idea carried over from the last film was the notion of killing Data, since Spiner had been saying for years there would come a point where the actor out-aged the ageless android.

By this point, the diminishing box office from the previous feature, coupled with the lackluster response to *Voyager*, led to the common conclusion that the franchise was showing its age. It might be time to wind down operations, either temporarily or for good.

As a result, Berman wanted *Star Trek: Nemesis* to be more for the fans than the general audience, and he ensured that there were plenty of overt moments for them to enjoy. The film featured the overdue wedding of Riker and Troi, as well as the return of Wil Wheaton as Wesley Crusher, back in Starfleet uniform for the nuptials.

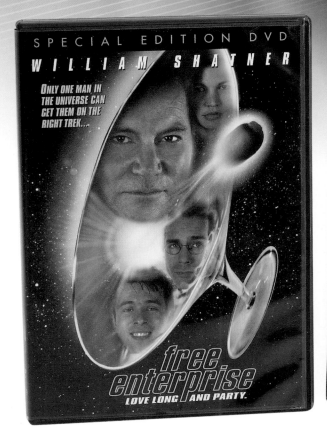

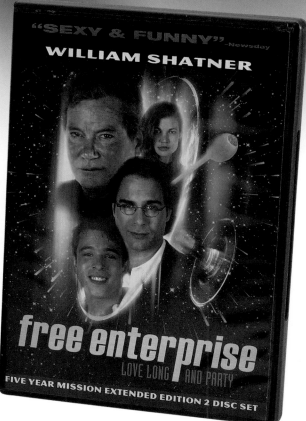

Journalist-turned-producer Mark A. Altman went on to make the semiautobiographical *Free Enterprise*, a valentine to the show, with his friend, cowriter and director Robert Meyer Burnett. William Shatner starred as a bizarre version of himself.

Whoopi Goldberg appeared as Guinan but, oddly, while Majel Barrett was on hand as the computer voice, she was not on screen as the bride's mother, Lwaxana Troi. On the other hand, Kathryn Janeway (Kate Mulgrew), just back from the Delta Quadrant in the finale of *Voyager*, showed up, promoted to admiral.

With a story in place, Berman was ready to hire a crew, but Paramount intervened, insisting the producer use director Stuart Baird, to whom the studio owed a film. The newcomer, without bothering to watch a single episode or film, asked for redesigned phasers and other props, seeking a more realistic look. And where Frakes took things darker than the TV series in *First Contact*, Baird went further, even requiring Okuda's computer displays be completely redone.

The story logic in the script was deeply flawed. Rick Sternbach pointed out a serious issue: at the climax, Data was to destroy Shinzon's ship, the *Scimitar*, by firing a phaser at a warp core relay, one of several affixed to the bridge. The designer noted how little sense that made, so the script was altered so that Data destroyed the *Scimitar*'s thalaron generator instead.

If Spiner wanted out, for legitimate reasons, it made little sense to introduce B4, an early prototype for Data, and set things up to make it appear Data could live on through his "brother." And while Stewart may have enjoyed joyriding in a ground-based vehicle on Kolarus III, it also violated the Prime Directive, a bit of business that annoyed fans. And how could a story set on Romulus not even acknowledge Spock's unification work?

Baird cast newcomer Tom Hardy as Shinzon, but a bald head was about all he had in common with Stewart, making the clone notion hard for audiences to accept. Ron Perlman played Shinzon's viceroy, with *Starship Troopers'* Dina Meyer as Commander Donatra. Behind the camera, Baird brought in many people new to the franchise, although some key crew were retained, including Herman Zimmerman for the production design. Michael Westmore created the makeup

once again, gaining inspiration from the German silent classic *Nosferatu* for the Remans' look. Drexler and Eaves also returned to design the Romulan and Reman vessels, notably the massive *Scimitar*.

The $60-million production started shooting on November 28, 2001, and wrapped March 9, 2002. Baird proved he was a no-nonsense director, unaccustomed to the decade-plus camaraderie that had developed among the cast. Sirtis later regaled convention audiences with tales of the cast cracking one another up before a take, angering Baird. LeVar Burton chafed that Baird called him "Laverne" for the first six weeks of production and that the director didn't know that Geordi was human.

Digital Domain provided the impressive visual effects, which at least made the movie pretty to look at. The five-hundred-plus effects shots were a record for the film series. Jerry Goldsmith returned, and as it turned out, *Nemesis* was one of his final scores before passing away.

The movie was reviled by fans and critics alike, ruining the odd-even pattern. A mere 37 percent of professional critics liked the movie, according Rotten Tomatoes. Most focused on the aging, over-exposed franchise.

Opening on December 13, 2002, it was easily trounced at the box office by the superior seasonal competition: *Harry Potter and the Chamber of Secrets*, the Bond film *Die Another Day*, and *The Lord of the Rings: The Two Towers*. As a result, the film took in a paltry worldwide $67.3 million, financially a disaster for Paramount. It marked the end of the *Enterprise*'s career on the big screen—at least under the creative control of Rick Berman.

Brent Spiner, Marina Sirtis, Patrick Stewart, and Tom Hardy at a public appearance in Germany promoting the upcoming release of *Nemesis*.
*Associated Press*

# CHAPTER 15
# DEEP SPACE NINE

The Playmates Toys crew of *Deep Space Nine*, from left: Julian Bashir, Kira Nerys, Benjamin Sisko, Jadzia Dax, and Odo.

The success of *TNG* was not lost on Hollywood and very quickly, all manner of first-run syndicated fare was suddenly broadcast. Their ratings and profits owed much to Roddenberry and Paramount's efforts.

Paramount chairman Brandon Tartikoff wanted a second *Star Trek* series to cash in on the franchise's renewed popularity. He met with Rick Berman in 1991 and suggested that if Roddenberry's concept was "*Wagon Train* to the stars," the new series would be based on a different western, *The Rifleman*, about a father and son living on the frontier. Intrigued, Berman sat down with Michael Piller, and they began brainstorming the new series, without directly involving the ailing Roddenberry. When the creator passed away that October, the concepts were still far from complete, but he had reportedly blessed the idea of another show.

The idea would be to debut in January 1993, halfway through *TNG*'s sixth season and become the primary televised *Star Trek* when the *TNG* cast graduated to the features. If successful, the pattern could be repeated with successive shows.

Piller determined to make the new series vastly different than its predecessor, first by making the frontier a fixed point: a space station. He reviewed *TNG* episodes to find interesting alien races to populate the station along with Starfleet crew, so there was a constant set of personalities to spark stories and conflicts. While Roddenberry insisted humanity had evolved beyond personal issues, he never said that applied to other races, so Piller included a Trill, then a Ferengi for comic relief, and so on.

The Starfleet presence would be headed by Benjamin Sisko, a father accompanied by his son, Jake. His wife was killed during the battle of Wolf 359, as depicted in the *TNG* story "The Best of Both Worlds," and he took the post to grieve and raise his son in what he expected was relative peace. Avery Brooks, a stage performer seen on television as Hawk in the adaptation of Robert B. Parker's *Spenser* novels,

Two of the great non–Starfleet characters of *Deep Space Nine* from Playmates Toys, Quark (left), the Ferengi bartender and shady businessman, and Garak, the exiled Cardassian and simple tailor.

was cast as Sisko. Originally envisioned as a cross between Kirk and Picard, Brooks gave a far more military bearing to Sisko at the outset, before beginning the character's spiritual journey across the seven seasons. Young Cirroc Lofton was cast as his son Jake.

The Cardassians, who had annexed Bajor, served as the source for the initial stories, which Piller and Berman hoped would feature Michelle Forbes as the Bajoran Ensign Ro, transferred to the new station. The actress, though, rejected the offer in favor of film work, so the part was rewritten into Major Kira Nerys, performed by dancer-turned-actress Nana Visitor.

Similarly, Famke Janssen, who played a Trill in "The Perfect Mate," was invited to reprise the role on the new show, but she too refused the part. It was rewritten as Jadzia Dax and given to the attractive Terry Farrell.

Colm Meaney, though, jumped at the chance for a more prominent role, bringing his Miles O'Brien from the *Enterprise* to space station Deep Space 9 as its new chief engineer, along with his wife Keiko and daughter Molly. And when they cast Siddig el Fadil (who later changed his name to Alexander Siddig) as the station's doctor Julian Amoros (renamed just

Playmates Toys nine-inch version of Gul Dukat.

While Piller wrote the pilot, other *TNG* staff was asked to make the move to the new show, including Ira Steven Behr and Peter Allan Fields. Herman Zimmerman was brought over to supervise the station's design and construction. By then it was determined the station was Cardassian in origin and he was directed to make it as alien as possible. He would ultimately earn an Emmy nomination for his first season efforts. Quark's bar, for example, was designed without any internal lighting, challenging director of photography Marvin Rush to light the set from the outside.

"No one person created the station," Zimmerman admitted later. Rick Sternbach, Rick Berman, Mike Okuda, and Ricardo Delgado all contributed ideas to help make the station look as different as possible. "No one on the art department staff was the least bit afraid to accept an idea from somebody else."

The series quickly gained a reputation as representing the dark side of *Star Trek*. Some of that came from the physical esthetic, but it later earned the description from the tenor of the stories. As we met the station's inhabitants, the Cardassians had just left Bajor, abandoning their processing station, and leaving the planet strip-mined and hurting. Starfleet took possession of Deep Space 9 and was on hand to help the Bajoran people rebuild, while maintaining a presence to keep the Cardassians from coming back. An underground resistance movement named the Maquis rose up to continue the fight against the Cardassians, a thread that carried not only through this series but into *Voyager*. The region of space became valuable when it was learned in the pilot that a stable wormhole existed nearby, granting instantaneous access to the Gamma Quadrant.

By being set in a fixed point, the writers could explore the characters and their respective cultures more deeply, making each distinctive and memorable. Much of the modern-day *Star Trek* mythos was explored and shaped through the stories told on this series. While Picard said, "Let's see what's out there," *DS9* looked inward. Sisko discovered he

before the pilot shot to Bashir), the pairing of an Irishman and a Brit seemed perfect to the writers.

The Ferengi, Quark, was assigned to Armin Shimerman, who played the first such alien in "The Last Outpost" and was accustomed to the latex and fake teeth. Less comfortable was René Auberjonois, who was given the part of the stoic station constable Odo, envisioned as the outsider looking in on humanity, much as Spock then Data were in their respective series. The theatrical-trained actor rose to the challenge and the character quickly became a fan favorite.

As for the antagonistic Cardassians, the first choice for Gul Dukat didn't meet the producers' expectations, and he was quickly replaced by Marc Alaimo, who previously played Gul Macet on *TNG*. He turned the villain into a conflicted, multilayered character, elevating the part beyond imagining.

*Above:* Nana Kira Visitor, a dancer turned actress, greets a fan at a 1996 convention. © *Mark Peterson/Corbis*

*Right:* Fans of the *Star Trek* films and TV series visiting *Star Trek: The Experience* dressed in Ferengi and drill-thrall outfits. *Time Life Pictures/Getty Images*

was the Bajorans' Emissary, the spiritual figure who would lead the people to their destiny, a role he neither sought nor accepted. This conflict began an examination of religious ideals and beliefs that Roddenberry thoroughly eschewed in the previous series (and Shatner ham-fistedly explored in the fifth film).

In the pilot, we learned that noncorporeal beings, called the Prophets by the Bajorans, inhabited the wormhole. They communicated with Sisko or others through a series of ancient Orbs, which had become Cardassian booty and needed to be reclaimed. The entire notion of these beings and the religious orders on Bajor fueled countless storylines.

Piller and the writing staff took chances, letting story arcs run for many episodes before devoting entire seasons to specific stories, notably the Dominion War. In fact, Piller credited eventual producer Behr with pushing the series in that direction, letting the consequences of actions from one episode be explored in future installments. While the *TNG* status quo

Sisko in disguise as a Klingon (left) and Worf's brother Kurn from Playmates Toys.

remained relatively fixed for the length of the series and feature films, *DS9*'s setup changed with startling regularity.

The series arrived amid cautious optimism from the fans, but the critics recognized the new show arrived in sharper shape than its predecessor. They appreciated the cast's depth and skill, while noting the scripts were strong. Fans were won over, and across the series' life, its popularity grew until as many people debated the merits of *TNG* vs. *DS9* as they did the original series vs. *TNG*.

*DS9*'s ratings were strong enough to allow the series a full seven seasons, but they were never as strong as *TNG*, meaning that the show was always deemed less successful in Paramount's eyes. Rick Berman was so focused on the overall franchise and film series that he pretty much let the producers do as they pleased. He did voice his disapproval of the entire Dominion War aspect, which is why it was hardly reflected in the *TNG* movies. When Paramount formed its own network, UPN, and announced it would be anchored by *Voyager,* it meant less attention and promotion for *DS9,* which may be why the series was able to take as many creative risks as it did.

One wrinkle was its obvious comparisons with Warner Bros.' *Babylon 5*. Its creator J. Michael Straczynski first showed his concept of a space station in a dark universe to Paramount and posted online that he felt *DS9*'s first season borrowed heavily from his pitch. However, he never filed a lawsuit. Instead, there was some rivalry going back and forth, with Walter Koenig gaining a recurring role on the opposing science fiction series. As a goodwill gesture, Majel Barrett guest starred on *Babylon 5* in a role written for her.

What would Roddenberry have thought of the new show? Barrett thought he too would have disliked the Dominion War, but had budgets in the 1960s allowed, he would also have shown armed conflicts. D. C. Fontana pointed out the Great Bird was a World War II combat pilot and would have appreciated the series' themes.

Ron Moore, who came across from *TNG* and contributed some of *DS9*'s strongest episodes, said in 2002, "I think *Deep Space [Nine]* was the show that really took *Star Trek* as far as you could take it. . . . It just says, 'OK, you think you know what *Star Trek* is, let's put it on a space station, and let's make it darker. Let's make it a continuing story, and let's continually challenge your assumptions about what this American icon means.' And I think it was the ultimate achievement for the franchise. Personally, I think it's the best of all of them, I think it's an amazing piece of work."

## NEW FRIENDS AND OLD

Slowly, the writers solidified characters as they got to see how the actors interpreted their parts and where there was chemistry between performers. As a result, the Bashir/O'Brien friendship grew quickly as did the Quark/ Odo rivalry.

Larger themes were also slowly explored, such as the revelation in "Rules of Acquisition" that something called the Dominion ruled the Gamma Quadrant. The second season ended with the arrival of the fearsome Jem'Hadar, foot soldiers for the Founders, who were the Dominion

Playmates Toys Jem'Hadar warrior.

and of the same race as Odo. Their goal was to impose order on the galaxy, and now that they knew of the Alpha Quadrant, they intended to extend their reach through the Wormhole. Of course, Sisko and Starfleet had something to say about this.

The third season was all about gearing up for a conflict Starfleet didn't want, or was necessarily prepared for after various Borg attacks. Sisko was given the battleship *Defiant* to help protect the wormhole and the station. Like a chess game, pieces were strategically moved as the Dominion allied themselves with the Cardassians, and the Federation strengthened their alliance with the Klingons and later the Romulans. Another darkening shade for Starfleet was the revelation of Section 31, the covert espionage branch of Starfleet Intelligence that sought to manipulate events, going so far as to recruit Bashir to help them from time to time.

The series benefitted from the largest pool of recurring characters in any of the series. There were various Bajorans, Cardassians, Vorta (the cloned mouthpieces for the Founders), Klingons, Ferengi, and so on. The large, silent Morn (named in honor of the *Cheers* character Norm) could be found in his regular seat at Quark's in almost every episode, a reassuring presence. The most interesting of the recurring players might well have been Elim Garak, the Cardassian tailor who was also a spy. As portrayed with smarmy élan by Andrew J. Robinson, he quickly became a fascinating, enigmatic manipulator, especially during the Dominion War.

The Ferengi became more than just a joke, displaying a complex, rich, and yes, funny, culture. Their sense of family, as demonstrated by Quark, his brother Rom (Max Grodénchik), and nephew Nog (Aron Eisenberg), also deepened our appreciation of them. Nog and Jake's friendship demonstrated the Vulcan philosophy of Infinite Diversity in Infinite Combinations in action, while Nog's struggles after losing a leg during the Dominion War also showed how one overcame adversity.

Patrick Stewart guest-starred in the pilot, allowing Sisko to confront Picard, who as Locutus, was responsible for his wife

Micromachines *Deep Space Nine* series, clockwise from the top: Deep Space 9, Cardassian *Galor*-class cruiser, Federation *Danube*-class runabout, and a Ferengi *D'Kora*-class Marauder.

Jennifer's death. It was clearly a tense handoff, signaling this was to be a different series.

While *TNG* was cautious about bringing back concepts or characters from the original series, the new show seized the opportunity with relish. In the second season's "Blood Oath," they united the first series' prominent Klingons—Kor, Koloth, and Kang—and tied to them to Jadzia's previous Trill host, Curzon Dax. A year later, "Crossover" reintroduced viewers to the parallel universe first seen in "Mirror, Mirror." Subsequent visits between universes gave the performers, notably Visitor, a chance to stretch. Barrett's Lwaxana Troi turned up a few times as well.

When *TNG* ended its series run, it was decided to relocate Worf to the station, stirring things up among the regulars and giving the writers a chance to explore more of the Klingon culture. As a result, Worf became a pivotal figure during the Dominion War, on hand to bring down the weak chancellor Gowron (Robert O'Reilly) in favor of the honorable General Martok (J. G. Hertzler). He also got to romance Jadzia, marrying her before Terry Farrell chose to leave the series when her

Sisko sits in the *Defiant's* command chair, which, in this Playmates Toys incarnation, is a few sizes too big.

# THE MANY UNIVERSES OF *STAR TREK*

Steve Roby

There's a lot more to *Star Trek* than TV series and movies. Books, comics, and games by the hundreds have made a multimedia phenomenon with few peers. Since 1967 there hasn't been a year without at least some *Trek* literature of some kind.

The *Star Trek* novels can generate furious fan debates, over adult relationships, gay and straight; political subtexts (left, right, and other); diversity; militarism; and the way the books have moved beyond series finales and movies. Janeway's death may be the most hotly debated single event in the books, but fans also continue to argue whether *Enterprise* should have left Trip Tucker dead, and whether the *Destiny* trilogy's massive Borg invasion and its changes to the *Star Trek* universe were too drastic. Fans also argue the merits of book-only series like *New Frontier* (over-the-top action and humor), *Starfleet Corps of Engineers* (tech mysteries and human drama), and *Vanguard* (*Trek* for pay cable).

Then there are the lost books, the ones that got away. Gene Roddenberry's *The God Thing* was first announced in 1976. Walter Koenig, Susan Sackett, Michael Jan Friedman, and David Alexander all tried expanding the incomplete novel, but it's never been published. Dozens of novels and nonfiction books never appeared, some officially announced, scheduled, and written, including four novels set in the new movie continuity.

Nonfiction books have been just as varied. There are biographies, autobiographies, behind-the-scenes books, episode guides, trivia quizzes, art books, and technical manuals. Academics have studied *Star Trek* and race, gender, sexuality, religion, politics, and fan activities (conventions, fan fiction, and costuming). Some books offer *Star Trek*–inspired management tips, daily affirmations, recipes, and relationship advice; others teach Klingon, the world's fastest-growing artificial language.

The comics have their own rich history. The earliest were obviously aimed at children, sometimes produced by people who'd never seen the show. The second attempt wasn't well-received, in part due to license constraints limiting the comics to concepts from the first movie. Things finally changed in 1982 with *Star Trek* comics aimed at the same audience as the movies and TV series, with more complex plots and characterization. In fact, for the twenty-fifth anniversary, DC released *Debt of Honor*, a hardcover graphic novel by acclaimed *X-Men* writer Chris Claremont and artists Adam Hughes and Karl Story, which won several industry awards.

Since then there have been standalone stories and epic serials, crossovers and new original series, like *Early Voyages* and *Starfleet Academy*. The 2009 *Star Trek* movie has inspired several new comic series.

For some, reading isn't enough. Why not lead a starship into battle or explore a strange new world yourself? *Star Fleet Battles* developed a complex set of rules for starship combat and a new, very different extrapolation of *Star Trek* history due to its limited license—original series *Star Trek* only. Three other companies have produced different takes on *Star Trek* role-playing games, all of them still having devoted followings. It's not necessary to be a gamer to enjoy the inventive, creative sourcebooks, either; *Star Trek: Enterprise* even borrowed concepts from one game's Andorian reference book.

The dozens of video games created over the years have included console and PC games, shooters and simulators, even a popular computer game adaptation of *Star Fleet Battles*. Games range from text only to filmed segments with familiar cast members. Some even have their own novel and comic tie-ins.

Now there's *Star Trek Online*, the massively multiplayer online role playing game (MMORPG) that allows players to take command of their own starship and experience ship battles and planetary adventures decades after *TNG*. Fans argue over the game's connection to other tie-ins and the overarching storylines, but the game appears to be a solid success.

*Star Trek* is a vast and wonderful multimedia phenomenon. There are many strange new worlds waiting to be explored.

*Steve Roby, a librarian in Ottawa, Canada, has been a* Star Trek *fan since childhood, and his addiction to* Star Trek *books led him to create the Complete Starfleet Library website.*

Voyageur Press collection

*Left:* To celebrate *Star Trek*'s thirtieth anniversary, *Star Trek: Deep Space Nine* produced the beloved "Trials and Tribble-ations," carefully integrating the new crew into footage featuring the original stars from "The Trouble with Tribbles." The flawless production was a charming success, which spawned some special Playmates Toys. From left, in their period costumes, Jadzia Dax, Benjamin Sisko, and Odo.

contract was up. Jadzia was given a glorious death, and the Trill symbiont was allowed to live on in Ezri Dax, with Nicole deBoer joining the show.

Creatively, the series avoided the clichés plaguing the previous series. Worlds visited were not variations on Earth; the holodeck did not become a recurring problem. In fact in later seasons, the holodeck became a home away from home for the crew as they grew fond of Vic Fontaine, the Las Vegas showman who became a counselor of sorts. Former *The Time Tunnel* star James Darren was initially wary when offered the role, but when he saw how rich the potential was, he signed on and enjoyed himself. At conventions, he entertained fans with a short set of standards he sang on the show.

Two of the show's later episodes stand out as among the best that *Star Trek* produced across the various series. "Far Beyond the Stars" honored science fiction's pulp origins with a story set in the 1950s featuring fevered writer Benny Russell (Brooks), whose stories about a space station in the future were seemingly driving him mad. It was a strong, honest examination of the rampant racism of the day, impressing the cast both with its writing and Brooks's direction.

Perhaps the most technically challenging and creatively satisfying episode was "Trials and Tribble-ations," *DS9*'s salute to *Star Trek*'s thirtieth anniversary. Technology first pioneered in *Forrest Gump* showed that modern-day actors could be seamlessly added to footage from the original series. A light-

hearted sequel to "The Trouble with Tribbles" was the perfect vehicle for this technique, allowing the cast to dress in original series uniforms and interact with the first cast. Although angered at not being asked to script the sequel, "Tribbles" author David Gerrold made a cameo, seen collecting tribbles overrunning a corridor.

## SEASON BY SEASON

The twenty-episode first season quickly established the new status quo but took the time to ensure every character had a show or two to spotlight them. There were also direct ties to *TNG* to solidify the series in fans' minds. As a result, we had the one and only appearance of Q, alongside Picard's foil, Vash (Jennifer Hetrick). Where Picard argued with Q, Sisko simply punched out the omnipotent figure.

Piller explained that the intention of the first season was "to do stories that bring in fans of *TNG*. If you create a space station that is at the crossroads of the universe, then you basically have the justification for bringing in old friends from past episodes. Their ships would normally come through this crossroads, and we felt that was a good way to bring viewers to the show. I think by the second season, we were looking more at standing on our own two feet, and we hadn't been entirely satisfied. When we really started doing stories about our space station, and really made it unique to itself, that's when the series, I think, really became special."

*Above:* After leaving, saying their good-byes to Picard in "Qpid," Vash and Q went off to adventure together. Later, when Vash ended up on Deep Space 9, so did Q, in the episode "Q-Less." And Playmates issued the *DS9* versions of the characters.

*Below:* GTI scanned and collected every *Star Trek* comic from 1966–2005 and released them on a DVD, instantly completing people's collections.

**STAR TREK** ™
**THE COMPLETE COMIC BOOK COLLECTION**

*U.S.S. ENTERPRISE NCC-1701*

- Every comic book July 1967 through October 2002*
- Over 500 complete printable comic books
- All annuals
- (1) One DVD-ROM

WIN MAC
DVD-ROM SOFTWARE

*No comic books were published from 2003 - 2006

OGY INC.

Things definitely solidified in the second season, which featured a nice bit of foreshadowing, with three different references to the Dominion before they were introduced. Looking back, writer Robert Hewitt Wolfe noted, "By the second season we knew how to do the right things, I think with more consistency, and we started to nail them more often. And we also started to develop the Dominion arc, and to really understand more about the Prophets and Bajor and understand the relationship with the characters. So it just became a stronger show."

The writers took delight in putting their characters through painful stories, notably O'Brien who earned a subgenre called "Let's torture O'Brien" as seen in "Armageddon Game," "Whispers," and "Tribunal." Auberjonois also visited Piller to note the season was light on Odo's observations about man—something the showrunner agreed with. "For me," the actor said, "that was an important discovery, and I was particularly glad that my relationship with the writers and producers is such that I felt comfortable to go to them."

The mirror universe was quite the showcase for Visitor, as the other reality's cold and sexy Intendant, in charge of the mirror space station, still known by its Cardassian name, Terok Nor. "Nana just had a great time," Wolfe recounted. "She just vamped the hell out of it and just went nuts, but in the same kind of fun way that George Takei did in the original mirror universe show. . . . Avery got to do that, too, in the first one."

The show and its follow-ups showed that not every crewman was an exact opposite. "Regular O'Brien is brash and confident," Wolfe explained. "He's vulnerable; there's a certain humanity to him, but he's opinionated. A lot of the changes came from the premise—humans were on the short end of the stick in the mirror society. You've got people like Sisko, the pirate captain, who was more of a criminal, willing to defy authority. He had people protecting him up in the power chain. Then you had someone like Smiley [O'Brien's nickname in the mirror

Bajoran earrings, traditionally worn on the right ear, symbolized their religious faith. *Voyageur Press collection*

universe], who was really as low as you could get. He had to be very deferential and he was not a brave man. Sisko barely survived because he had the Intendant's protection. Smiley didn't have that. His ability to be unnoticed and necessary was keeping him alive."

The third season was when things really took off, partly because Paramount was launching *Voyager* and *Generations* was being released. In fact, the first ten episodes aired without competition from another *Trek* series for the first time. As it turned out, while some stations ran *TNG* and *DS9* back to back on Saturday nights, others picked one over the other. Some countries only bought one series to air at a time, often picking *TNG* then *Voyager* until circling back to begin running *DS9*, making some of the continuity confusing to foreign fans.

During production of the third season, Piller left the show to focus on *Voyager* with Jeri Taylor, so Behr became the new Executive Producer and began taking more chances with the content. He was cognizant that fans were underwhelmed with some of the stories, including those focusing on the religious aspects, hence the addition of the *Defiant* complete with cloaking device, over Berman's objections. Ron Moore also arrived from *TNG* and was a strong addition to the writing team as the crew geared up for war.

It was the season Auberjonois got to first direct an episode, followed by Brooks, and Jonathan Frakes came over to guest star in one episode then direct three others. Additionally, to quiet critics who complained, Sisko was finally promoted from commander to captain, putting him on equal footing with Kirk and Picard.

The initial plan was to end the season with the revelation that there were changelings on Earth. However, in a rare instance of interference in the storytelling, Paramount insisted on no cliffhanger so the plans were changed.

**B**ehr kicked things into higher gear with season four as the Klingons invaded the Cardassian Union and galactic politics

moved to the forefront. To increase fan loyalty, Michael Dorn arrived as Worf, at Rick Berman's suggestion, in response to Paramount's request for something big to shake things up. "In the beginning it was difficult to integrate this new character," Wolfe said, "but that was good because it challenged us, and made us re-examine the show in a whole new light. How do we make this guy work? How do we bring him in? How does he change the relationships for all of our characters? He stirred up the whole thing again, gave the whole show a second phase. Suddenly, there's Worf and we've got to deal with him and his issues, and suddenly there's Klingons everywhere. That brought a new flavor to play with."

Other additions to the growing ensemble included Gul Dukat's daughter, Tora Ziyal (Melanie Smith), who would later romance Garak, much to her father's displeasure. We visited Earth this season, meeting Sisko's father (Brock Peters, last seen in *Star Trek VI* as Admiral Cartwright). Sisko also deepened his friendship with freighter captain Kasidy Yates (Penny Jerald Johnson).

Perhaps the most obvious change that season was Sisko's new pate. Brooks preferred having a shaved scalp, but the producers initially insisted on some hair so viewers saw Sisko, not Hawk. Paramount had no problems with the actor's desire to revert to baldness, and the new look was well-received by cast, crew, and fans alike.

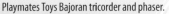
Playmates Toys Bajoran tricorder and phaser.

When *Star Trek: The Next Generation* wrapped production, the producers asked Michael Dorn to bring the stoic Worf to *Deep Space Nine* to freshen the series. © *Julie Dennis Brothers/Corbis*

*Ella Pearson*

*Voyageur Press collection*

The fifth season saw further changes. Executive producer Behr reflected, "We only recovered our equilibrium in the middle of the fifth season following another meeting with the studio in which we said, 'How about making the Klingons our friends again? You'll see them as much as you want, but we want to get back to the Dominion.' While I like having brought Worf onto the show, and I love some of the things that he brought along, I think it had a fairly substantial impact that wasn't all for the good. It took us way off from where we'd intended to go and it was slow going getting back."

Old secrets also came to the fore that year, changing how viewers saw some of their favorite characters, notably Odo. There were still some lighter moments, such as Worf's blossoming romance with Jadzia, and his role as Cyrano de Bergerac, aiding Quark in whispering sweet nothings in his ex-wife Grilka's ear. The O'Briens somehow managed time to add Kirayoshi to their family. Bashir's friends learned he had been genetically enhanced as a child in violation of the law.

The season ended with the Cardassians retaking the station, although Dukat found Sisko had left behind his beloved baseball. It was a message: Sisko would be back.

Season six picked up three months later, and the opening half-dozen episodes detailed Sisko and company retaking the station. Wolfe left the series while Bradley Thompson and David Weddle joined as story editors. Hans Beimler became Behr's writing partner, as everyone waited for a decision from Paramount whether or not this was to be the final season. The year saw one of the series' strongest episodes, "In the Pale Moonlight," which saw Sisko break many of his convictions to engineer a scenario that brought the Romulans into the Federation/Klingon alliance.

Terry Farrell's decision to leave meant substantially changing the plans for the final episode, in which originally the Prophets would have been destroyed. It did, though, see Dukat getting possessed and get embroiled in Bajoran religion. The story also left Sisko with a sense of failure. It was a downbeat conclusion to a season that saw him embrace becoming the Emissary and lead the victorious campaign against the Dominion.

All the other regular cast signed on for a final season, although it had become clear by now the "ugly stepchild" was not destined for the silver screen. Once more, the show had to share the spotlight, this time with not only *Voyager* but also *Insurrection*. The concluding episodes did allow the writers to explore another facet of Trill life, as Nicole deBoer's unprepared Ezri struggled with her unwanted symbiont.

"Going into season seven, we knew everything was canted towards the end," Moore said. "We were seeing plot threads and characters and where they were going. Even in the stand-alones, we could see that the tapestry was getting woven tighter and tighter. So we had to be careful, especially on the stand-alones."

The final season did tidy up all the character arcs and story threads, and concluded with a rousing two-hour story that properly brought down the curtain on the most ambitious of the series. The final day of shooting was April 20, 1999, and members of the crew, along with recurring players (most of whom skipped their latex appliances), gathered in period suits and dresses to fill the audience of Vic's Lounge. It was a happy but bittersweet day, and just before midnight, filming ended.

Knowing that there were no features planned, Pocket Books asked Paramount Licensing for permission to continue the stories in novel form. As a result, editor Marco Palmieri guided a series of books that effectively became the eighth season, and advanced all the players. Prior to that, actors Andrew J. Robinson and J. G. Hertzler each contributed to the prose line, the former with the acclaimed *A Stitch in Time*.

# CHAPTER 16

# VOYAGER

A mouse pad featuring *U.S.S. Voyager*.
*Voyageur Press collection*

The holographic Doctor (left) and Captain Janeway in a twenty-third-century uniform for *Voyager*'s *Star Trek* thirtieth anniversary episode, "Flashback," which placed her on Captain Sulu's *Excelsior*, both from Playmates Toys. *Voyageur Press collection*

United Paramount Network launched as a new national network on January 16, 1995, five days after another new national network, Warner Bros' The WB, launched. What UPN had that The WB lacked was a starship.

Since arriving at Paramount in 1991 after thirteen years at Universal, Kerry McCluggage had launching a network at the top of his to-do list. At the time, *TNG* was rewriting the rules for first-run syndication, and plans were being drawn up to maximize the franchise with a second series. Imagine, McCluggage, argued, if it anchored the new network, eerily echoing Barry Diller's plans nearly two decades earlier.

While the network notion took shape, Paramount television forged ahead and launched *DS9* in January 1993. By then, it was clear the new network was likely to become a reality, and McCluggage needed a new *Star Trek* series to appeal to men. On October 26, 1993, Paramount Communications and Chris-Craft Industries jointly announced UPN, which would feature the fourth iteration of *Star Trek*. While that took some pressure off *DS9*, it doubled the burden felt in

Rick Berman's office. It was made clear: the new show had to be wonderful.

Berman, Piller, and Jeri Taylor brainstormed how to create a fourth show and still be fresh. Among the earliest decisions was that the time had come for a female captain, soon followed by the notion of sending the starship to a previously unexplored portion of the universe, forcing the crew to face new situations, while challenging the writers not to resort to the tried and true antagonists.

*Voyager* would be a new breed of starship, an exploratory vessel that could actually land on planets, which it did in six episodes. Additionally, its nacelles would swivel into position before going to warp, making for a neat visual.

If they were going to send a ship full of people far from home, Taylor explained to me at the time, they wanted to bring along their favorite species, which meant having not only humans but Vulcans, Klingons, and others on hand. Since they were challenging stereotypes, it was also deemed time for the first black Vulcan.

Color Slide Film

this side toward screen

COLOR
TRANSPARENCY

PROCESSED BY
DYNACOLOR

The fans were largely skeptical of *Star Trek: Voyager*, but it slowly gained a following, lasting seven seasons on the new UPN network. Here, the crew celebrates its centennial episode in August 1998. *From left:* Tim Russ, Robert Picardo, Ethan Phillips, Kate Mulgrew, Jeri Ryan, Robert Beltran, Roxann Dawson, Garrett Wang, and Robert Duncan McNeill. *Associated Press*

"It took a long time, it took us weeks, even to come up with a cast of characters," Taylor said, "because we found that so many wonderful characters had already been done and we didn't want to repeat ourselves. We'd come up with an idea then say, 'No, that's too much like Data,' or Odo or Worf. To find the right balance of characters really took a long time."

Once the trio began fleshing out their ideas, they shared them with the production teams on *TNG* and *DS9* so seeds could be sown into both shows. The initial tensions would be formed by *Voyager* going after a Maquis vessel, with both ships inexplicably sent hurtling deep in the Delta Quadrant. The Maquis objected to the way the Federation settled a dispute with the Cardassians, and they took it upon themselves to fight back, being branded criminals by the authorities. *DS9* showed members of Starfleet resigning their commissions to join the Maquis, as so it made sense that the Maquis ship had ex-Starfleet on hand.

The pilot story was devised to cripple the Maquis ship and force the disgruntled crew aboard the starship, where everyone would have to try to live in harmony as they sought a way home. Hanging over their heads was the notion that, barring a miracle, they faced a seventy-year journey, meaning most of the crew would be dead before *Voyager* returned to Federation space.

It was a strong and bold notion, one that was filled with potential drama and conflict. Genuine differences of opinion would keep both sides from trusting one another when trust was all they had.

At least that's what was promised in the pilot. By the second episode, all the tension was gone.

"When testing was done on *DS9*, the results told us that audiences were unhappy that the characters on board the space station didn't always get along," Michael Piller wrote. "And they complained that the 'station doesn't go anywhere.' In other words, they were asking for more of *TNG*. We made

*Voyageur Press collection*

a few adjustments to *DS9*, but the real impact of that research was on the creation of *Voyager*. It was decided early on that it would be a ship-based show and there were to be no serious conflicts between the characters because *that's what the fans wanted*."

By instantly depriving the writers of an interesting—and fresh—source of drama, it quickly proved a challenge to differentiate the series from *TNG*.

Taylor, though, optimistically saw possibilities. She said, "We felt a need to create an avenue for new and fresh storytelling. We are forced into creating a new universe. We have to come up with new aliens, new situations. We knew we were taking some risks. We decided, in a very calculated way, to cut our ties with everything that was familiar. This is a dangerous thing to do. There is no more Starfleet, there are no more admirals to tell us what we can and cannot do, there are no Romulans, no Klingons, no Ferengi, no Cardassians. All those wonderful array of villains that the audience has come

*Star Trek* fan Chris Skinner (left) of California poses for a photo with fellow fan Eric Hall of Utah at the fifth annual official *Star Trek* convention at the Las Vegas Hilton August 19, 2006. *Ethan Miller/Getty Images*

to love and hate at the same time will no longer be there. This is a tricky thing to do."

Piller knew that after the slightly more introspective *DS9*, he was ready for a more action-oriented show and tried to pour all of those notions into the pilot script.

To bring the two sides together, the ship would need a very special kind of captain and a great deal of thought went into creating and casting Elizabeth Janeway.

"The search for the captain was a long and difficult one," Taylor recalled. "This is the person that gets the white-hot glare of publicity as the first female ever to head one of the *Star Trek* series and she had to be just right."

Berman added, "We didn't want to just create a captain and cast it with a female. We wanted to create a female captain who was a captain that was somewhat more nurturing and a little bit less swashbuckling than someone like Captain Kirk,

a little bit less sullen than someone like Captain Sisko, and a little bit more approachable than Captain Picard."

French-Canadian-film actress Geneviève Bujold captured the producers' imaginations and she was given the part, asking that the captain be renamed Nicole. She proved difficult to deal with, as she didn't want to do press for the new series. Unfortunately since *Voyager* was headlining a brand new network, there was higher than normal interest from the media. After two days of filming in September 1994, she ran to her trailer in tears. Director Winrich Kolbe and Berman sent her home. "This was a woman who, in no way, was going to be able to deal with the rigors of episodic television," Berman observed.

The producers had to scramble and recast the role, auditioning Erin Gray, Karen Austin, and Chelsea Field, as well as briefly considering changing the role back to a male captain, before settling on Kate Mulgrew, then perhaps best

# PITCHING IN SPACE: WRITING FOR *STAR TREK*

*Lisa Klink*

I was one of many writers who benefitted from *Star Trek*'s open script submission policy. I sent in a *TNG* spec script and was invited to pitch to *DS9*. I ended up pitching to the show four times, and three times to *Voyager*, before I sold a story to *DS9* and wrote the script. That was "Hippocratic Oath." What I enjoyed most about that script was the chance to put two of our heroes, Bashir and O'Brien, in direct conflict with each other about how to handle being prisoners of the Jem'Hadar. Neither one was wrong, exactly, but their backgrounds and experience gave them very different perspectives. I'll never forget going to the soundstage as they were filming my episode. I looked around at the set they'd built and thought, "I made this happen." It was amazing.

That episode got me a staff writer job on *Voyager*. It was a great place to start. Most of the writers and crew had been working in the *Trek* universe for a while, and everyone really knew what they were doing. We knew that we probably wouldn't get cancelled anytime soon, which is rare in television. It was also great to work on the same lot where the show was shooting. I could walk over to the set anytime. Since then, I've worked on several shows that filmed in a different country, so I never got to know the cast and crew.

The first episode I wrote for *Voyager* was called "Resistance." It was a spin on the Don Quixote story, where Janeway meets a sweet and noble alien who is on an imaginary quest. We cast an Oscar-winning actor as the alien—Joel Grey. I found out later that various *Trek* shows had been trying to get him to do a guest spot with no luck, but he liked this role well enough to sign on. That was the best compliment I could imagine. He was great in the episode, really heartbreaking.

I was less pleased with the trailer advertising my episode. It took a brief moment from the show when Janeway distracts a guard by pretending to be a prostitute and made it seem like the whole episode was about whether Janeway would sleep with the guy to save her crew. Infuriating.

Everybody loved writing for the Doctor, mainly because Robert Picardo could make anything funny. He also got some of the best lines because the Doctor was the "outsider" character, like Data in *TNG* or Odo in *DS9*, trying to act human and sometimes failing miserably. He could be rude or wildly inappropriate in a way the straight-laced Starfleet officers couldn't. Seven of Nine got to do that, too, because she'd been a Borg so long she didn't know how to consider other people's feelings.

Our least favorite episodes to write were usually the dreaded "bottle shows." These were the money-saving episodes that had to take place entirely on our regular sets, with minimal guest characters and special effects. I actually enjoyed the one I wrote, called "Scientific Method." Aliens had invaded the ship and were experimenting on the crew without their knowledge. Seven of Nine could see them because of her Borg technology, but couldn't let on that she saw them. In one scene, she's in the turbolift and one of the aliens pokes a long needle into her eye. She has to keep a straight face and just take it. It was creepy and fun.

Even now, people are impressed when I tell them I worked on a *Trek* show. It's nice to be even a small part of that universe.

*Lisa Klink went from writing for* Star Trek *to writing for a variety of other television shows and comic books.*

Playmates Toys issued a number of alternates for characters in their *Voyager* collection. At left is Tom Paris in a transitional form as he mutates into an amphibian—and that's just the beginning—in "Threshold," arguably the oddest *Voyager* episode ever. At right is the much less odd Chakotay in his Maquis clothes before joining the Starfleet crew on *Voyager*.

Forge, became the Vulcan science officer Tuvok; newcomer Garrett Wang was added as navigator Ensign Harry Kim; and *China Beach* alum Robert Picardo was the holographic doctor (named Doc Zimmerman in the bible and early press materials, although the character remained nameless in the series). Two Delta Quadrant residents joined the ship in the pilot: the nomad Talaxian, Neelix, played by stage and screen actor Ethan Phillips, and Kes, an Ocampan with a nine-year life span, portrayed by Jennifer Lien.

The pilot guest-starred Armin Shimerman as Quark, since *Voyager* paused at Deep Space 9 before heading on their mission of exploration. The delays and costs associated with the reshoots, plus the ambitious special effects, resulted in a two-hour pilot costing $23 million, the single most expensive television production at the time.

While work began on *Voyager*, UPN was lining up affiliates, competing market after market with the WB. Meantime, Paramount was selling *Voyager* as a first-run syndicated show to those markets that lacked a UPN affiliate, which was internally seen as robbing from the new network.

## SEASON BY SEASON

The crew almost immediately found new enemies in the Kazon, who turned out to have franchises located in their section of the Delta Quadrant and were frequent opponents for the first two seasons until the starship managed to leave them in their rear viewscreen. As recurring opponents, they lacked the culture of the Klingons or the charm of the Cardassians. A fiercer race, the Hirogen were hunters who trolled the quadrant in search of fascinating prey, such as the starship. They proved strong enough to recur from seasons four through seven. One of Mulgrew's favorite races was the Vidiians, who stole organs from other living beings merely to survive.

The series continued production through May 1995, choosing to save four episodes for the second season.

known as the title star of *Mrs. Columbo*. She accepted the part but asked that Nicole be renamed Kathryn.

"Kate, I think, remarkably deliver[ed] a feminine nurturing side and at the same time, a sense of strength and confidence. And that's just what we were looking for and I think that we've gotten it in spades," Berman later said. Mulgrew reported for her first scenes on September 19, just over a week after Bujold left the production. After a few days, it was determined her hair needed attention and the tight bun style was incorporated, requiring additional reshoots.

Fortunately, the rest of the casting proved easier. Robert Beltran (*Eating Raoul*) was signed as the rebellious first officer Chakotay; singer/dancer Roxann Biggs-Dawson was the half-human/half-Klingon engineer B'Elanna Torres; *TNG* guest star Robert Duncan McNeill played helmsman Lt. Tom Paris; Tim Russ, who previously auditioned to play Geordi La

Voyager's star-crossed lovers, the Talaxian Neelix (left) and Kes the Ocampan, from Playmates Toys. *Voyageur Press collection*

Playmates Toys issued the character Seska in her two "versions": a Bajoran from the Maquis who joined *Voyager's* Starfleet crew (left) and a Cardassian operative. *Seska as Starfleet, Voyageur Press collection*

"*Voyager* by the end of its first season settled into credible, but not impressive, ratings territory. It was by far the most-watched program on the network, but for Paramount it was a ratings disappointment," wrote Susanne Daniels and Cynthia Littleton in *Season Finale*, a history of the rival new networks. It was, though, the only UPN inaugural series to survive to a second season.

As the show began its sophomore year, and the ship meandered towards home, the Starfleet/Maquis tensions flared with less frequency. Fueling the conflict was Chakotay's second in command, Seska (Martha Hackett), who wound up betraying him. Beyond that, character relationships firmed up as Neelix and Tuvok forged an odd bond, and Harry and Tom Paris deepened their bromance. More significantly, the first hints of the Paris/Torres romance were seen, as were further sparks between Janeway and Chakotay.

UPN's overall ratings continued to flounder, as did the critical response to *Voyager*. Fans liked it but didn't *love* it, and no character had broken out in the way Spock or Data had by this point in their respective series. In an effort to boost ratings, Q made the first of many appearances, and at least the byplay between John de Lancie and Mulgrew made for fun watching. Still, Q could have returned the ship home in a heartbeat if he had wished to, but always found an excuse to prolong their journey.

The third season began with four episodes held back from the previous year. The Doctor gained a mobile emitter (from the twenty-ninth century), which allowed him to venture out of sickbay, and it was during this season that Picardo's performance captivated audiences and writers alike. The ship made it through the Nekrit Expanse, but this concerned Neelix because the ship was now in unfamiliar territory.

The crew of *Voyager* faced many hostile forces while stranded in the Delta Quadrant, including the Swarm (left) and the Borg, from Playmates Toys. This particular Borg, Seven of Nine, was liberated and became a member of the crew in a more human form. *Voyageur Press collection*

It was at this point that *Voyager* found the Borg, in "Blood Fever," and they were to remain a repeat nemesis until the finale. This allowed the series to begin developing its own internal mythos. Q's return in "The Q and the Grey" also helped in this regard. The series also began relying on more two-parters to give the show a sense of scope, with the most effective being "Year of Hell," which many fans felt should have been more like what the series should have been all along: a real dramatic struggle against failing systems and frayed nerves. Writer Bryan Fuller revealed that the two-parter was planned as a season-long arc, but the plan was rejected by Paramount, who preferred their starships spit-polished.

Picardo told *Star Trek Magazine* of one episode that wound up never getting produced: "They . . . have a comic story in mind in which some alien computer hacker hijacks the holographic Doctor's program and actually steals him off the ship! He's held hostage with a zany alien family, which should be fun."

One of the best received episodes of the series was "Flashback," the show's contribution to *Star Trek*'s thirtieth anniversary. Not only did it provide some much needed backstory for Tuvok, but it also seamlessly added the Vulcan to the bridge of the *U.S.S. Excelsior* at the time of *Star Trek VI*. George Takei guest-starred as Captain Sulu, and Grace Lee Whitney made an appearance as First Officer Rand, a nice continuity treat for the fans. A small part was written for Nichelle Nichols to bring her in on the fun, but she declined. Uhura was dropped late in the scripting process, although Michael Ansara's Kang did appear.

When Paramount asked for the special episode, Brannon Braga already had a Tuvok story in the works that was easily reworked to accommodate Sulu. Russ reveled in the part, altering some dialogue to be consistent with Vulcans through the years, although he disliked the twenty-third century uniforms. In addition to rebuilding the older starship bridge in just two weeks, director David Livingston also tracked down and rehired some of the extras from the film, including Boris Krutonog. Livingston enjoyed the technical challenges along with working with the veteran cast, but the faster-paced *Excelsior* scenes left the episode five minutes short, requiring two scenes—Tuvok's breakfast with Neelix, and the meditation scene between Tuvok and Kes—to be added.

The fourth season required the producers to shake things up to goose the ratings and return some heat to the series. UPN, by then, had improved overall, but only slightly, so there was a struggle to build the audience, as well as recapture fans who were just not engaged by the series. It was decided to add a new cast member, but budgetary constraints meant someone had to go. At first, Berman targeted Garrett Wang, who had a testy relationship with the production. However, when *People* named him one of the "Fifty Most Beautiful People in the World," his job was saved. As a result, Berman selected Jennifer Lien as the one to leave.

Taylor later observed, "These things are never cut-and-dried. It's never one thing. I think Jennifer had a wish to move on, and that coincided with some thinking here. There has not been any rancor or unpleasantness about it . . . I know she will go on to a wonderful career . . . and I will miss her very much." Mulgrew was the most upset cast member when gentle Lien left the ensemble.

"I will say that there were definitely uncomfortable feelings among the cast, which is totally understandable," Braga said. "We let Jennifer Lien go, and brought someone new on, and that's bound to cause some unsettled feelings. There were rough spots here and there, but it's nothing worth noting. Everyone was very professional."

The magazines made a big deal over the addition of Jeri Ryan as Seven of Nine, a Borg who was to be rescued and added to the *Voyager* complement. Her skintight catsuit and minimal Borg appliances seemed to emphasize both her beauty and curves. A jolt of sex appeal was the presumed prescription to bring viewers back to the series. Seven arrived during the fourth season opener "Scorpion, Part II" and Kes departed an episode later, but first gifted the starship's crew by telekinetically moving the ship 9,000 light years closer to home.

Much of the season was devoted to Seven's integration with the crew, as the writers paired her with different characters to see where there might be chemistry. As a result, she and Harry Kim formed a friendship, and Janeway took the woman under her wing. "[Mulgrew and Ryan] brought out such great things from each other," Fuller said. "The legacy of *Voyager*, really, is that relationship. And I know that the fan base was very critical of Janeway, but I loved that character and I loved Kate Mulgrew. I think she's a fantastic actress." Later, Seven's close friendship with the Doctor was allowed to flourish, letting them dominate the final seasons. When the Seven-centric stories continued during the fifth year, Beltran began

Facsimile script for "Flashback," celebrating *Star Trek*'s thirtieth anniversary. The ambitious episode guest-starred George Takei, Grace Lee Whitney, and Michael Ansara, setting the story during the time of *Star Trek VI: The Undiscovered Country*. *Voyageur Press collection*

complaining loudly about diminished stories for Chakotay and having little to do as an actor.

Pocket Books had created a Klingon holiday "Day of Honor," the Klingon equivalent of Yom Kippur, around which editor John Ordover built a four-book series. He mentioned the notion to Jeri Taylor, who by then had already written two original *Voyager* novels, figuring she might see the merit in the idea. For the first time, an episode inspired by the book series was created, featuring B'Elanna Torres.

The other big change in the fourth season came when the Doctor contacted the Alpha Quadrant in "Message in a Bottle," confirming the crew of *Voyager* had survived.

At the end of the year, Taylor left the franchise, never quite comfortable with the production team. Braga replaced her as executive producer, and he continued the pedestrian storytelling. He did darken the tone somewhat, beginning with "Night," when Janeway experienced a months-long ennui. Braga saw to it every character had a crisis of confidence throughout the season, even letting Harry Kim get in trouble for defying orders for the first time.

A highlight of the fifth season was the return of the Borg Queen (last seen in *First Contact* but now played by Susanna Thompson). She was a fitting opponent for Janeway, and the two women would tussle for the remainder of the series. Meantime, both Borg and *Voyager* were further plagued by Species 8472, introduced in "Scorpion," which existed in something called "fluidic space."

The sixth was the show's first season without competition from *DS9*, which had ended the previous May. With the ship that much closer to home and further away from the Delta inhabitants they'd met, the writers introduced many new races this season, which also led to the show feeling less like the internally consistent previous seasons. The Hirogen and Borg did make appearances, as did the Vidiians.

Kes made a poorly received one-off reappearance in an attempt to tie off her character's story, and Dwight Schultz guest-starred as Reg Barclay in "Pathfinder," which established real-time communication with Starfleet. *Voyager* was now no longer the isolated starship originally conceived.

While Seven remained the predominant focus of storylines, it was Janeway, Tuvok, and Torres who boarded a Borg vessel to help an underground Borg Resistance group in the season cliffhanger.

Having limped to a seventh season, it was clear the show was reaching its end, especially with UPN and Paramount already talking about creating a replacement *Star Trek* series. Braga left *Voyager* to spend the year developing what would become *Enterprise*. As a result, new showrunner Kenneth Biller was left to wrap up the character arcs and bring the ship home. This led to the use of familiar races, from the Hirogen to the Ferengi, making appearances. It was decided to give Neelix a happy ending and let him be reunited with his Talaxian people in "Homestead," but not before Janeway named him a Federation ambassador.

In one story, which could be considered a victory lap, Chakotay tripped through time to seal fractures, which allowed him and the audience to revisit the previous seasons, letting us see the Kazon and Seska one final time. Q came back for a last bow, in time to have a child and saddle Janeway with babysitting the appropriately named q.

As if to address Beltran's complaints about Seven getting too much screen time, an out-of-leftfield romance between Chakotay and Seven was kindled. Meantime, Paris and Torres finally married, and B'Elanna gave birth just as the starship re-entered the Alpha Quadrant in the two-hour finale, "Endgame." This saw Alice Krige return to her Borg Queen role, and Mulgrew play two versions of Janeway, in a time-twisting tale that felt all too familiar. By the time the ship staggered home, they reported they had made first contact with over 400 separate races, a distinguished record. For that and, it seems, merely surviving, Janeway was promoted to vice admiral, as seen in *Nemesis*.

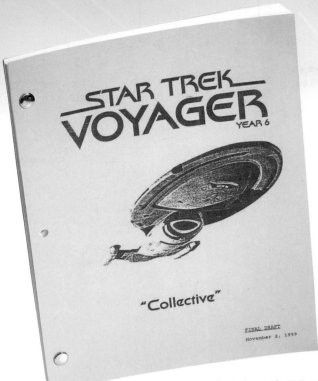

Facsimile script for "Collective," a sixth season episode involving the discovery of five young Borg who are no longer connected to the Borg Collective. *Voyageur Press collection*

Hallmark's *U.S.S Voyager* light-up ornament. *Voyageur Press collection*

And with that, a promising but ultimately disappointing *Star Trek* series wound down. The show was plagued by lacking the courage of its convictions, resetting the status quo way too often, and not making the antagonists challenging enough. Similarly, it allowed itself to play favorites with the characters, and the writers fell into bad habits.

Nineteen episodes relied on holodeck or holoemitter problems for plots, and the use of fake 1930s movie serial *Captain Proton* and stereotypical Irish village Fairhaven for stories grew tedious. Another thirty-three episodes saw one or more members of the crew possessed in some manner. An additional five saw *Voyager* destroyed, only to have the starship restored. Despite Janeway saying, "Since my first day on the job as a Starfleet captain, I swore I'd never let myself get caught in one of those God-forsaken paradoxes," there were seventeen episodes that used time travel as an element, including the finale, which of course echoed *TNG*'s time-tossed ending, and the show's hundredth episode, "Timeless," which saw LeVar Burton reprise his role as a future version of Geordi La Forge.

Looking back, Fuller lamented, "If you had told me [before working on *Voyager*] that my career was going to be thirty years of writing *Star Trek*, I would have been thrilled. But then having worked the show for a while and starting to bump up against some of the parameters of things that we couldn't do, I started to feel frustrated because I wanted to write more character stuff and have those great character moments. I began to feel a little stifled by the reset button at the end of the day, because there was so much stuff happening in the characters' worlds that I wanted to see how they would grow from those experiences.

"For example with B'Elanna Torres and 'Barge of the Dead,' what happens when somebody has a religious experience? Because *DS9* was so serialized, the edict on *Voyager* was very reactionary to that serialization, so that at the end of the episode, there was a history-eraser button and we moved forward with the next adventure.

"I wanted to take more risks, just in terms of the storytelling, in terms of the genre . . . *DS9* did that in spades. They took Starfleet to war. They took the Federation to war, which is

STAR TREK

THE KOBAYASHI ALTERNATIVE

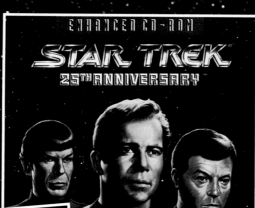

ENHANCED CD-ROM

STAR TREK

25TH ANNIVERSARY

STAR TREK

JUDGMENT RITES

SPECIAL CD-ROM EDITION

GAME DISC

STAR TREK
THE NEXT GENERATION

"A Final Unity"

Spectrum
HoloByte

STAR TREK™

STARFLEET
ACADEMY™

STAR TREK
KLINGON™

STAR TREK
BORG

THE INTERACTIVE MOVIE

STAR TREK
THE NEXT GENERATION

INTERACTIVE
TECHNICAL MANUAL
U.S.S. ENTERPRISE™ NCC-1701-D

THE OFFICIAL STARFLEET VIRTUAL TOUR
Debut Product for Apple® Computer QuickTime® VR
Featuring the Voices of JONATHAN FRAKES & MAJEL BARRETT RODDENBERRY

STAR TREK
THE NEXT GENERATION®
COMPANION
A SERIES GUIDE AND SCRIPT LIBRARY

MacOS

STAR TREK THE NEXT GENERATION

KLINGON
HONOR GUARD

MICRO PROSE

MacSoft

STAR TREK
DEEP SPACE NINE
HARBINGER™

1 OF 2

VIACOM
NEWMEDIA

STAR TREK: DEEP SPACE NINE®
The saga continues...

THE FALLEN
STAR TREK

STAR TREK
DEEP SPACE NINE
COMPANION
A SERIES GUIDE AND SCRIPT LIBRARY

* INCLUDES VIDEO TRAILERS FOR

STAR TREK
VOYAGER
ELITE FORCE

STAR TREK
ELITE FORCE II

TEEN
T

ritual

ASPYR    ACTIVISION

THE
STAR TREK®
ENCYCLOPEDIA
A Reference Guide to the Future
VERSION 3.0

WINDOWS®/MACINTOSH® CD-ROM

From MICHAEL OKUDA and DENISE OKUDA

DELUXE
STAR TREK®

New with 3
New Starship
Classes: AKIRA,
OBERTH and
PROMETHEUS

Now Send 2
of Your Ships
on a Mission
Together!

DON'T DREAM IT. BUILD IT.

STARSHIP CREATOR

Windows® 95/98 and MACINTOSH®

7 New Missions

Star Trek fans are known as early adopters, so it's no surprise the franchise has been a rich source for computer games. The various series inspired a wide range of tie-in software, from early text-based games to first-person shooters, ship-to-ship battles, reference works, and even a game show. *Kobayashi Alternative*, Steve Roby collection; *Tactical Assault*, Ella Pearson

SOUND SOURCE
INTERACTIVE
STAR TREK®
THE GAME SHOW
THE ULTIMATE TRIVIA CHALLENGE SPANNING OVER 30 YEARS OF STAR TREK

ENGINEERING    MEDICAL

ENGINEERING
OPERATIONS

500
UNITS

WITH YOUR
HOST, Q

NINTENDO DS™

STAR TREK
TACTICAL ASSAULT™

NTR-K7E-USA

Bethesda
a ZeniMax Media company

EVERYONE
E

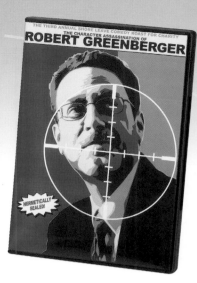

*Star Trek* authors use their status to raise money for the American Red Cross. Author David Mack produced three elaborate roasts of fellow authors Keith R. A. DeCandido, Michael Jan Friedman, and Robert Greenberger from 2009–2011 at Shore Leave.

huge and dramatic and really gutsy—because the Dominion attacked San Francisco. That's great! It's just really impactful and dramatic and a little more embracing of the genre."

The show was good to its cast, letting Picardo, Russ, Dawson, and McNeill take turns behind the camera, while it welcomed actors-turned-directors Burton, Jonathan Frakes, and Andrew J. Robinson. Dawson has since gone on to a successful directing career while McNeill has directed and produced, notably NBC's geek spy series *Chuck*.

# MERCHANDISE FLAGS

As a new millennium began, it was clear interest in *Star Trek* had been fairly well exploited, with toys, games, cards, comic books, novels, and even holiday ornaments crowding fans' homes. But as *DS9* left the air and *Star Trek: Insurrection* left a sour taste in many fans' mouths, the weekly constant was *Voyager*, which was lackluster in execution. The resulting drop in interest led to merchandisers scaling back. For example, the volume of *Voyager* novels was far lower than for its predecessors, despite executive producer Jeri Taylor penning two of them. After the show ended its run, there was lower demand to continue the crew's adventures, although Pocket attempted new stories in 2003 and 2004, which were not well-received by the fans. Characters from the series were then poached for other crews, with Tuvok joining Will Riker aboard the *U.S.S. Titan* in a series of original novels set after *Nemesis*. Janeway was even killed off in a *TNG* novel, *Before Dishonor* by Peter David. A new series of *Voyager* novels, penned by Kirsten Beyer, has

seen the ship return to the Delta Quadrant at the head of a fleet. In *The Eternal Tide*, after much fan anticipation, Beyer brought Janeway back.

The books remained one of the strongest aspects of the licensing efforts. When Microsoft approached Pocket Books about launching a series of eBooks, it was clearly aimed at the demographic that were the *Trek* fan core. Editor John Ordover and writer Keith R. A. DeCandido conceived a series set around the mentioned, but never seen, Starfleet Corps of Engineers. The *Star Trek: SCE* series launched in 2000 and was rebranded *Corps of Engineers* in 2006 before the line ended in 2007. Characters from other elements of the franchise were included, such as Sonya Gomez, a *TNG* engineer.

Mixing original and established characters in a new environment had proven to be a successful formula for Pocket Books, which previously launched *Star Trek: New Frontier* in 1997. Set in a distant portion of the Federation with a new ship, the *Excalibur*, it also lifted characters from *TNG*, such as Elizabeth Shelby and Robin Lefler. Under author Peter David, the stories explored different facets of galactic politics and problems.

More recently, *Star Trek: Vanguard* told stories concurrent with Kirk's adventures aboard the *Enterprise*, but in another sector of space. Under authors David Mack, Kevin Dilmore, Dayton Ward, and Marco Palmieri, it spanned nine volumes.

Novels featuring the crews from *TNG*, *DS9*, and *Voyager* developed interweaving continuities as each series went off the air. As a result, readers can enjoy the further adventures of their favorite characters over a decade after they last were seen on screen.

*Voyageur Press collection*

*Voyageur Press collection*

*Voyageur Press collection*

# CHAPTER 17

# ENTERPRISE

The main crew of the *Enterprise* NX-01 around the tactical station, from Art Asylum. From left, T'Pol, Jonathan Archer, Malcolm Reed, Charles "Trip" Tucker III, and Travis Mayweather. Hoshi Sato and Dr. Phlox were not issued in their regular uniforms.

*Star Trek* fan Luis Valentine of New York talks to a friend on his communicator/phone while walking through the exhibit area at the fifth annual official *Star Trek* convention at the Las Vegas Hilton on August 17, 2006. *Getty Images*

In May 1994, before the first *TNG* film opened, Rick Berman said, "People ask, 'Can you make too many trips to the well?' I think the answer is, yes you can. But I think we've been careful that the most recent trip, *Voyager*, won't be that one-too-many-trips. We try to keep all these series different and that's good for everybody to skew a little differently on each of the series. And as long as we can keep them interesting to us and keep them challenging to us, I think they'll work with the audience."

By 2000, though, it was clear the audience had other ideas.

UPN and Paramount were clearly unhappy with how *Voyager* had performed as a series and continuation of the *Star Trek* franchise. By that point, UPN and The WB were merging into The CW, and former WB exec Dean Valentine was running the new network According to Daniel and Littleton, Valentine tried to persuade Kerry McCluggage not to rush into a new series, but the Paramount boss was adamant.

Paramount ordered the fifth iteration of *Star Trek* from Berman in spring 2000 as *Voyager* was filming its sixth season. He was initially apprehensive about going back to the well one more time, but the studio insisted, so Berman tapped Brannon Braga to help him develop it. As a result, Braga left *Voyager*'s final season to devote himself to conceiving the new show, which was set to debut in September 2001.

Berman indicated he wanted a more action-oriented series, closer in feeling to Kirk's original five-year mission. That led to a series of conversations that resulted in a conclusion that the new series would explore the birth of the Federation, some 150 years prior to Kirk's era. Effectively, the series would occur not long after the events of *First Contact*, which

The *Enterprise* NX-01 from the Johnny Lightning
"Legends of Star Trek" series fires its phase cannons.

showcased the first human use of warp drive, catching the Vulcans' attention. As a result, the series would mix the familiar (actual days and dates rather than stardates) with the futuristic (Klingons, Andorians).

The executive producer envisioned spending the first season following the building of the first warp-capable starship, *Enterprise* NX-01, but that idea was scrapped as taking too long and keeping the characters from the hoped-for action. In the internet-era and with no Roddenberry around to leak details that he disapproved of, the producers successfully kept their plans to themselves, until fans heard in February 2001 that Herman Zimmerman and John Eaves had been hired to design the early days of space travel. They were quickly followed to the show by Michael Westmore, Michael Okuda, Ronald B. Moore, and Marvin Rush, bringing their wealth of *Trek* knowledge to the new production.

Their biggest challenge was going to be giving the series a retro look while letting Kirk's 1960s-era starship

still look futuristic. There would have to be little touches to connect it all, such as the color-stripping on the uniforms for specialization identification and sound effects. But clearly, phasers were out, and while it was decided the transporters were still needed as a storytelling shortcut, they were not going to work all that securely.

The series bible took shape over the months, with the starship captain first named Jackson then Jeffrey and finally Jonathan Archer. A big name actor was needed to anchor the show and *Quantum Leap* star Scott Bakula was hired.

At the CW's upfront presentation in May, fans finally learned the show was to be named simply *Enterprise*, without the usual *Star Trek* prefix. Supposedly this was to attract viewers who might be put off by the history of the franchise, although, as Daniel and Littleton pointed out, "the iconography, starships, and futuristic jargon [would be] a dead giveaway to any viewer who hadn't been living in a cave for the past forty years."

The remainder of the cast was announced days later and it included many unfamiliar names, such as Connor Trinneer as Trip Tucker; Jolene Blalock as the Vulcan subcommander T'Pol; Dominic Keating as security chief Malcolm Reed; Anthony Montgomery as helmsman Travis Mayweather; and Linda Park as communicator Hoshi Sato. Veteran character actor John Billingsley rounded out the cast as the Denobulan Dr. Phlox.

A week after the series was formally announced, production on "Broken Bow," the two-hour opener, began. It featured an uncredited cameo from James Cromwell, reprising his Zefram Cochrane role from *First Contact*.

The new series debuted on September 26, earning very strong ratings with an estimated 12.54 million viewers, offering CW executives some hope. Those expectations were quickly dashed as the negative professional and fan reviews spread, and ratings shrank week after week.

Fans weren't sure which angered them more, the lack of *Star Trek* in the title, or the use of the song "Where My Heart Will Take Me" as a theme. Fans scoffed at the slow starship needing just days to travel to the Klingon planet Qo'noS, and they questioned why these Klingons resembled the movie versions, not those seen in the original series (a point finally addressed in the fourth season episodes "Affliction" and "Divergence").

The show did take some chances, humanizing Archer by having him bring Porthos, his beagle, along for the ride, and making the Vulcans appear villainous as they were impeding humanity's entry in the galactic neighborhood. A new antagonistic race, the Suliban, were introduced and worked better than their equivalents on *Voyager*, the Kazon, ever did.

Not all the storytelling risks paid off. Braga's introduction of an underlying arc, the Temporal Cold War, was not well received at all. He said the "nifty" idea was added at Paramount's insistence, while Berman felt that the idea of time travel allowing events to be constantly reset gave the production team plenty of new storytelling opportunities.

Archer in space suit from Art Asylum.

*Voyageur Press collection*

# THE NEVER-ENDING *TREK*: RISK WAS ITS BUSINESS

*Mark A. Altman*

The amazing thing about the original *Star Trek*, which seems to get lost in the sands of time now, is how truly groundbreaking the show was at the time. Despite the fact that it lifted some of its paradigm from MGM's sci-fi marvel *Forbidden Planet*, which unspooled with a ponderous seriousness except when Robby the Robot was onscreen, there was so much about *Star Trek* that was completely fresh and new. While most of the sci-fi of the 1950s and 1960s was either dystopian meditations on H-Bomb fears or kitsch, *Star Trek* was remarkably inventive and utopian. It worked as contemporary metaphor, dealing with some of the most divisive social issues of the time, including Vietnam, racism and poverty in the wake of Lyndon Johnson's Great Society, but was also incredibly prescient, maybe not of the twenty-third century, but at least of the twenty-first. It anticipated everything from cell phones to personal computers, big-screen TVs to the iPad, to something as mundane as grocery store sliding doors. It looked and sounded like nothing else on television, anchored by the iconic performances of William Shatner and Leonard Nimoy as the stewards of a franchise that would endure and flourish for decades. And most successfully of all it harnessed the hopefulness and optimism of Kennedy's New Frontier as the warp core of its journey. It's not an accident that J. J. Abrams chose to revisit this *Trek* series for his reboot; it provided the richest canvas and colors, literally and figuratively, to work from, which is why the series remains so utterly engaging even after many of its visual effects, prosthetics, and stories ("The Way to Eden," anyone?) have dated.

And if there's a reason that subsequent *Trek*s have never achieved the lofty heights of the original series, it's largely because they never took the risks the original did in terms of reinventing the television medium, and anticipating the leaps forward in technology that made the original *Trek* a marvel to behold. *TNG*, for all its bells and whistles, was a simple updating on the format and archetypes of the original. The holodeck was as close as *TNG* came in attempting to presage a future technology, and it was misused as a contrived plot device endlessly. All the other bells and whistles remained the same: tricorders, transporters, and phasers. The most imaginative reinvention of the formula was the conceit that the crew traveled with their families, a concept that was quickly dispensed with when it proved untenable to working with the established formula. One of the reasons I find the series so hard to watch today is its static camera and color palette that mires it in the blandness of the 1990s. It failed to anticipate the type of storytelling and style that would help the medium achieve new heights in the first decade of the twenty-first century and in the genre with shows like *Battlestar Galactica*.

*DS9* was far more ambitious in its plotting, and was a byproduct of the L.A. Riots of the early 90s. Its simple message: "Can't we all just get along?" But unlike its progressive storylines and deep bench of supporting characters, *DS9* was stuck in the five act and a teaser structure of 1960s *Star Trek* and, while less flatly lit, edited, and scored than *TNG*, still failed to create a new esthetic for the series to match its attempts at taking the franchise in a new direction. By the time the lethargic *Voyager* and *Enterprise* made it out of drydock, they suffered from the Xerox Syndrome, being a copy of a copy of a copy. Each degraded the original premise further with an ensemble of characters that seemed all too familiar.

Ultimately, *Enterprise*'s biggest problem, was an adversity to risk. Already hampered with being a prequel where we knew the outcome before it even started, *Enterprise* looked like it took place years *after* the original, and it failed to take advantage of the franchise's biggest strength, its voluminous and deep continuity, until its final season. It was also an opportunity to revisit the traditional story structure and look of a *Trek* series and could have actually been a throwback to the faux-1960s Tomorrowland look rather than yet another iteration of the *Trek* series of the previous two decades. By the end, *Trek*'s failure to continually reinvent the helm, er, wheel, helped lead to a growing disinterest in the franchise among anyone but the most ardent superfan. A series that had started as space opera, writ large, had not so suddenly lost its voice. Thankfully, there's J. J. Abrams who is truly introducing the floundering franchise to the real next generation.

*Mark A. Altman graduated from genre journalist to writer/producer of* Free Enterprise *(1999), the award-winning comedy classic, starring Emmy Award winners Eric McCormack and William Shatner.*

## SEASON BY SEASON

The first season slowly explored the core characters, establishing a triumvirate between Archer, Trip, and T'Pol, that allowed the writers to explore various themes and points of view. Once more, a Vulcan was the outsider looking in on humanity, while Phlox was her opposite, reveling in all cultures.

We learned plenty about the Vulcans of the era as well as the Andorians. It appeared the two races distrusted one another less than two centuries after meeting. Imperial Guard commander Shran (*DS9* veteran Jeffrey Combs) was introduced and became a fan favorite, recurring in all four seasons.

Despite mediocre ratings, *Enterprise* was renewed for a second season and the crew traveled further from home, meeting Tholians, unseen Romulans, and new races, including the Kriosians and Arkonians.

The show was still figuring out its voice, but fans were being critical, especially of the smarmy scenes between Trip and T'Pol set in the decontamination chamber, where a gel had to be applied to the naked body. Despite the soft lights, steam, and close-ups, the hoped for eroticism fell flat, especially in "A Night in Sickbay."

Things remained unsettled and unsatisfactory, so the producers changed gears as the season wound up. The final episode changed the playing field, reflecting the national mood post-9/11 (which had occurred as the show's first episode featuring the Andorians was in production). The alien Xindi attacked Earth, destroying sections of the American continents from Florida (killing Trip's sister in the process) all the way to Venezuela. Archer was assigned to take the NX-01 into the Delphic Expanse to stop them.

The third season was designed to be mostly about the Xindi conflict. But there were other changes afoot. The show was renamed *Star Trek: Enterprise* to reclaim lost fans, and

The Klingon courier Klaang from Art Asylum. Klaang crash landed on Earth in the *Enterprise* premiere episode "Broken Bow."

Silik of the Suliban Cabal from Art Asylum. He was a recurring opponent for Captain Archer from the premiere to the fourth season.

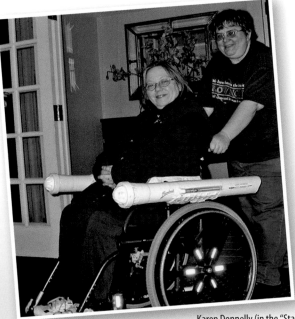

Karen Donnelly (in the "Starchair") and Jennifer Morris attend the 2006 Farpoint convention in Timonium, Maryland. *Blair Learn*

Leonard Nimoy and William Shatner went from rivals to warm friends and produced *Mind Meld*, a two-man documentary about the impact the *Star Trek* experience has had on the franchise's two most celebrated participants. Here they talk privately while autographing copies of the DVD. *Associated Press*

added a dose of testosterone in the form of the military assault command operations (MACOs) led by new recurring player Steven Culp.

It took everything the *Enterprise* crew had, and Archer lost people along the way, but the five races comprising the Xindi were finally stopped once and for all. But, before our heroes could arrive home safely, they found themselves tossed back in time to an alien-controlled Nazi Germany in the season cliffhanger "Storm Front."

Manny Coto came to the series having grown up on the original series but being young enough to prefer *Lost in Space*. He became a fan through the reruns, which in turn led him to read the works of Harlan Ellison, Jerome Bixby, and James Blish. "*The Making of Star Trek* really was the first book that made me realize, 'Wow, this could be a profession and a damn fun one,'" he said in an interview for this book. After graduating from the American Film Institute, he wrote and directed the horror movie *Doctor Giggles*, as well as episodes of *Tales from the Crypt* and the 1995 revival of *The Outer Limits*. It was his work creating the little-remembered *Odyssey 5* that caught Braga's attention, which led to him joining the *Enterprise* staff during the third season.

"When I got there," Coto recalled, "they'd had the first two seasons and the response hadn't been that great. For season three, Brannon wanted to really mix it up and he wanted to do a season-long arc. I think it was the first time *Star Trek* had done something like this, make a whole season-long story arc of interlocked episodes. So the idea was to make it darker and edgier, just one entire huge story of *Enterprise* going into the Delphic Expanse to search for the Xindi.

"I think we were pretty successful. It certainly gave the show a lot more energy, and I think some of the better episodes started appearing in season three. That's similar to *TNG*: the first two seasons of that I always thought were kind of unwatchable."

George Takei (center), Johanna Miller Lewis, chair of the history department at the University of Arkansas in Little Rock (right), and Richard Yada, of Little Rock, walk past a memorial erected for the inhabitants of a Japanese-American World War II interment camp in Rohwer, Arkansas, in 2003. Takei was four when he, his parents, and two younger siblings were ordered from their Los Angeles home and taken by railroad under armed guard to the camp after the bombing of Pearl Harbor. *Associated Press*

Despite the strongest writing yet, the ratings continued to disappoint, so the CW cut the episode order by two, to twenty-four. Even reworking the theme music didn't help. Its core fan following was worried about cancellation, but on May 20, 2004, a fourth season was confirmed. Although in an eerie echo of the original series, it was moved to Friday nights.

Coto was placed fully in creative control, and he quickly wrapped the cliffhanger, dispatching the Temporal Cold War at the same time. "I always thought that *Enterprise* could have a lot more fun with tying into the original series, which is what I was always a huge fan of," Coto said. "So I thought, 'If this is a precursor to the original series, wouldn't it be fun to use it as a real stepping stone to see how the Federation was built, and tie into some of the earlier episodes?'

"I thought it would be fun to do a series of three episode arcs, where you end up with little mini-movies if you put them all together. That would allow us to develop more complex plots and deal with grander themes. And also it'd help,

because on season four, the budget was cut a little bit. By doing these arcs, we were able to re-use sets for multiple episodes." Joining him, as story editors, were popular *Star Trek* novelists Judith and Garfield Reeves-Stevens.

The emphasis on the show's prequel premise was emphasized with tales including Brent Spiner guest starring as Dr. Ari Soong, an ancestor to Data's designer, Noonien Soong. The story had two purposes: to show the path to Data's creation and to create a genetic plot point that could then be used to explain the varying Klingon appearances. In that same story, the supermen of Khan Noonien Singh's time were also revisited.

Coto also addressed another of the fans' complaints about *Enterprise*. "Brannon's idea was that [the Vulcans seen on *Enterprise*] were Vulcans who were closer to the Vulcans that existed before Surak brought logic to Vulcan. I thought it'd be fun to do a three-episode arc where you actually bridged the *Enterprise* Vulcans with the Vulcans we were used to seeing

Self-avowed *Star Trek* fan Jason Alexander— partially assimilated—appeared with a cadre of Borg at at the opening of the Borg Invasion 4D attraction at *Star Trek: The Experience* in Las Vegas in 2004. The new attraction featured live actors and a 3D film in a motion simulator theatre containing sensory seats, choreographed to the film, that probed and poked the viewer's back. *Associated Press*

on the original series. You have a situation where this group of Vulcans who were trying to get back to the old ways clash with the Vulcans that were in charge now."

Perhaps the best story of the season was a two-parter set in the mirror universe, complete with its own version of the credit sequence that relayed the history of the alternate timeline. Explaining what happened to the *U.S.S. Defiant* from the original series episode "The Tholian Web," it was loved by cast and crew alike, particularly when they had the chance to work on a re-creation of the original *Constitution*-class bridge.

Alumni directors for the show included LeVar Burton, Michael Dorn, Roxann Dawson, and Robert Duncan McNeill.

The ratings had not matched the improved critical reception, and cancelation was confirmed on February 2, 2005. Political and sports pre-emptions hurt the fourth season after its October debut, and while an increasing percentage of audiences were digitally recording the show to watch later, such results were not yet factored into the ratings.

Fans tried to "Save *Enterprise*," hoping to raise $30 million to finance a fifth season, and Washington, D.C. lobbyist Dan Jensen tried a politically packed petition, getting Florida Congressman Mark Foley to sign on.

The final episodes' focus took the crew to Earth to deal with a xenophobic terrorist group. On May 13, "These are the Voyages . . ." brought down the curtain. Guest starring Jonathan Frakes and Marina Sirtis, it was set aboard the *Enterprise*-D with Commander Riker reviewing holographic footage of the first *Enterprise*'s final mission. Controversial with the fans, it was the lowest-rated episode of the series. Much of the *Enterprise* cast were angered by sharing their final screen minutes with *TNG* performers, feeling it took away from their own closure.

"I think a lot of fans and people said that it was a little bit of an insult to *Enterprise* because you had to bring in the *Next Generation* characters," Coto recalled. "I always looked at it as the previous episodes, about Peter Weller's character wanting aliens off the Earth, as the finale for *Enterprise*. Because we knew that *Enterprise* was going off the air, and that there would be no *Star Trek* replacing it, it was the end of the eighteen-year franchise. I think the final episode was Brannon and Rick's idea of ending the franchise itself, at least in its current incarnation.

"I didn't have a problem with the way they approached it and I kind of enjoyed the episode. I actually don't understand the huge fan backlash over it. I thought it was charming, I thought it was emotional at the end and I thought it was a cool idea, looking back on *Enterprise* through a holodeck."

Coto had ideas for a hoped-for fifth season, possibly including the seeds of the Romulan War (which wound up being played out in novels by Michael A. Martin). Shran was also considered for a regular berth on *Enterprise*. Other ideas included a Kzinti story, using Larry Niven's aliens from the animated "The Slaver Weapon," the construction of Starbase 1, and more trips through the mirror. The Reeves-Stevens and Alice Krige even conceived of a Borg Queen origin tale, while writer/producer Mike Sussman wanted to introduce T'Pol's father. There was even a possible story featuring the character of Flint encountered in the original series' third season.

One of Coto's best ideas for the series never came together. "We had concocted a really cool mirror universe story," Coto

An ailing Jimmy Doohan received his star on the Hollywood Walk of Fame in August 2004, flanked by his dear friends and fellow castmates. *Associated Press*

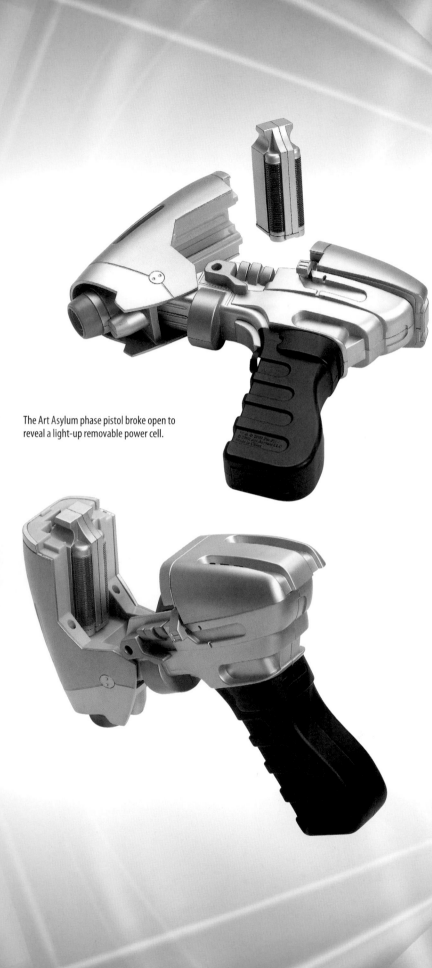

The Art Asylum phase pistol broke open to reveal a light-up removable power cell.

recalled. "*Enterprise* comes across a pocket universe where the evil Kirk from the mirror universe is residing. I don't remember exactly how we worked in a temporal loop, but it would have been a two-parter for Shatner to star in and play Tiberius. We had lunch with Shatner; myself and Brannon and Rick, and pitched him the idea, which he really thought was great. But ultimately, Paramount wouldn't pay for what he wanted, which was a lot, but not outrageous considering how legendary it would have been. I think it was a great lost opportunity. It would have been a spectacular two-parter.

"I really enjoyed just having lunch with Shatner and watching him. He had just gotten a cell phone at the time and he was trying to figure out how it worked—it looked like Captain Kirk trying to figure out his cell phone. If I had a video of it, I think it would have been one of the greatest viral videos of all time."

Technically, *Enterprise* spent its money well, and it had strong set designs and digital effects. It was the first of the *Trek* series to be produced in widescreen as that became the new television standard. On October 15, 2003, the show began being broadcast in high definition and was filmed on digital video a year later.

Matching the diminished interest in the series, there were just two video games tying in with the show and only five novels from Pocket Books published alongside the series. By then, overall *Trek* book sales were down resulting in the line being halved to a dozen or so books a year. In 2007, post-*Enterprise* novels began, rewriting the events of "These Are The Voyages . . .," eliminating Trip's death and setting them before the Romulan War took place.

## A NEW BEGINNING

According to Manny Coto, he was "trying to get Rick to try to start up a new series before *Enterprise* ended. I don't know if Paramount had any appetite for it or what Paramount's thinking, I just thought that if there could be

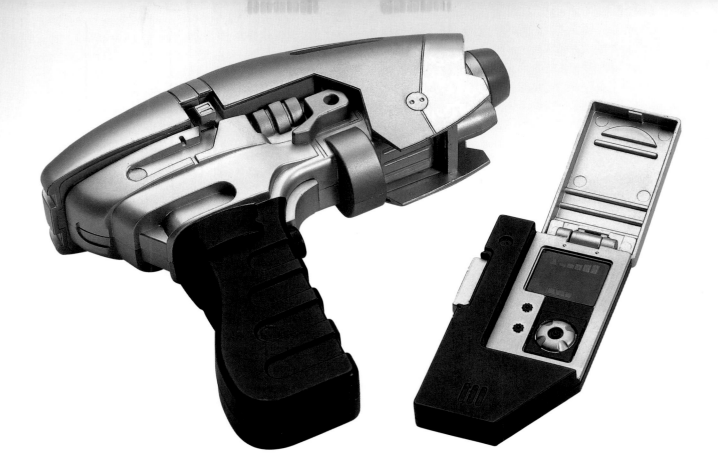

forty-five [variants of] *C.S.I.*, I think there could be a *Star Trek* on the air."

While there was no discussion of a sixth TV series, on the heels of *Enterprise*'s cancellation, Paramount President Donald DeLine commissioned an eleventh feature film from Berman and McCluggage. *Star Trek: The Beginning* was to be written by Erik Jendresen (*Band of Brothers*) and was to be the connection between Archer's era and Kirk's, using the Romulan War of 2156–61 as the impetus. Envisioned as the first of a trilogy, clearly the scope was to be epic, focusing on Tiberius Chase, an ancestor of Kirk.

The lack of main characters from a previous version of the franchise (although Shran was in the script, as was Vulcan ambassador Skon, Sarek's father) and the overall down cycle of interest in the franchise ultimately led Paramount to cancel the project. Briefly, plans for an animated version, also featuring Chase but now set in the twenty-ninth century, were considered but abandoned.

Jendresen was quite vocal in his support of the project and noted Berman was being eased out in favor of McCluggage becoming the franchise's new overseer.

However, the time had come to let *Star Trek* get some rest.

Art Asylum's models of the phase pistols and communicators used by the crew of the *Enterprise*.

# CHAPTER 18

STAR TREK

# *REBOOTED*

The two Spocks—Zachary Quinto and Leonard Nimoy— meet at Comic-Con in San Diego in 2007. Fans went berserk. *Associated Press*

Zachary Quinto and Chris Pine in uniform for the new production of *Star Trek*, which was a fresh take on Gene Roddenberry's initial concept. *Jill Greenberg/Corbis Outline*

In 2005, around the time that *Enterprise* was winding down, Paramount split into two divisions: Viacom and CBS Corporation, each taking control of aspects of *Star Trek*. Paramount president Gail Berman won eighteen months to revive *Star Trek* as a feature film before CBS took a shot at a new television series.

Everyone saw the property as too valuable to abandon, but it was also clearly in need of rest and rethinking. Rick Berman, who had been caretaking Roddenberry's creation since 1991, was relieved of command. At this point, Paramount was making the third *Mission: Impossible* film with the Bad Robot Productions group, comprising genre wunderkind J. J. Abrams, screenwriting partners Roberto Orci and Alex Kurtzman, and *Lost* producers Damon Lindelof and Bryan Burk. Gail Berman approached them with the idea of rebooting *Star Trek*. Most were fans, although for Abrams *Star Trek* was all about Kirk and Spock.

As had been proposed several times before, the story they came up with would feature Kirk, Spock, and McCoy meeting at Starfleet Academy. Orci and Kurtzman were huge *Trek* fans, crediting inspiration from not only the various television series, but also the novels *Prime Directive*, *Spock's World*, and *Best Destiny*. To be respectful of *Star Trek*'s long history, they conceived of using Leonard Nimoy's Spock to connect the original series to the relaunched franchise, then creating an alternate reality for the new crew and starship. Since Spock was last seen on Romulus, it naturally led the writers to use the underutilized Romulans, even though they had been the villains in the most recent movie.

Abrams's role as producer was revealed on April 20, 2006, and the screenplay was developed between August and December 2006. After reading a draft, Abrams accepted Paramount's offer to direct as well.

# TO SEEK OUT NEW FANS AND NEW WORLDVIEWS

*Kalliope Dalto*

I found *Star Trek* when I needed it most. Just over five years ago, as a lonely and studious middle school student of twelve, I lived every day on a kind of hand-to-mouth basis: if no teachers picked on me, if none of my classmates spoke to me, if I got all my work done and everyone left me alone, the day was a success. I didn't have a single friend, but I preferred it that way. Needless to say, I was supremely unhappy, even though I'd be hard pressed to tell you why: I had my books, my imagination, and my pride; why shouldn't that be enough? I rarely voiced my dissatisfaction to any adult, but when I did, I was often met with this dread response: "Enjoy it! This is the best time of your life!" I began to wonder what was wrong with me.

Then I discovered *Star Trek*, and the strange new worlds within seemed so inviting. Those seventy-nine episodes in brilliant Technicolor filled my whole life. In a fifty-one minute vision I could be transported to a realm of storytelling in which every hardship was met with a balance of cool logic and unstoppable heart. What's more, *Star Trek* presented me with a measure of hope. By observing the irrepressible bonds of friendship and trust that Kirk, Spock, and McCoy shared, I learned that I wasn't quite as self-sufficient as I had liked to believe. I was desperate for a community like that of the *Enterprise* crew, in which I could feel loved and accepted and useful.

I can't pretend that *Star Trek* wrought an immediate overhaul of my terrible attitude or nonexistent social skills.

But it certainly was the first step. I came to recognize that my story was far from a singularity—there were other kids (and adults!) who were wondering what was wrong with them, and whether it was ever going to get better. *Star Trek* served as a communications channel. When my kind librarian, Janet Lukas, learned I had declared myself a fan, she put me into contact with a friend of her husband Robert, the incredible Howard Weinstein, who just happened to be a *Star Trek* novelist. My correspondence with him led to a fateful trip to the Shore Leave convention, which effectively shattered any remaining illusions I had about my own isolation. The *Star Trek* community, I found, is filled with people like me, reaching out to find understanding among other intelligent beings. I will never forget how amazed and humbled I was by the whole scene; somehow, that community that I had longed for had existed all along.

*Star Trek* is the hope of a happier, more challenging future. It is the hope that humanity will find unity and comfort even in the farthest depths of space. These hopes bind our beautiful, unstoppable fandom together; help us conquer our anxieties and live life in anticipation of boldly going where no man has gone before.

*Kalliope Dalto found* Star Trek *at age twelve and began attending college in fall 2012, curious to find "what's out there."*

From left, Chris Pine, director J. J. Abrams, and Zachary Quinto at a news conference in Tokyo publicizing the film. *Associated Press*

A new cast was needed: Zachary Quinto, one of the stars of NBC's *Heroes*, looked so much like Nimoy that he was a shoe-in for the role of Spock and was the first cast. Chris Pine overcame a bad audition to become the new James T. Kirk, and *Lord of the Rings*' Karl Urban uncannily channeled DeForest Kelley as McCoy. Zoe Saldana, who played a *Trek* fan in *The Terminal*, became Uhura. After directing Simon Pegg in *Mission: Impossible III*, Abrams thought he'd make a good Scotty. John Cho from *Harold & Kumar* won out as Sulu and *Alpha Dog*'s Anton Yelchin was tapped for Chekov. They were supported by Bruce Greenwood as Christopher Pike, and all opposed Eric Bana's Romulan miner-turned-terrorist Nero.

Majel Barrett recorded the computer voice, a nice link to her husband's legacy, just eight days before her death. *TNG*'s Wil Wheaton also provided background Romulan voices.

The new Capt. Christopher Pike, Bruce Greenwood, poses on the red carpet with Erin Melcher from the town of Vulcan, Alberta, before a special screening of *Star Trek* in Calgary, Alberta, May 6, 2009. *Todd Korol/ Reuters/Corbis*

A regular contributor to Abrams's projects, Scott Chambliss stepped in as production designer and thoroughly reimagined everything about Starfleet Academy and the *Enterprise*; the starship was executed along with the special effects by ILM. The fresh design requirements allowed modern-day technology to be extrapolated for a new future, from control panels to communicators and phasers. Michael Kaplan designed all the twenty-third-century costumes and uniforms. Abrams's frequent composer Michael Giacchino provided a score to the film, keeping Alexander Courage's theme for the end credits.

Filming lasted from November 7 through March 27, 2008. Locations included California's Bakersfield (standing in for Iowa) and Long Beach and Utah. A Budweiser plant in Van Nuys controversially became the *Enterprise*'s engineering section.

Claiming that the film would benefit from a summer opening, Paramount announced that the movie would open on May 8, 2009, rather than the originally planned Christmas Day 2008. One advantage to the extra time was that Alan Dean Foster, chosen by Orci and Kurtzman, could see the entire film before writing the novelization. On April 6, Austin's Alamo Drafthouse was supposedly screening *The Wrath of Khan* when the audience was surprised with a special advance screening of the new film, featuring appearances by the writers, producers, and Nimoy. The internet melted down that night as news spread: the movie was not just good. It was great.

Diehard traditionalists could still have Roddenberry's series to love while a new generation could fall in love with a new, optimistic vision of the future. The science was fuzzy, and the story logic didn't entirely hold up, but it was a breathless thrill ride.

Still, Paramount felt the need to heavily market the film, introducing a new generation of fans to the classic characters and premise. A teaser trailer showed the *Enterprise* being

THEY THOUGHT SPACE WAS THE FINAL
FRONTIER—THEY WERE WRONG.

QUIRK FICTION

# NIGHT OF THE LIVING TREKKIES

UNOFFICIAL! UNIMAGINABLE! UNBELIEVABLE! • BY KEVIN DAVID ANDERSON AND SAM STALL

*Above:* Kellogg's cereal premiums for the new film included uniform t-shirts in command yellow, science blue, and operations red. *Ella Pearson*

*Right:* Playmates Toys' replica of the reboot communicator.

*Left:* If there's a trend, you can bet that someone will find a way to work *Star Trek* into it. Kevin David Anderson and Sam Stall's mash-up of zombies and *Trek* conventions was published by Quirk Books in 2010.

Over the years the franchise has accumulated a wealth of soundtracks, a handful of audio dramas, and a sound effects album.

*Above:* Ecstatic fans on the red carpet for the Los Angeles premiere of *Star Trek* at the Grauman's Chinese Theatre on April 30, 2009, in Hollywood. *Getty Images*

*Below, from left:* A sampling of Burger King tie-in merchandise: McCoy, Scotty, Sulu, and the *U.S.S. Kelvin.*

built, followed by more expanded trailers outlining the story. Nokia, Verizon Wireless, Esurance, Kellogg's, Burger King, and Intel Corporation signed on as sponsors.

Critics and fans adored the fresh new take on the beloved series and the film was a box office smash, grossing $385.7 million worldwide. According to Rotten Tomatoes, this new film was 95 percent "fresh," the highest rating for any *Trek* film. It also ignited the largest merchandising wave in two decades.

It was the first *Trek* film nominated for Best Picture, taking home Best Makeup, the franchise's first Academy Award.

Above: A treasure trove of memorabilia, sets, props, and costumes were auctioned off at Christie's during a three-day sale in October 2006. The auction featured more than 1,000 lots from the archives of CBS Paramount Television Studios. *Associated Press*

Below: Walter Koenig talks with a Karen refugee at a refugee camp near the Thai-Myanmar border in July 2007. Koenig visited a medical clinic and refugees during a three-day trip to Mae Sot, 240 miles northeast of Bangkok, to bring attention to their plight. *Associated Press*

## THE SEQUEL

Though Orci and Kurtzman intended to have a screenplay for a sequel completed by Christmas 2009, a heavy Bad Robot development slate, and script and preproduction delays though 2010 and 2011, made it impossible to meet the originally announced June 29, 2012, release date. Finally, in spring 2011, a draft was completed. Meanwhile, Chris Pine had been cast as Jack Ryan in a new movie based on Tom Clancy's books. That film was scheduled to shoot in January 2012, forcing *Star Trek*'s release back to May 17, 2013, four years after the first film. This negated franchise momentum,

frustrating Paramount and their merchandising partners. When the Ryan film got delayed, *Trek*'s production date moved to mid-January 2012, finishing in May.

In September 2011, Abrams formally signed to direct the sequel, with Benicio del Toro announced as the unnamed antagonist. He failed to agree terms with Paramount in late 2011, and in 2012, a week before production began on January 12, Benedict Cumberbatch, the BBC's Sherlock Holmes, replaced him. Noel Clarke (*Doctor Who*), Alice Eve (*Sex and the City 2*), Nazneen Contractor (*24*), and Joseph Gatt (*Thor*) joined *Enterprise* guest star Peter Weller in the cast.

Bad Robot Productions' deal to handle the franchise gave Abrams vast approval rights over merchandising, notably novels and comics. As a result, members of the production team have been integral in creating IDW's comics. It led to a clever innovation: retelling some of the original seventy-nine episodes using the new franchise reality, with early issues seeded with clues to the second film. That series launched to acclaim in late 2011.

# FAN FILMS COME OF AGE

David Galanter

*Star Trek* fan films date back to the original series, when kids (or college students) took an 8mm movie camera, donned quickly rendered Starfleet costumes and turned their parents' backyard into the latest strange new world. If a scene of the *Enterprise* orbiting a planet was needed, a toy model hung from fishing wire and a painted globe had to suffice. In the last four-plus decades, however, things have greatly changed.

With the advent of *Star Trek*-like technology that puts supercomputers in the home and digital recording in the palm of one's hand, fan films have become full-fledged internet web-series with professional-quality full episodes.

Perhaps the two best known to create a new crew to helm a starship other than the *Enterprise* are *Starship Exeter* and *Starship Farragut*. *Farragut* took up where *Exeter* left off, telling stories of a *Constitution*-class Starfleet vessel along the same thematic lines of the original series. Both rebuilt classic *Star Trek* sets based upon the original blueprints, at great expense to the participants and creators, and their love for *Star Trek* is evident in every frame of both series. The *Farragut* team has gone so far as to also recreate the look and feel of the *Trek* animated series for two original animated episodes, and they view and sound almost indistinguishable from the original cartoons, other than characters and stories, of course.

Arguably the best of the fan films, and the show that broke new ground on many levels, is the one with which I'm most closely associated. James Cawley's *Star Trek: Phase II* (formerly *Star Trek: New Voyages*) rebuilt the *Enterprise* so closely to the original that when *Star Trek: Enterprise* needed assistance re-creating an original series era ship set and costumes, they sought out Cawley's help.

Longtime *Trek* writers D .C. Fontana and David Gerrold have been involved with *Phase II*, along with this humble *Trek* novelist

who was allowed to cowrite one of their episodes. I can say from personal experience that standing on that bridge or sitting in Kirk's chair gave new me perspective on how the original show was made, and how Kirk and his crew would have interacted.

Recasting the original characters of Kirk, Spock and McCoy, et al, the quality of Cawley's show was able to lure *Trek* actors George Takei and Walter Koenig to reprise their respective roles as Sulu and Chekov. Takei's episode was, in fact, nominated for a Hugo award and won an Online Video Award from *TV Guide*.

Enlisting professional actors, writers, crew, and costumers (Cawley himself worked under William Ware Theiss during his time on *TNG*)— often for low or no remuneration—has given *Phase II* a leg up in comparison to other fan-made concerns. The lighting, sets, props, and other production values are as high— or higher, given the show is shot in high definition—than the original series, and the special effects are modern movie quality, thanks to skilled professionals like Daren Dochterman, Tobias Richter, and the Digital Animation & Visual Effects School at Universal Studios, all working for their love of *Star Trek*.

Cawley's ability to garner support for a project on which no one can make money (the caveat under which CBS and formerly Paramount allow *Phase II* and other fan films to exist without breaking copyright and trademark restrictions) is not merely based on his vision to fulfill his childhood desire to be Captain Kirk on the *Enterprise*. It is the common ground that all *Star Trek* fans share: their desire to see the missions of their favorite crew and ship continue.

*David Galanter has written* Star Trek *fiction and an episode of* Phase II *in addition to co-owning ComicBoards.com and TVShowBoards.com.*

# CHAPTER 19 STAR TREK'S PLACE IN HISTORY

An *Enterprise* mural at the Outer Limits Coffee Shop, Best Western Space Age Lodge, in Gila Bend, Arizona. *Alamy*

Avery Brooks (Capt. Benjamin Sisko of *Deep Space Nine*) and William Shatner appearing at a panel for *The Captains* at San Diego Comic-Con. Shatner directed and produced *The Captains*, in which he interviews fellow *Star Trek* captains Patrick Stewart, Brooks, Kate Mulgrew, Scott Bakula, and Christopher Pine. © Karl *Polverino/ ZUMA Press/Corbis*

Since its debut in 1966, several generations of viewers around the world found themselves inspired by *Star Trek*'s optimistic view of the future. They grew up studying science or engineering or filmmaking. Countless people can cite the episode, novel, or character that proved to be the life-changing encounter that put them on a new course. As a result, this can arguably be the most influential television program of all time, helping to shape the world we currently live in.

*Star Trek* can now be streamed on Netflix and Hulu, or on CBS-owned websites. It and the spinoffs continue to air on broadcast television while countless other series have vanished into the dustbin of history. Somewhere around the world, episodes continue to be broadcast almost every hour of the day and night, much as most weekends there is a convention being held featuring performers from one of the series.

And the original series continues to make headlines. In November 2011, after a forty-three-year ban, German audiences finally got to watch "Patterns of Force," the episode where the *Enterprise* found a world patterned after Nazi Germany. Channel ZDF broadcast the episode in a late night time slot without fanfare or controversy.

William Shatner hosted a two-hour documentary that gave *Star Trek* credit for much of the modern-day look and feel of our electronic tools. He's not far wrong because, after all, people designing user interfaces and hardware grew up on Wah Chang's prop designs. The computer data discs the crew used were clearly forerunners of floppy discs, and the communicator inspired the clamshell cell phone. And can't you see Uhura using a Bluetooth earpiece?

When Gene Roddenberry and company began studying cutting-edge technology, they anticipated the far-future while influencing the near-future, bringing things almost full circle. Jeffries's bridge design was studied for military vessels and sickbay's diagnostic beds have become a reality.

Much as today's filmmakers were raised on the revolutionary Marvel Comics of the 1960s and have made movies inspired by those tales, technicians, programmers, engineers, special effects artists, makeup artists, writers, and teachers have taken the lessons from the five series and have applied them in their careers. The original cast continues to marvel at the numerous people who have credited their work as the inspiration for career choices, notably many who actually became astronauts. NASA was smart enough to

*(Continued on page 244)*

# THE ENTERPRISE IN SPACE

*Mario Runco Jr.*

When I was growing up, back in the 1950s, science fiction was not a mainstream entertainment genre. Indeed, it was considered a form of entertainment meant only for children, the seminal films *The Day the Earth Stood Still* (1951) and *Forbidden Planet* (1956) notwithstanding. I saw both of these for the first time at around the time of the start of space race when the Soviets launched Sputnik in 1957. It didn't take much more than seeing those films and the country's new found interest in space for me to know what I wanted to do. I'd previously looked up at the stars on clear summer nights and wondered what was out there, and thought of one day visiting those distant points of light. The launch of Alan Shepard as the first American into space sealed the deal on my interest in space exploration, but to a nine-year-old, really going to do that seemed as impossible as traveling faster than the speed of light. In the interim, I would have to settle for science fiction books from the likes of Arthur C. Clarke and other media to vicariously satisfy that desire.

The first television space exploration series I remember was a show called *Space Angel* (1962–64). The show was an animated series whose technical content and stories were done pretty well for such an early series, but it left much to be desired. Then came the Irwin Allen production *Lost in Space* (1965–68), which provided hope that there might be a decent space exploration series on television. However, that hope was quickly dashed after the first few weeks of episodes when it became apparent that it would be nothing more than a guy in the monster suit of the week. The show probably should have been called "Marooned on Monster Planet."

A year later *Star Trek* debuted on television, but it had an uphill battle in gaining acceptance, especially on the heels of the disaster that was *Lost in Space*. In any case, *Star Trek* along with Stanley Kubrick's movie *2001: A Space Odyssey* (1968) were breaths of fresh air after the previously childish way the film industry, and especially television, generally

The crew of STS-54, space shuttle *Endeavour*: (left to right) Donald R. McMonagle, pilot; Mario Runco Jr., mission specialist; John H. Casper, commander; Susan J. Helms, mission specialist; and Gregory J. Harbaugh, mission specialist. *NASA*

handled science fiction. *Star Trek* ultimately tapped into the huge reservoir of frustrated science fiction fans and became a must-watch each week, delivering an intelligent, scientific approach to the genre that was sorely needed. Each week the show would vicariously take a generation of Earth-bound space explorers farther out into the galaxy.

I remember even participating in the write-in campaign to NBC when it was announced that the show would be canceled after only its second season. The write-in campaign gave us fans a reprieve for a year, but alas the damage done by its predecessor took its toll and by 1969, after being moved in its third season to Friday nights, the death knell for a television series, it went into reruns.

I remember the extreme disappointment I felt with the buffoons at NBC who originally thought the show was "too cerebral," and who arguably made the biggest corporate decision blunder of all time in canceling the show. I continued to watch the show in reruns during my college years, and in 1972, I attended the first *Star Trek* convention in New York with the hope that something might come of it in bringing back the show. The animated series (1973–74) that followed was a glimmer of hope, and I'm glad I went.

A few years later, when I was in Officer Candidate School in the Navy, after a hard day of classes and physical training, almost every weary candidate would cram into their company wardrooms with their respective company classmates from 5:00–6:00 p.m. to watch *Star Trek* and get more "training." The odd thing was that the mess hall opened at 5:30 p.m. but hardly anyone would go, even though most everyone was famished by that time of the day. It was only after the final words from Kirk, Spock, Scotty, or McCoy were uttered and the closing theme music started did practically the entire class go over to eat. It truly was a phenomenon to behold: All these educated, military trainees glued to the set to watch episodes that most of us had seen before. There was

*Left:* Helms, an unnamed Klingon, and Runco. *NASA*

*Opposite:* Runco performs flight tests of the *Enterprise*-A aboard the *Endeavour*. *NASA*

something about watching it together in that environment that made it special and brought us closer together as a team. The folks in the mess hall never really did figure out why the candidates would only come in en masse a half hour after they opened.

Subsequently, during my time in the Navy I really started seriously thinking that I could actually possibly become an astronaut and years later, in 1987, I was fortunate enough to be selected, after applying several times. Having had the honor and privilege of really traveling into space on my three space shuttle missions, STS-44, 54, and 77 (*Atlantis* for the first one and *Endeavour* on the later two), I have to say that in large part my motivation was wanting "to boldly go where no man has gone before."

On my second mission the connection was complete as I brought with me, as far as I know, the first *Star Trek* vessels to have actually flown in space: a die-cast *Enterprise* (NCC 1701-A) model and Franklin Mint pewter models of the *Enterprise* (NCC-1701) and a Klingon battle cruiser. Unlike the pewter models, I had access to the *Enterprise*-A onboard and was able to perform and video actual "space flight tests." That was cool! Thank you Gene Rodenberry for having the vision.

*Mario Runco Jr. was a New Jersey state trooper before joining NASA in 1987. A veteran of three space flights (STS-44 in 1991, STS-54 in 1993, and STS-77 in 1996), Runco has logged over 551 hours in space, which includes a 4.5-hour spacewalk during his STS-54 mission.*

(Continued from page 239)

recruit Nichelle Nichols to attract more minorities into their astronaut corps during the 1970s.

More impressive are the steps towards turning hypothetical scientific concepts into reality. Purdue University engineers created a theoretical design for a cloaking device that used an array of tiny needles radiating outward from a central spoke, which resembled a round hairbrush. Light would bend around the object being cloaked so background objects would be visible. It used nano-technology, which seemed far-fetched when first seen in *TNG*. Other ideas like transparent aluminum, tricorders, phasers, and even tractor beams are all inching their way from fiction to fact.

While the television series was initially considered a failure in 1969, it went on to rewrite the expectations of networks, film studios, and merchandisers. The reruns ignited fresh interest in the show, leading to spinoffs, conventions, merchandise, and everything leading up to the book you are reading. When *TNG* came along, it launched a wave of first-run syndication, paving the way for entirely new distribution methods for original material, long before such programming became a staple on basic channel channels.

Similarly, almost every genre television show to follow tried to ape the merchandising bonanza, from action figures to novels. But, since the first James Blish book through today,

*Above:* While in D.C. for a NASA event in February 2012, Nichelle Nichols paid a visit to the Oval Office to meet President Barack Obama, who admitted to having had a crush on her when he was growing up watching *Star Trek*. *White House photo*

*Right:* In 1999, the thirty-third anniversary of *Star Trek*, the United States Post Office issued a thirty-three-cent first class stamp featuring the *Enterprise*. *Alamy*

no other franchise has published original fiction for so long without interruption, nor matched the number of nonfiction books about the show.

*Star Trek* spawned countless lines of dialogue and concepts that have been used and adopted by people around the world. One of the best known is the "Curse of the Red Shirt." Given that the color was worn by security personnel, it made the most sense that they suffered the highest casualty rate. According to Paula Block and Terry Erdmann, 73 percent of the crewmen to die in service wore a red shirt. As a result, referring to cannon fodder characters as "red shirts" has seeped into the vernacular.

Newspapers and magazines have all borrowed lines from the series, so when you hear "boldly go" or "warp speed" there is no explanation necessary. Half the jokes on CBS's brilliant comedy *The Big Bang Theory* feel like they are based on *Star Trek* and don't need explanation. Generations of nonfans have been exposed often enough to "get it." No other show has given rise to a brand new language, Klingon, which has been used to perform stage works or rewrite Shakespeare. You can even have Google translate English into Klingon, with several phrases added to the Oxford English Dictionary. Heck, an entire episode of *Frasier* was built around the Klingon language.

Music cues from the original series, along with familiar sound effects, have found their way into countless movies and television programs. References to the show have crept into dialogue, such as the lines Quentin Tarantino contributed to *Crimson Tide*, while characters, such as those on *The Big Bang Theory* and Xander from *Buffy the Vampire Slayer*, were allowed to be fans. It has become a fitting tribute that cast members have appeared on other genre shows, like Koenig on *Babylon 5* or Nichols and Takei in *Heroes*. In 2005, Takei, who has parlayed his familiarity from *Trek* better than his peers, came out as a proud gay man, married his longtime partner and advocated for equality at countless opportunities.

Kevin Parker as Col. Amar Koloth, a.k.a. the Homeless Klingon. *Stephen Lesnik*

Merchandise inspired by the
original series is still popular.

The *Trek* franchise's decades-long history
makes it an obvious subject for Mattel's line of
Scene It? trivia games.

The York Maze, the largest maize maze in the world, inspired by the fortieth anniversary of *Star Trek*. Features include the *Enterprise*, a Borg cube, and a giant image of Spock's head. *Alamy*

No other television series has spawned not just one but two feature film documentaries—*Trekkies* and *Trekkies 2*, from *TNG* actress Denise Crosby. Then there are the love letters to *Star Trek* in the form of *Free Enterprise*, an independent film sending up Shatner and the fans; and the big-budget *Galaxy Quest*, which many consider the best *Star Trek* feature film of them all. Other shows have paid their tribute, sometimes with tongue-in-cheek, including *Futurama*, *The Simpsons*, and *Family Guy*. *Trek* phrases and characters have appeared in pop songs too voluminous to even try and recount, with some novelty songs becoming hits on Dr. Demento's syndicated radio show.

And every new generation of hardware and software tends to include something from Roddenberry's universe among its earliest features. When customized fonts were added to computers, you could suddenly make signs worthy of the *Enterprise* bridge. You could trick out your desktop to make *Enterprise* sound effects, or use audio clips as alarms. Early Hallmark ornaments with voice chips of course included ones with Kirk and Spock. As apps became popular for cell phones and then tablets, *Star Trek*–oriented ones were among the best sellers. After all, your tablet can now resemble the PADDs seen on Picard's *Enterprise*.

As home video became popular, you could buy all the episodes on video cassettes, only to replace them on DVD, and then replace them again on Blu-ray. And fans did, generating untold millions in profit for Paramount.

The town of Riverside, Iowa, decided to proclaim itself the future birthplace of James Kirk, based on Roddenberry indicating that is where he would be born in *The Making of Star Trek*. The Riverside City Council moved to make the claim in 1985, ultimately receiving the Great Bird's blessing. Abrams honored that by having the *Enterprise* being constructed just outside Riverside where Kirk was living.

Tourists to Vulcan, Alberta, in Canada can see a statue of the movie-era *Enterprise*, and Las Vegas tourists used to include *The Star Trek Experience* as a must-see attraction in between trips to the gambling tables.

Clearly, *Star Trek* has become part of the fabric of life around the world.

# STAR TREK'S

# *FUTURE*

Cryptic Studio's *Star Trek Online* game pushes into *Trek*'s future, set thirty years after *Nemesis*. The massively multiplayer game puts players in the center seat as starship captains.

*Left:* Kirk Williams, owner and only driver for Capt. Kirk Enterprises, an interstate cargo trucking company he started on 2007, shows off his Freightliner rig complete with a painting of the *Starship Enterprise* on the trailer. *Associated Press*

*Above:* Brynley T. Dolman wears a Scotish kilt while dressed as Klingon at the 63rd World Science Fiction Convention and 2005 Eurocon. *Corbis*

Whither *Star Trek?*

It's safe to say that it isn't going anywhere, as it's too deeply entrenched in the global social construct. And like most things, it will wax and wane in popularity. As a pop culture phenomenon, it was eclipsed in the 1960s by *Batman* and the Beatles, but proved to be as enduring after gaining the reputation as the television show that wouldn't die.

It did almost die in the 1970s when Paramount couldn't make up its mind what to do with its property, wasting years when new adventures could have been told. With few exceptions, the executives in charge of the studio merely saw the franchise as something to be exploited for all it was worth. As a result, it lacked a strong champion to protect its creative interests, so the inevitable movie and related merchandise were haphazard.

That began to change when Harve Bennett arrived, followed by Rick Berman. While Roddenberry knew what he wanted from his ship and crew, he was less adept at executing that vision as a movie producer or overseer of the growing integrated licensing world that has been dubbed transmedia. While Lucasfilm kept a tight handle on the internal continuity between the movies, novels, comics (books and strips), role playing games, and the like, Paramount appeared less interested in managing a creative universe. It fell to editors and writers of books and comics to handle that, with Rick Sternbach and Mike and Denise Okuda cementing many of the details in works like the various technical manuals, *Encyclopedia* and *Chronology*.

Now it's all controlled through J. J. Abrams's Bad Robot Productions and that's perhaps for the best, long-term. They have breathed new life into a franchise that was allowed to be worn down, so much so it was in danger of becoming nothing more than the butt of the joke, a cliché-ridden concept too hokey to be taken seriously.

The collector's edition of *Star Trek Online* included special packaging, a collectible pin, guest passes, and a hardcover manual with artwork.

At least, that's what the cynics have been saying since Shatner himself parodied his fans with the infamous "Get a Life" sketch on *Saturday Night Live*. But the reality is that the concept endured for a reason. Ever since the show debuted, people have tried to explore the reason for its success and durability. Time and again, it goes back to Roddenberry's belief that mankind will make it to the stars. It won't be easy—in fact, there will be a lot of strife before we get there (Colonel Green, the Eugenics War, World War III), but it will be worth it because there are wonders to behold.

When America was torn by a generation gap and an unpopular war in Vietnam, here was a show that said we'll survive and thrive, meet other races, and make a difference in the universe. Kirk repeatedly met superior races and demonstrated mankind's compassion and moral strength. Our potential, the shows told us, was unlimited, and we continue to need that reminder. We'll continue turning to *Star Trek* for that reminder, and it was that very optimism that Abrams recognized when it was his turn in the center seat.

*Star Trek* lives!

Authors Kevin Dilmore (in Christopher Pike mode) and Dayton Ward perform at a celebrity roast at the Shore Leave convention. Every blink of the light was a guaranteed laugh getter. *Jen Snyder*

*Voyageur Press collection*

# ACKNOWLEDGMENTS

When editor Grace Labatt called and offered me this assignment, I greeted it with a mix of excitement and dread. This was a lot of history to research and pack into a tight word count on an even tighter deadline. At the time, I was completing my graduate studies and spent the vast majority of my days interning at a high school. But how could I refuse?

I first encountered *Star Trek* when I caught my father watching an episode during the original series run and later asked to try one on my own. I was hooked. I first wrote about the show for my junior high school newspaper and have been writing about it ever since. I was there for the first convention, went on to volunteer for the next four, and it was a heady experience to be a guest speaker at a *Trek* con in 1981. *Star Trek* has been a part of my personal and professional life, complete with editing the comic book adaptations for eight years plus all the fiction I wrote for Pocket Books. Barely a year goes by without my writing something for or about the series.

I had the support of encouragement of my pals, and the additional support of my local Democratic Town Committee, which allowed me to pawn off my campaign direction to others. I said yes to Grace. She then pulled a bait and switch, handing me over to Scott Pearson, who is not only my friend but Grace's colleague, so he helped me shape the book. His insights and knowledge proved instrumental.

Since this was designed to trace not just the history of the series but its fervent fans, I reached out to many friends, most of whom came through with anecdotes and answers to a set of questions. While space considerations prevented most of their words from being used, their stories helped shaped the narrative. I want to thank Bob Ahrens, Mark Altman, Lorraine Anderson, Kirsten Beyer, T. Alan Chafin, Linda Deneroff, David R. George III, Devra Langsam, Marc Lee, Bill Mumy, Susan Olesen, Renfield, John Scheeler, Steve Wilson, and Sandy Zier for their contributions and memories. My old high school friend Andrew Scholnick came through with some great early convention pictures, while Steve Lesnick and Jen Rohrbach Snyder provided us with thousands of more modern images.

While *Star Trek* may be the most written about show ever, there remain no books about *Enterprise* so I thank Manny Coto for making himself available to talk about the show (with a tip of the cap to Brian K. Morris for ably handling the transcription). As it was, there are so many conflicting accounts in the various histories and memoirs, I felt like a referee sorting through what may actually have occurred since 1964. The accounts in this book are as accurate as I could make them and any errors that may be found are strictly of my own making.

When the words began to resemble tribbles in volume, my long-distance pal Paul Simpson and Howard Weinstein, one of my oldest friends, both volunteered to help me tighten chapters. This book would not be here without their tireless help and support.

Given the crushing schedule from October 2011 through January 2012, there was no way this could have happened had my wife Deb not given me her blessing. She shared me with the future and for that I cannot thank her enough.

COLOR TRANSPARENCY

PROCESSED BY
DYNACOLOR

Color Slide Film

this side toward screen

# BIBLIOGRAPHY

Abramowitz, Rachel. *Is That a Gun in Your Pocket? The Truth About Female Power in Hollywood*. New York: Random House, 2000.

Alexander, David. *Star Trek Creator: The Authorized Biography of Gene Roddenberry*. New York: Roc Books, 1994.

Asherman, Allan. *The Star Trek Compendium*. New York: Pocket Books, 1986.

——. *The Star Trek Interview Book*. New York: Pocket Books, 1988.

——. *The Making of Star Trek II: The Wrath of Khan*. New York: Pocket Books, 1982.

Ayers, Jeff. S*tar Trek: Voyages of the Imagination*. New York: Pocket Books, 2006.

*CAVU Forty-Two G*. Goodfellow Field, San Angelo, TX: Class 42-G, US Army Air Corps. 1942. pp. 70. http://aafcollection.info/items/detail.php?key=105 (accessed September 29, 2011).

Danhauser, Curt. Curt Danhauser's Guide to the Animated Star Trek. www.danhausertrek.com/AnimatedSeries/Main.html (accessed November 12, 2011).

Daniels, Susanne, and Cynthia Littleton. *Season Finale*. New York: HarperCollins, 2007.

Erdman, Terry. *Star Trek Deep Space Nine Companion*. New York: Pocket Books, 2000.

Engel, Joel. *Gene Roddenberry: The Myth and the Man Behind Star Trek*. New York: Hyperion Books, 1994.

Gerrold, David. *The World of Star Trek*. New York: Ballantine Books, 1973.

Gross, Edward, and Mark A. Altman. *Captains' Logs: The Unauthorized Complete Trek Voyages*. New York: Little Brown, 1995.

Kiker, Edward B. "Soldiers of Vision: We Don't Stop When We Take Off the Uniform." *Army Space Journal*, Winter/Spring 2004, 1F. http://www.smdc-armyforces.army.mil/Pic_Archive/ASJ_PDFs/ASJ_VOL_3_NO_1_Y_FLIP_1.pdf (accessed September 29, 2011).

Meyer, Nicholas. *The View from the Bridge*. New York: Plume Books, 2009.

The Museum of Broadcast Communications, s.v. "Roddenberry, Gene" (by Susan Gibberman), http://www.museum.tv/eotvsection.php?entrycode=roddenberry (accessed September 29, 2011).

Nemecek, Larry. *Star Trek: The Next Generation Companion*. New York: Pocket Books, 2003.

Nichols, Nichelle. Archive of American Television interview with Nichelle Nichols. By Stephen J. Abramson. www.emmytvlegends.org/interviews/people/nichelle-nichols (accessed October 1, 2011).

Nimoy, Leonard. *I Am Spock*. New York: Hyperion Books, 1995.

Porter, Alan J. *Star Trek: A Comics History*. New Castle, PA: Hermes Press, 2009.

Reeves-Stevens, Judith & Garfield. *The Making of Star Trek: Deep Space Nine*. New York: Pocket Books, 1994.

Ruditis, Paul. *Star Trek Voyager Companion*. New York: Pocket Books, 2003.

Sackett, Susan. *Inside Trek: My Secret Life with Star Trek Creator Gene Roddenberry*. Tulsa, OK: Hawk Publishing Group, 2002.

Sackett, Susan, and Gene Roddenberry. *The Making of Star Trek: The Motion Picture*. New York: Pocket Books, 1979.

Snyder, J. William, Jr. "*Star Trek*: A Phenomenon and Social Statement on the 1960s." www.ibiblio.org/jwsnyder/wisdom/trek.html (accessed September 29, 2011).

Solow, Herbert F., and Robert H. Justman, *Inside Star Trek: The Real Story*. New York: Pocket Books, 1996.

Whitfield, Stephen E., and Gene Roddenberry. *The Making of Star Trek*. New York: Ballantine Books, 1968.

# INDEX

# ABOUT THE AUTHOR

Robert Greenberger was given his first comic at age six. Since then, he has been a passionate fan of the medium, directly leading him to his reading science fiction and watching *Star Trek*. He wrote and edited for his various school newspapers, serving as Editor-in-Chief of *Pipe Dream* at Binghamton University.

Bob's professional career began at Starlog Press where he created *Comics Scene*, the first nationally distributed magazine to cover comic books, comic strips, and animation. He then joined DC Comics as assistant editor, rising to full editor and eventually switched to the administrative side of the company, ultimately to the role of Manager-Editorial Operations.

In 2000, Bob left DC for a job as Producer at Gist Communications and then returned to comics in 2001, as Marvel Comics' Director-Publishing Operations. In 2002, he went back to DC Comics as a Senior Editor in its collected editions department. Bob joined *Weekly World News* as Managing Editor until its demise in 2007. Since then he has been a fulltime freelance writer and editor, including News Editor at ComicMix.com.

As a freelancer, Bob has written numerous *Star Trek* novels and short fiction, in addition to short works of science fiction and fantasy. His adult nonfiction includes *The Essential Batman Encyclopedia*, *The Batman Vault*, and *The Art of Howard Chaykin*. He also cowrote *Stan Lee's How to Write Comics*. His fiction includes *Iron Man: Femme Fatales* and the award-winning novelization of *Hellboy II: The Golden Army*.

With fellow *Star Trek* authors Peter David, Michael Jan Friedman, Glenn Hauman, Aaron Rosenberg, and Howard Weinstein, he helped found Crazy 8 Press, a digital publishing hub. Partnered with David and Friedman, he has most recently written a comic book, novellas, and novel based on 2013's *After Earth* feature film.

In 2012, he obtained his Masters of Science in Education, intending to become a high school English teacher.

He makes his home in Fairfield, Connecticut, with his wife Deb and their dogs Dixie and Ginger. Their daughter Kate lives in Maryland.

For more information, see his website, www.bobgreenberger.com.

*Jerome K. Moore*